MW00584355

HARVARD EARLY MODERN AND
MODERN GREEK LIBRARY

EDITED BY

PANAGIOTIS ROILOS, DEMETRIOS YATROMANOLAKIS

C. P. CAVAFY

HEMMGL 1

HARVARD EARLY MODERN AND
MODERN GREEK LIBRARY

Series Editors: Panagiotis Roilos, Demetrios Yatromanolakis

Harvard Early Modern and Modern Greek Library is the only series of books which, through both original text and English translation, makes accessible to scholars and general readers the major works of Greek literature and thought produced in the last millennium, from the late eleventh century to the present. Each volume offers a reliable Greek text together with an accurate and literate English translation on facing pages. The editors/translators provide wide-ranging introductions as well as explanatory notes and selective bibliographies. This groundbreaking series presents current scholarship in a convenient and elegant format, aiming to make this substantial component of postclassical European literature available to researchers and students from a broad range of disciplines.

Advisory Board

C. P. CAVAFY

POEMS

THE CANON

EDITED BY

DEMETRIOS YATROMANOLAKIS

TRANSLATED BY

JOHN CHIOLES

HARVARD EARLY MODERN AND MODERN GREEK LIBRARY
HARVARD UNIVERSITY
DEPARTMENT OF THE CLASSICS
DISTRIBUTED BY HARVARD UNIVERSITY PRESS
CAMBRIDGE, MASSACHUSETTS
2011

Library of Congress Cataloging-in-Publication Data

Cavafy, Constantine, 1863-1933.
[Poems. English & Greek. Selections]
Poems : the canon / C. P. Cavafy ; edited by Demetrios Yatromanolakis ;
translated by John Chioles.
    p. cm. -- (Harvard Early Modern and Modern Greek Library; 1)
Includes bibliographical references and index.
Greek with English translation on facing page.
ISBN 978-0-674-05326-7
1 Cavafy, Constantine, 1863-1933--Translations into English. I. Roilos, Panagiotis.
II. Yatromanolakis, Demetrios. III. Title.
PA5610.K2A6 2011
889.1'32--dc22
                                                            2011020208

Contents

Foreword

Harvard Early Modern and Modern Greek Library is the only series of books which, through both original text and English translation, makes accessible to scholars and general readers the major works of Greek literature and thought produced in the last millennium, from the late eleventh century to the present. Each volume offers a reliable Greek text together with an accurate and literate English translation on facing pages. The editors/translators provide wide-ranging introductions as well as explanatory notes and selective bibliographies. This new series presents current scholarship in a convenient and elegant format, aiming to make this substantial component of post-classical European literature available to researchers and students from a broad range of disciplines.

C. P. Cavafy (Konstantinos Petrou Kavafis) is one of the most influential Greek poets. The history of the reception of his poetry and of his figure in world literature is labyrinthine and multifaceted. He was born, lived, and died in Alexandria (1863–1933), with brief periods spent in England, Constantinople, and Athens. Cavafy set in motion the most powerful modernism in early twentieth-century European poetry, exhibiting subtle truths about eroticism, history, and philosophy—an inscrutable triumvirate that informs the Greek language and cultures in all their diachronies. The Cavafy Canon plays with the complexities of ironic Socratic thought, suffused with the honesty of unadorned verse and the intricacy of metonymic modalities.

Being the only eminently bilingual translator of Cavafy's poems, John Chioles has set himself to the task of tracing and deciphering the multileveled subtleties of the Greek original. His succinct introduction and notes comment on aspects of Cavafy's 154 poems that constitute what is known as his Canon. Based on a thirty-year, continuous scholarly and literary interaction with Cavafy's poetry and its Greek and western European intertexts, Chioles has produced a most

authoritative and exceptionally nuanced translation into English of
the complex linguistic and poetic registers of Cavafy's Canon.

Panagiotis Roilos
Demetrios Yatromanolakis

Introduction

If we seek to clarify Cavafy's poetry using the poet himself as guide, we risk doing him an injustice. His often-quoted comment that he wrote three kinds of poems (philosophical, historical, and erotic) is an ironic smokescreen, partaking as much of truth as of an "apostrophic smile"—that is to say, a harmless half-truth. The apostrophic smile of irony was not only a part of his poetry, but also a part of his life. Strict demarcations simply do not pertain to his writing. He is not an "Aristotelian reader" of his own poetry; rather, he may be thought of as a proto-existentialist, using more a certain Platonic social relativism in his approach to shaping character and action in a virtually dramatic sense. In the erotic domain, the poet is not far from an ethical world that guides a unique compassion for the "other," for the lover and for the beloved; and that partakes as much of philosophy as of eroticism, if not of history as well—a kind of history as understood by the ancients: of time and suffering in tragedy, of time as a river never to be captured.

What clarifies Cavafy's stance on these matters is the fact that the voice of the poem is not identical with the voice of the poet. And so the degree to which proximity between the two voices comes and goes and has to do with the historicity of his Greek world—ancient, proto-Christian, Byzantine, and modern—is the degree to which the poet achieves the depth of thought he seeks. Identity—even proximity—between the two voices localizes history and fails to universalize thought, including the eroticism of the enclave of history and philosophy, as Cavafy would see it. In this rather complex notion of poeticizing, the poet would "infuse" his unique Greek category of metonymy, working at once with the "hidden and the open" forces at play.[1] Thus, the various types of rejected poems suffer the fate of

---

[1] Panagiotis Roilos's groundbreaking book *C. P. Cavafy: The Economics of Metonymy* (Chicago and Urbana 2009) is the first study of metonymic discursive strategies in Cavafy's work.

"localized thought" that the poet put aside as an experiment in the "confessional" mode of his writing. This would seem to be what lurks behind Cavafy's stance as concerns his position on private printings, re-printings, and the correction of various sheaves and broadsheets of his poems in order to give them as presents to friends and acquaintances.

But more than that, the poet appears to want to unify his sexuality with his thought, together with the historicity that defines him as a Greek poet in the continuum of Greek poetry that uses open and closed forms of metonymy. And very much within that continuum, he works to center a unified principle, as much to personalize his poetic world as to objectify it—with the latter being of paramount importance. That is why his *personae* look in both directions, Janus-faced, toward the poet, and at once away, to a world that eroticism and history define, while they partake of philosophy.

This philosophical/universality principle, in the various categories of the surviving poems, is profoundly revealing in *The Canon*, comprising of 154 poems, the only ones Cavafy wanted to represent his life's work. The various other categories of poems (most of which were found among his papers after his death) present a serious dilemma for scholars and critics; these are the so-called *Unpublished* (or *Hidden) Poems* and *Rejected Poems,* along with a small group known as *Unfinished Poems,* together with a handful of prose poems.

Whatever may be said of these works, one thing is certain: Cavafy did not wish them to be included in his wider canon of work. But in fact, something even more complicated may be at play here. The poet keeps hidden the fact that these are "sketches" or "drafts" of ideas that may possibly have come together for him in other more accomplished poems, which took their place in the canon. As sketches, these are not identifiable as might be the drafts of a painter. They are, therefore, naturally mistaken as the "real thing." The poet's rejection of them was an expression of true wisdom. And yet what does it mean for a poet to refuse a poem's place in his own canon—what does the poet wish to tell us with that refusal? We might best understand his position by looking at one of his rejected poems ("Hidden Things") that has nevertheless captured the imagination of critics and students of the poet's work after his death:

> From all I did and all I said,
> let them not seek to find who I was.
> It stood an obstacle in my way this, altering
> my actions and my way of life.
> This stood an obstacle in my way, stopping me
> all the times I wanted to speak out.
> My most unnoticed actions,
> discreet writings, the ones most disguised—
> from these alone they'll understand me.
> But maybe it's not worth so much care,
> all this effort just to know what and who I am.
> A long time from now—in a more perfect world—
> some other made like me will appear
> and, to be sure, he will act freely.

This is, by any account, a fine representative poem of the confessional mode; it functions as a reflectively philosophical trope whose poetic value leans to one side, thus creating a maudlin reality without the respite of the "other side"—irony or the obverse meaning of metonymy, the tools of Cavafy's trade. Irony proper is easily identifiable; the poet uses it most frequently to explore the paradoxical nature of reality—and, most eloquently, the great poems abound with this type of irony: from "Awaiting the Barbarians," to "Myres, Alexandria, A.D. 340," to "On the Outskirts of Antioch," among many others.

And so, as a rule of thumb, that which is missing from the rejected poems is the second side of the argument, one of the two parts of the dialogic imagination of the Socratic irony, the "yes" and the "no" of "*Che fece ... il gran rifiuto.*" And this is the case—in some more, in others less—for all those poems that Cavafy himself rejected. And it is so with "Hidden Things," as unique and poignant an autobiographical piece as it may be. In irony, whatever stable values may be in the poem are normally undermined; and so the sense of relativism in the erotic domain comes to the foreground. This is, in large part, how Cavafy's great poems function. "Hidden Things" keeps every part of its thinking at a distance—essay-like; it will not allow an opening to the other side, hence the poet keeps it among his "unpublished" poems. In the great poems, on the other hand, such as in "Awaiting the Barbarians," both irony and metonymy are in the foreground; and while irony is everywhere visible, the intent with metonymy is to create an abstract term for the term itself—in other words, to communicate reality through abstraction. The notion of "misnomer" or "change of name" lurks in the background to show the Greek origin of the term metonymy. In Cavafy's use of metonymy we are easily transported to the Hellenistic and proto-Christian eras, along with a trans-historical motion of a sensual world, oscillating between present and past.

Each in its own way, Cavafy's great poems are quietly shocking in their genius because they "cut to the quick." They do not settle for local prurience or autobiographical revelations, as did the "confessional poetry" of the mid-twentieth century: Cavafy's poems of the *Canon* are themselves time and suffering and beauty, personified in their metonymic force—a fact that places the poet at once smack into a Hellenistic and a postmodernist tradition of his own making, with an avant-garde approach to the world around him. The poet stays clear of metaphors as well as a variety of figures that inform the various forms of modernist poetry. In his easy use of *irony* and his immensely complex use of *metonymy,* Cavafy opens a new world for Greek and modernist poetry of post twentieth-century Europe and America.

———

In the early hours of the morning, at two o'clock, Cavafy died of a stroke in the Greek hospital at Alexandria. It was the dawn of his seventieth birthday, April 29, 1932. The day before, he had reluctantly taken Holy Communion. Unable to speak, he gestured for pen and paper and drew a circle and placed in the middle of the circle a period. And so the Greek-Alexandrian poet, whom the British novelist E. M. Forster had only the year before called an admirable thinker and poet, was no more.

Despite the fact that during his lifetime his work never appeared in book form by a publishing house, his reputation as "a poet's poet" had traveled far and wide in the last several years of his life. By 1926 he was greatly honored in Greece and abroad, when the famous composer/conductor Dimitris Mitropoulos set ten of his poems to music. (This complements the setting to music, some sixty years later, of his choice of ten of Cavafy's poems by the current, well-known composer/conductor Theodore Antoniou.)[2]

In the early decades of his life Cavafy shaped his poetry to complement a persona, built around a trans-historical Greek identity. In the early years, his sexual identity was not so much hidden as it was spread out across the map of his poetry and of his historical world. In later years, he located his identity in the humble life of his ancient Alexandria, a city that defined all his walks of life: his real life and the life of his imagination through Greek history and landscape.

———

After the death of his father in 1870, the family business collapsed, and the large Cavafy family, under the care of Harikleia, their mother, moved to various places, from England to Constantinople and back to Alexandria. The series of deaths that beset them followed after the demise of his oldest brother Peter-John, who died at age forty in

---

[2] In the early 1980s the composer Theodore Antoniou had written music to ten poems of the Cavafy canon. They were to be sung at the Tanglewood Summer Festival, and he needed English text to replace the Greek and to fit to his music. I undertook that daunting task with some trepidation and began counting notes and syllables, paying heed to the composer's musical rhythms, and to Cavafy's free, relaxed iambs, while giving the English text its exact and appropriate sense—so to do justice to the Greek verse. The result was remarkable. I discovered that translating Cavafy's poetry had more to do with length of sound, of rhythm, and accented line than any complex prosody. It was this result that led me to complete his "Canon."

1891, followed at the end of that decade by Harikleia's death in 1899. Giorgos died in 1900, the second oldest, born in 1850; then Aristides died in 1902. During these years, from 1888 on, Constantine focused mainly on his poetry, which he wrote in Greek, English, and French. He had also acquired a journalist's card for the Alexandrian newspaper *Telegraphos*. He wrote some essays at this time, notably one with the title "Give back the Elgin Marbles."

In 1905 Constantine visited Athens, his third trip to the renowned city in as many years. He had by then acquired a small group of artists and intellectuals as admiring friends, among them the attractive Ion Dragoumis, who was to write two seminal articles in the Athenian press on Cavafy's poetry during those crucial years of the new century—crucial for Greek and for modernist poetry. And it was here that tragedy befell Cavafy once again: his brother Alexander who had, for the second time, traveled with him to Athens, died in August of that year, after contracting typhoid fever. And later, his brother Paul, who had been living in France, the fifth in line of the brothers, died in 1920.

In 1922 Cavafy's civil service job at Alexandria's Irrigation Department—Third Circle—of the Ministry of Public Works came to an end: he resigned with a small pension. And it was in the following year, 1923, that the poet experienced being alone in the world, without any immediate family, after the death of his sixth and last brother, John, born in 1861, a mere two years younger than himself. It was at this time that the poet wrote out his will, appointing Alekos Sengopoulos the main heir and executor of his literary work and his estate. The poet was by now acquiring a quiet renown, both in Athens and in London. In Athens, a large group of Greek artists and intellectuals, some sixty of them, signed a manifesto, defending Cavafy's poetry against slanderous critics. In London, his cause was taken up by T. S. Eliot, who published the poem "Ithaca" in his magazine, *Criterion,* in 1924. By 1926 Cavafy became the recipient of The Order of the Phoenix by the Greek government; he was subsequently appointed to the international committee for the Rupert Brooke memorial statue that was erected on the island of Skyros. And, with the intervention of E. M. Forster, several writers responded with great interest in his work; among these were Arnold Toynbee and T. E. Lawrence.

By the early 1920's Cavafy's work acquires a different kind of maturity: it reveals a level of complexity in thought and "looseness" in prosody; a sure-footedness with historical subject matter; and a revelation and openness with the erotic world that he has been creating for himself for several decades. His "Greater Greece" does not only extend from Alexandria, Constantinople, and Athens, but the expanse begins internally, with a history that is more akin to the ancient historians, and with philosophical ethics alongside the openness of Socratic Eros. Cavafy abhorred Gibbon as a historian—the poet's notion of history was of an entirely different order. He had to find the historian in himself through his own poetry, rather than apply a historical order of the historians of his time. Choosing the persons from history that suited his thought, he created his own version of a historical continuum from late antiquity and the proto-Christian era. And in that choice, his main tool of expression was a sometimes humble, sometimes sharp form of "colloquial" expression which we call "irony"—one of the more eloquent Greek words with which to cover all sorts of intellectual "twists and turns," from Homer to Sokrates to Michael Psellos and Theodoros Prodromos to Cavafy.

In conclusion, here the poet Giorgos Seferis speaks about Cavafy in his "Letter to a Foreign Friend":

> He is a mythologist with an astonishing feeling for history … One is never quite sure when one reads him whether a youth who works in a poor black-smith's shop in contemporary Alexandria will not turn up in the evening at one of the dives where subjects of Ptolemy Lathyros are holding revels, or if the favorite of Antiochos Epiphanes has not in mind to discuss with the King the outcome of

Rommel's operation on Libya. Surrounded with tombs and epitaphs—it is Cavafy I am speaking of—he lives in a huge cemetery, where with torment, he invokes endlessly the resurrection of a young body; of an Adonis who, as the years pass, seems to change and become vilified by a love ...[3]

As maker of myths, Cavafy conveys an ethical world, which is consistent with the entire sweep of Greek philosophy. Seferis might have also added: "knowledge as *mnêmosynê*" brings forth that astonishing feeling for persons in history; and that is what turns the poet into a maker of myths, responsible for the release of the idea into philosophical and poetic expression.

---

[3] G. Seferis, *On the Greek Style: Selected Essays in Poetry and Hellenism*, trans. R. Warner and T. D. Frangopoulos (Boston 1966), 175.

Editor's Note

The present edition is partly based on a critical edition I am preparing of the 154 poems that constitute what is known as Cavafy's "Canon." That critical edition includes a detailed apparatus criticus with the different readings and revisions/corrections presented in Cavafy's manuscripts and printed texts. No critical edition, with apparatus criticus, has appeared so far. George Savidis's 1963 two-volume edition and its subsequent revised and expanded versions (see his 1984 one-volume edition [Ποιήματα, 1897-1933, Athens 1984] and the 1991 revised two-volume edition [see Bibliography]) are useful. They do not, however, report variants or revisions/corrections, and each of these editions offers different versions of the orthographic idiosyncracies of Cavafy's poetic language. For example, the word κομμάτι is spelled as κομάτι or as κομμάτι in different editions of Savidis.[1] Savidis does not explain that in some manuscripts/printed texts Cavafy spells it as κομάτι, while in others as κομμάτι; since no apparatus criticus or text-critical notes are provided, careful readers are left puzzled by this apparent discrepancy in his editions. Similar problems occur when one notices that:

a) in his 1984 edition, Savidis prints the form ἔδωσε in line 31 of the poem Ἰθάκη and in line 18 of Ἀπὸ τὴν σχολὴν τοῦ περιωνύμου φιλοσόφου, παρέδοσαν in line 34 of Ἡ κηδεία τοῦ Σαρπηδόνος,

---

[1] It is worth observing that Cavafy spells participles like κρυμένη/μισοκρυμένα (in Μιὰ νύχτα line 2 and in Ὅταν διεγείρονται line 4, respectively) with single μ—contrary to the widely established spelling with double μ. See θαμένη in Ἡ πόλις line 4, ἀναμένη in Πολυέλαιος line 6, κομένα in Ἐν τῇ ὁδῷ line 2, ἀναμένα in Κεριά lines 2 and 10, σκυμένος in Ἕνας γέρος line 2 and in Ρωτοῦσε γιὰ τὴν ποιότητα— line 5, ἐπιστραμένο in Τὰ ἄλογα τοῦ Ἀχιλλέως line 11 (but cf. ἐπιτετραμμένον μένοντες in the poem Σ' ἕνα βιβλίο παληό— line 10), θαμένος in Εὐρίωνος τάφος line 4, ἀναθρεμένοι in Εἰς Ἰταλικὴν παραλίαν line 4 (8), ἀναμένη in Στὸ πληκτικὸ χωριό line 10, προκομένους and κατεστραμένος in Ἂς φρόντιζαν lines 21 and 32.

παρέδοσε in line 6 of Ὁ καθρέπτης στὴν εἴσοδο, and διέδοσε in line 31 of Εἰς τὰ περίχωρα τῆς Ἀντιοχείας;

b) whereas, in his 1991 edition, he prints the forms παρέδοσαν, παρέδωσε, and διέδωσε in the last three poems, but no explanation is provided; and

c) in his 1963 edition, he prints ἔδωσε and ἔδοσε in Ἰθάκη and in Ἀπὸ τὴν σχολὴν τοῦ περιωνύμου φιλοσόφου, respectively. Again, no text-critical notes are provided.

Another similar case is the phrase μὲς στήν/μὲς στές (or μὲς στό/μὲς στά, etc.), which appears as μὲς τήν/μὲς τές in certain manuscripts.[2] Finally, in certain cases the use of grave accent differs from Savidis's 1963 edition to his 1984 edition. Unfortunately, there is no systematic study of the grammar of Cavafy's linguistic registers (as, on the contrary, there is a grammar of the language, for instance, of Alkaios and Sappho), which, although it would not need to be as detailed as that of Eva-Maria Hamm's *Grammatik zu Sappho und Alkaios* (Berlin 1957), would considerably help critical editors and scholars of Cavafy.

Since this is not a critical edition, but rather a reader's text with facing translation, I have refrained from providing an apparatus criticus with variants and revisions/corrections.

Demetrios Yatromanolakis

---

[2] Note that in his 1984 edition and, even more significantly, in his 1991 revised edition, Savidis prints μὲς τὲς λειτουργικὲς φωνὲς καὶ συμφωνίες in line 6 of Στὴν ἐκκλησία, while in his 1963 edition he prints μὲ τὲς λειτουργικὲς φωνὲς καὶ συμφωνίες. These observations by no means attempt to undermine the importance of the most useful editions and scholarly work by Savidis (see, especially, his Οἱ Καβαφικὲς Ἐκδόσεις (1891–1932). Περιγραφὴ καὶ Σχόλιο: Βιβλιογραφικὴ Μελέτη, Athens 1966), but intend to emphasize the need for a critical edition that includes an apparatus criticus with the variants and revisions/corrections found in Cavafy's printed texts and manuscripts.

Bibliography

EDITIONS

Cavafy, C. P. [Kavafis, Konstantinos Petrou]. *Ποιήματα*. Ed. R. Sengopoulou. Alexandria 1935.

———. *Ἀνέκδοτα Πεζὰ Κείμενα*. Ed. M. Peridis. Athens 1963.

———. *Πεζά*. Ed. G. A. Papoutsakis. Athens 1963.

———. *Ἀνέκδοτα Ποιήματα*. Ed. G. P. Savidis. Athens 1968.

———. *Costantino Kavafis: Εἰς τὸ Φῶς τῆς Ἡμέρας*. Ed. R. Lavagnini. Palermo 1979.

———. *Ἀνέκδοτα Σημειώματα Ποιητικῆς καὶ Ἠθικῆς*. Ed. G. P. Savidis. Athens 1983.

———. *Ἀποκηρυγμένα Ποιήματα καὶ Μεταφράσεις*. Ed. G. P. Savidis. Athens 1983.

———. *Τὰ Ποιήματα*. 2 vols. Ed. G. P. Savidis. Revised edition. Athens 1991. [First edition 1963].

———. *Κρυμμένα Ποιήματα*. Ed. G. P. Savidis. Athens 1993. [Revised edition of Cavafy 1968].

———. *Ἀτελῆ Ποιήματα*. Ed. R. Lavagnini. Athens 1994.

———. *Τὰ Πεζά*. Ed. M. Pieris. Athens 2003.

SELECT TRANSLATIONS

Numerous translations of C. P. Cavafy's poetic work have appeared in the past decade, but the reliability of several of them is sometimes undermined by a somewhat tenuous comprehension of the subtleties and complexities of the original Greek texts.

Dalven, R. *The Complete Poems of Cavafy*. With an introduction by W. H. Auden. Expanded edition. New York 1976.

Keeley, E. and P. Sherrard. *C. P. Cavafy: Collected Poems.* Ed. G. Savidis. Revised edition. Princeton, N. J. 1992.

Sachperoglou, E. *C. P. Cavafy: The Collected Poems.* Oxford 2007.

SELECT BOOKS AND ARTICLES

Anton, J. P. *The Poetry and Poetics of Constantine P. Cavafy: Aesthetic Visions of Sensual Reality.* Chur, Switzerland 1995.

Bowra, C. M., "Constantine Cavafy and the Greek Past," in *idem, The Creative Experiment,* London 1949, 29–60.

Caires, V. A. "Originality and Eroticism: Constantine Cavafy and the Alexandrian Epigram," *Byzantine and Modern Greek Studies* 6 (1980): 131–55.

Cavafy, C. P. [Kavafis, K. P.]. Αὐτόγραφα Ποιήματα *(1896–1910).* Τὸ Τετράδιο Σεγκοπούλου σὲ Πανομοιότυπη Ἔκδοση. Ed. G. P. Savidis. Athens 1968.

Colaclides, P. "Ἡ Γλῶσσα τοῦ Καβάφη," in Πρακτικὰ Τρίτου Συμποσίου Ποίησης, Athens 1984, 119–46.

Dallas, G. Καβάφης καὶ Ἱστορία: Αἰσθητικὲς Λειτουργίες. Athens 1974.

———. Καβάφης καὶ ἡ Δεύτερη Σοφιστική. Athens 1984.

Daskalopoulos, D. Βιβλιογραφία Κ. Π. Καβάφη *(1886–2000).* Thessalonike 2003.

Dimaras, K. Σύμμικτα, 3: Περὶ Καβάφη. Athens 1992.

Faubion, J. D. "In Passing: Cavafy's Ontology of the Emotions and the Theoretico-poetics of Liminalism," in Roilos 2010, 20–49.

Haas, D. *Le problème religieux dans l' oeuvre de Cavafy: Les années de formation (1882–1905).* Paris 1996.

———. "Around the Revisions of Cavafy's 'Σ' ἔνα βιβλίο παληό—' ('In an Old Book—'), 1922–1929," in Roilos 2010, 245–262.

Ilinskayia, S. Κ. Π. Καβάφης: Οἱ Δρόμοι πρὸς τὸ Ρεαλισμὸ στὴν Ποίηση τοῦ 20οῦ Αἰῶνα. Athens 1983.

Jakobson, R. and P. Colaclides. "Grammatical Imagery in Cavafy's Poem 'Θυμήσου Σῶμα' ...," Linguistics 20 (1966): 51–59.

Karampini-Iatrou, M. Ἡ Βιβλιοθήκη Κ. Π. Καβάφη. Athens 2003.

Keeley, E. Cavafy's Alexandria. Princeton, N.J. 1996.

Liddell, R. Cavafy: A Critical Biography. London 1974.

Peri, M. Quattro saggi su Kavafis. Milan 1977.

Pieris, M. Χῶρος, Φῶς καὶ Λόγος: Ἡ Διαλεκτικὴ τοῦ "Μέσα"-"Ἔξω" στὴν Ποίηση τοῦ Καβάφη. Athens 1992.

Roilos, P. C. P. Cavafy: The Economics of Metonymy. Chicago and Urbana 2009.

———. (ed.). Imagination and Logos: Essays on C. P. Cavafy. Cambridge, Mass. 2010.

———. "The Seduction of the 'Real': Personification and Mimesis in C. P. Cavafy," in Roilos 2010, 219–244.

Savidis, G. P. Οἱ Καβαφικὲς Ἐκδόσεις (1891–1932). Περιγραφὴ καὶ Σχόλιο: Βιβλιογραφικὴ Μελέτη. Athens 1966.

———. Μικρὰ Καβαφικά. Vol. 1. Athens 1985.

———. Μικρὰ Καβαφικά. Vol. 2. Athens 1987.

Sedgwick Kosofsky, E. "Cavafy, Proust, and the Queer Little Gods," in Roilos 2010, 1–20.

Tsirkas, S. Ὁ Καβάφης καὶ ἡ Ἐποχή του. Second edition. Athens 1971.

———. Ὁ Πολιτικὸς Καβάφης. Athens 1971.

Vayenas, N. "The Language of Irony (Towards a Definition of the Poetry of Cavafy)," Byzantine and Modern Greek Studies 5 (1979): 43–56.

———. (ed.). *Συνομιλῶντας μὲ τὸν Καβάφη: Ἀνθολογία Ξένων Καβαφο-γενῶν Ποιημάτων*. Thessalonike 2000.

Yatromanolakis, D. "The Numismatics of *Poiêsis*: Art, Money, and Authority in Ezra Pound and C. P. Cavafy," in Roilos 2010, 71–89.

Yourcenar, M. *Présentation critique de Constantin Cavafy, 1863–1933. Suivie d' une traduction intégrale de ses poèmes par M. Yourcenar et Constantin Dimaras*. Paris 1958.

ΠΟΙΗΜΑΤΑ

Η ΠΟΛΙΣ

Εἶπες· «Θὰ πάγω σ᾿ ἄλλη γῆ, θὰ πάγω σ᾿ ἄλλη θάλασσα.
Μιὰ πόλις ἄλλη θὰ βρεθεῖ καλλίτερη ἀπὸ αὐτή.
Κάθε προσπάθεια μου μιὰ καταδίκη εἶναι γραφτή·
κ᾿ εἶν᾿ ἡ καρδιά μου—σὰν νεκρός—θαμένη.
Ὁ νοῦς μου ὡς πότε μὲς στὸν μαρασμὸν αὐτὸν θὰ μένει.
Ὅπου τὸ μάτι μου γυρίσω, ὅπου κι ἂν δῶ
ἐρείπια μαῦρα τῆς ζωῆς μου βλέπω ἐδῶ,
ποὺ τόσα χρόνια πέρασα καὶ ρήμαξα καὶ χάλασα.»

Καινούριους τόπους δὲν θὰ βρεῖς, δὲν θά ᾿βρεις ἄλλες θάλασσες.
Ἡ πόλις θὰ σὲ ἀκολουθεῖ. Στοὺς δρόμους θὰ γυρνᾶς
τοὺς ἴδιους. Καὶ στὲς γειτονιὲς τὲς ἴδιες θὰ γερνᾶς·
καὶ μὲς στὰ ἴδια σπίτια αὐτὰ θ᾿ ἀσπρίζεις.
Πάντα στὴν πόλι αὐτὴ θὰ φθάνεις. Γιὰ τὰ ἀλλοῦ—μὴ ἐλπίζεις—
δὲν ἔχει πλοῖο γιὰ σέ, δὲν ἔχει ὁδό.
Ἔτσι ποὺ τὴ ζωή σου ρήμαξες ἐδῶ
στὴν κώχη τούτη τὴν μικρή, σ᾿ ὅλην τὴν γῆ τὴν χάλασες.

Note: Cavafy's way of spelling Greek words is sometimes personal or idiosyncratic. See, for example, his use of ἡ for the nominative plural of the article ἡ.

THE CITY

You said, "I will go to another land, another sea,
a different city will be found for me, better than this;
here it's written: in each endeavor I am condemned;
and my heart (as of the dead) is buried.
My mind (how long) in this withering world, how can it last?
Wherever I turn to look, wherever my eyes rest,
I see ruins, the charred ruins of my life here,
after so many years gone by, barren and spent."

New lands will not be yours to find, you will not find other seas.
The city will follow you everywhere. You'll wander the streets,
these same streets, grow old in the same neighborhoods—
in the same houses you'll turn a soft pallor and gray.
You'll end up in this city. As for other things, other places,
cease your hoping—no ship exists for you, no road is left.
Just as you've torn your life apart in this patch of earth,
you've turned it to a wasteland the whole world over.

Η ΣΑΤΡΑΠΕΙΑ

Τί συμφορά, ἐνῶ εἶσαι καμωμένος
γιὰ τὰ ὡραῖα καὶ μεγάλα ἔργα
ἡ ἄδικη αὐτή σου ἡ τύχη πάντα
ἐνθάρρυνσι κ' ἐπιτυχία νὰ σὲ ἀρνεῖται·
νὰ σ' ἐμποδίζουν εὐτελεῖς συνήθειες,
καὶ μικροπρέπειες, κι ἀδιαφορίες.
Καὶ τί φρικτὴ ἡ μέρα ποὺ ἐνδίδεις
(ἡ μέρα ποὺ ἀφέθηκες κ' ἐνδίδεις),
καὶ φεύγεις ὁδοιπόρος γιὰ τὰ Σοῦσα,
καὶ πηαίνεις στὸν μονάρχην Ἀρταξέρξη
ποὺ εὐνοϊκὰ σὲ βάζει στὴν αὐλή του,
καὶ σὲ προσφέρει σατραπεῖες καὶ τέτοια.
Καὶ σὺ τὰ δέχεσαι μὲ ἀπελπισία
αὐτὰ τὰ πράγματα ποὺ δὲν τὰ θέλεις.
Ἄλλα ζητεῖ ἡ ψυχή σου, γι' ἄλλα κλαίει·
τὸν ἔπαινο τοῦ Δήμου καὶ τῶν Σοφιστῶν,
τὰ δύσκολα καὶ τ' ἀνεκτίμητα Εὖγε·
τὴν Ἀγορά, τὸ Θέατρο, καὶ τοὺς Στεφάνους.
Αὐτὰ ποῦ θὰ σ' τὰ δώσει ὁ Ἀρταξέρξης,
αὐτὰ ποῦ θὰ τὰ βρεῖς στὴ σατραπεία·
καὶ τί ζωὴ χωρὶς αὐτὰ θὰ κάμεις.

SATRAPY

What a pity, cut out as you are
for beautiful and grand works,
this unjust fate of yours always denies you
encouragement, never brings you success;
a pity, your cheap habits become obstacles,
your petty ways, your indifference.
And what a dreadful day when you give in,
(the day you let yourself go and give in),
and leave on foot on the road to Sousa
to reach the monarch Artaxerxes,
who graciously places you in his court
and offers you satrapies and such things.
And you, you accept them in despair,
all these that you'd rather not have.
Your soul craves and weeps for other things;
the City's tribute and the Sophists' praise,
the rare, the priceless acclaim: the Agora—
a speaking forum, the Theatre, the Crowns of Laurel.
How can Artaxerxes give you these,
where will you find them inside the satrapy;
and without them, what kind of life will you live?

ΣΟΦΟΙ ΔΕ ΠΡΟΣΙΟΝΤΩΝ

> Θεοὶ μὲν γὰρ μελλόντων, ἄνθρωποι δὲ γιγνομένων,
> σοφοὶ δὲ προσιόντων αἰσθάνονται.
>
> Φιλόστρατος, *Τὰ ἐς τὸν Τυανέα Ἀπολλώνιον*, VIII.7.

Οἱ ἄνθρωποι γνωρίζουν τὰ γινόμενα.
Τὰ μέλλοντα γνωρίζουν οἱ θεοί,
πλήρεις καὶ μόνοι κάτοχοι πάντων τῶν φώτων.
Ἐκ τῶν μελλόντων οἱ σοφοὶ τὰ προσερχόμενα
ἀντιλαμβάνονται. Ἡ ἀκοὴ

αὐτῶν κάποτε ἐν ὥραις σοβαρῶν σπουδῶν
ταράττεται. Ἡ μυστικὴ βοὴ
τοὺς ἔρχεται τῶν πλησιαζόντων γεγονότων.
Καὶ τὴν προσέχουν εὐλαβεῖς. Ἐνῶ εἰς τὴν ὁδὸν
ἔξω, οὐδὲν ἀκούουν οἱ λαοί.

THE WISE KNOW WHAT HAPPENS NEXT

Thus the gods know of future things, men of what happens
now, while the wise know of things to happen next.

Philostratos, *Life of Apollonios of Tyana*, VIII.7.

Mortals know the present turn of things,
what's to come is left the gods to know,
they who hold the long light of wisdom.
Of future time, wise men perceive
approaching things. Now and again,

while deep in contemplation, their hearing
breaks down. It comes to them,
the secret rumble of nearing events.
And they stop to look in awe. While on the street
outside, the masses hear nothing at all.

ΜΑΡΤΙΑΙ ΕΙΔΟΙ

Τὰ μεγαλεῖα νὰ φοβᾶσαι, ὦ ψυχή.
Καὶ τὲς φιλοδοξίες σου νὰ ὑπερνικήσεις
ἂν δὲν μπορεῖς, μὲ δισταγμὸ καὶ προφυλάξεις
νὰ τὲς ἀκολουθεῖς. Κι ὅσο ἐμπροστὰ προβαίνεις,
τόσο ἐξεταστική, προσεκτικὴ νὰ εἶσαι.

Κι ὅταν θὰ φθάσεις στὴν ἀκμή σου, Καῖσαρ πιά·
ἔτσι περιωνύμου ἀνθρώπου σχῆμα ὅταν λάβεις,
τότε κυρίως πρόσεξε σὰ βγεῖς στὸν δρόμον ἔξω,
ἐξουσιαστὴς περίβλεπτος μὲ συνοδεία,
ἂν τύχει καὶ πλησιάσει ἀπὸ τὸν ὄχλο
κανένας Ἀρτεμίδωρος, ποὺ φέρνει γράμμα,
καὶ λέγει βιαστικὰ «Διάβασε ἀμέσως τοῦτα,
εἶναι μεγάλα πράγματα ποὺ σ᾽ ἐνδιαφέρουν»,
μὴ λείψεις νὰ σταθεῖς· μὴ λείψεις ν᾽ ἀναβάλεις
κάθε ὁμιλίαν ἢ δουλειά· μὴ λείψεις τοὺς διαφόρους
ποὺ χαιρετοῦν καὶ προσκυνοῦν νὰ τοὺς παραμερίσεις
(τοὺς βλέπεις πιὸ ἀργά)· ἂς περιμένει ἀκόμη
κ᾽ ἡ Σύγκλητος αὐτή, κ᾽ εὐθὺς νὰ τὰ γνωρίσεις
τὰ σοβαρὰ γραφόμενα τοῦ Ἀρτεμιδώρου.

THE IDES OF MARCH

Fear, O my soul, fear this specious grandeur.
And if you cannot bridle your ambitions,
at least pursue them with caution,
hesitantly. And the higher you strive,
the more inquiring, the more watchful you must be.

And when you reach your summit, Caesar at last—
when you are anointed for the part of a famous man—
then, especially then, take care as you go out into the street,
a man conspicuous for his power and retinue;
and should it chance that someone from the crowd come near,
a certain Artemidoros, bringing a letter,
and saying in haste, "Read this at once,
there are urgent things here that concern you,"
do not fail to linger, don't fail to put off
every discussion or issue; don't fail to brush
aside all those who salute and bow
(you can see them later); let them wait, even
the Senate itself, and turn at once your attention
to the serious letter of Artemidoros.

ΤΕΛΕΙΩΜΕΝΑ

Μέσα στὸν φόβο καὶ στὲς ὑποψίες,
μὲ ταραγμένο νοῦ καὶ τρομαγμένα μάτια,
λυώνουμε καὶ σχεδιάζουμε τὸ πῶς νὰ κάμουμε
γιὰ ν' ἀποφύγουμε τὸν βέβαιο
τὸν κίνδυνο ποὺ ἔτσι φρικτὰ μᾶς ἀπειλεῖ.
Κι ὅμως λανθάνουμε, δὲν εἶν' αὐτὸς στὸν δρόμο·
ψεύτικα ἦσαν τὰ μηνύματα
(ἢ δὲν τ' ἀκούσαμε, ἢ δὲν τὰ νοιώσαμε καλά).
Ἄλλη καταστροφή, ποὺ δὲν τὴν φανταζόμεθαν,
ἐξαφνική, ραγδαία πέφτει ἐπάνω μας,
κι ἀνέτοιμους—ποῦ πιὰ καιρός—μᾶς συνεπαίρνει.

FINISHED

Amid the fear and the suspicions,
with unhinged mind and panicked eyes,
we melt down and make plans
how to avoid necessity,
the horror that threatens us.
Only we're mistaken, that's not what we find in our path;
the signs were all false
(either we didn't hear well or didn't understand).
A different disaster, one never imagined,
rapidly falls upon us, unexpected;
we're unprepared—no more time; it now drags us along.

ΑΠΟΛΕΙΠΕΙΝ Ο ΘΕΟΣ ΑΝΤΩΝΙΟΝ

Σὰν ἔξαφνα, ὥρα μεσάνυχτ᾽, ἀκουσθεῖ
ἀόρατος θίασος νὰ περνᾶ
μὲ μουσικὲς ἐξαίσιες, μὲ φωνές—
τὴν τύχη σου ποὺ ἐνδίδει πιά, τὰ ἔργα σου
ποὺ ἀπέτυχαν, τὰ σχέδια τῆς ζωῆς σου
ποὺ βγῆκαν ὅλα πλάνες, μὴ ἀνωφέλετα θρηνήσεις.
Σὰν ἕτοιμος ἀπὸ καιρό, σὰ θαρραλέος,
ἀποχαιρέτα την, τὴν Ἀλεξάνδρεια ποὺ φεύγει.
Πρὸ πάντων νὰ μὴ γελασθεῖς, μὴν πεῖς πὼς ἦταν
ἕνα ὄνειρο, πὼς ἀπατήθηκεν ἡ ἀκοή σου·
μάταιες ἐλπίδες τέτοιες μὴν καταδεχθεῖς.
Σὰν ἕτοιμος ἀπὸ καιρό, σὰ θαρραλέος,
σὰν ποὺ ταιριάζει σε ποὺ ἀξιώθηκες μιὰ τέτοια πόλι,
πλησίασε σταθερὰ πρὸς τὸ παράθυρο,
κι ἄκουσε μὲ συγκίνησιν, ἀλλ᾽ ὄχι
μὲ τῶν δειλῶν τὰ παρακάλια καὶ παράπονα,
ὡς τελευταία ἀπόλαυσι τοὺς ἤχους,
τὰ ἐξαίσια ὄργανα τοῦ μυστικοῦ θιάσου,
κι ἀποχαιρέτα την, τὴν Ἀλεξάνδρεια ποὺ χάνεις.

THE GOD ABANDONS ANTHONY

When suddenly, at the midnight hour, you hear
an invisible troupe of players passing by
with exquisite music, accompanying voices—
your compromising luck, your failed work,
your life's plans that proved deceptive—
don't mourn them now uselessly.
As one prepared long ago, one graced with courage,
say your goodbyes to her, the Alexandria that is leaving.
Above all, don't fool yourself, don't ever say
it was a dream, that your ears deceived you;
don't demean yourself with empty hopes like these.
As one prepared long ago, one graced with courage,
as befits your stature, one who took such a city,
go steadily closer toward the window,
and listen, and be deeply moved, but not with
the pleas of a coward and plaintive whines,
listen to the music, your parting comfort,
the exquisite organs of the secret players,
and say goodbye to her, the Alexandria you are losing.

Ο ΘΕΟΔΟΤΟΣ

Ἂν εἶσαι ἀπ' τοὺς ἀληθινὰ ἐκλεκτούς,
τὴν ἐπικράτησί σου κύτταζε πῶς ἀποκτᾶς.
Ὅσο κι ἂν δοξασθεῖς, τὰ κατορθώματά σου
στὴν Ἰταλία καὶ στὴν Θεσσαλία
ὅσο κι ἂν διαλαλοῦν ἡ πολιτεῖες,
ὅσα ψηφίσματα τιμητικὰ
κι ἂν σ' ἔβγαλαν στὴ Ρώμη οἱ θαυμασταί σου,
μήτε ἡ χαρά σου, μήτε ὁ θρίαμβος θὰ μείνουν,
μήτε ἀνώτερος—τί ἀνώτερος;—ἄνθρωπος θὰ αἰσθανθεῖς,
ὅταν, στὴν Ἀλεξάνδρεια, ὁ Θεόδοτος σὲ φέρει,
ἐπάνω σὲ σινὶ αἱματωμένο,
τοῦ ἀθλίου Πομπηΐου τὸ κεφάλι.

Καὶ μὴ ἐπαναπαύεσαι ποὺ στὴν ζωή σου
περιωρισμένη, τακτοποιημένη, καὶ πεζή,
τέτοια θεαματικὰ καὶ φοβερὰ δὲν ἔχει.
Ἴσως αὐτὴν τὴν ὥρα εἰς κανενὸς γειτόνου σου
τὸ νοικοκερεμένο σπίτι μπαίνει—
ἀόρατος, ἄϋλος—ὁ Θεόδοτος,
φέρνοντας τέτοιο ἕνα φρικτὸ κεφάλι.

THEODOTOS

If you are one of the truly chosen,
be careful how you manage to prevail.
No matter how much you are glorified, how much
your great exploits are praised in the cities
of Italy and Thessaly,
however many honors
your admirers decree for you in Rome,
neither your joy nor your triumph will last,
nor will you feel superior—superior indeed!—
when, in Alexandria, Theodotos brings you
upon a bloodied tray
pitiful Pompey's head.

And don't rest assured that in your life,
one constrained, settled, and boring,
that you know no such horrible spectacles.
Perhaps this very hour in some neighbor's
tidy house, enters—
invisible, bodiless—Theodotos,
bearing just such a shocking head.

MONOTONIA

Τὴν μιὰ μονότονην ἡμέραν ἄλλη
μονότονη, ἀπαράλλακτη ἀκολουθεῖ. Θὰ γίνουν
τὰ ἴδια πράγματα, θὰ ξαναγίνουν πάλι—
ἡ ὅμοιες στιγμὲς μᾶς βρίσκουνε καὶ μᾶς ἀφίνουν.

Μῆνας περνᾶ καὶ φέρνει ἄλλον μῆνα.
Αὐτὰ ποὺ ἔρχονται κανεὶς εὔκολα τὰ εἰκάζει·
εἶναι τὰ χθεσινὰ τὰ βαρετὰ ἐκεῖνα.
Καὶ καταντᾶ τὸ αὔριο πιὰ σὰν αὔριο νὰ μὴ μοιάζει.

MONOTONY

One monotonous day follows another
identical day. The same
things that happen will happen again—
the same moments finding us, the same ones leaving us.

A month passes, ushering in another month.
One can easily perceive what's coming:
yesterday's same boring things.
With tomorrow not resembling tomorrow at all.

ΙΘΑΚΗ

Σὰ βγεῖς στὸν πηγαιμὸ γιὰ τὴν Ἰθάκη,
νὰ εὔχεσαι νά 'ναι μακρὺς ὁ δρόμος,
γεμάτος περιπέτειες, γεμάτος γνώσεις.
Τοὺς Λαιστρυγόνας καὶ τοὺς Κύκλωπας,
τὸν θυμωμένο Ποσειδῶνα μὴ φοβᾶσαι,
τέτοια στὸν δρόμο σου ποτέ σου δὲν θὰ βρεῖς,
ἂν μέν' ἡ σκέψις σου ὑψηλή, ἂν ἐκλεκτὴ
συγκίνησις τὸ πνεῦμα καὶ τὸ σῶμα σου ἀγγίζει.
Τοὺς Λαιστρυγόνας καὶ τοὺς Κύκλωπας,
τὸν ἄγριο Ποσειδῶνα δὲν θὰ συναντήσεις,
ἂν δὲν τοὺς κουβανεῖς μὲς στὴν ψυχή σου,
ἂν ἡ ψυχή σου δὲν τοὺς στήνει ἐμπρός σου.

Νὰ εὔχεσαι νά 'ναι μακρὺς ὁ δρόμος.
Πολλὰ τὰ καλοκαιρινὰ πρωϊὰ νὰ εἶναι
ποὺ μὲ τί εὐχαρίστησι, μὲ τί χαρὰ
θὰ μπαίνεις σὲ λιμένας πρωτοειδωμένους·
νὰ σταματήσεις σ' ἐμπορεῖα Φοινικικά,
καὶ τὲς καλὲς πραγμάτειες ν' ἀποκτήσεις,
σεντέφια καὶ κοράλλια, κεχριμπάρια κ' ἔβενους,
καὶ ἡδονικὰ μυρωδικὰ κάθε λογῆς,
ὅσο μπορεῖς πιὸ ἄφθονα ἡδονικὰ μυρωδικά·
σὲ πόλεις Αἰγυπτιακὲς πολλὲς νὰ πᾶς,
νὰ μάθεις καὶ νὰ μάθεις ἀπ' τοὺς σπουδασμένους.

Πάντα στὸν νοῦ σου νά 'χεις τὴν Ἰθάκη.
Τὸ φθάσιμον ἐκεῖ εἶν' ὁ προορισμός σου.
Ἀλλὰ μὴ βιάζεις τὸ ταξεῖδι διόλου.
Καλλίτερα χρόνια πολλὰ νὰ διαρκέσει·
καὶ γέρος πιὰ ν' ἀράξεις στὸ νησί,
πλούσιος μὲ ὅσα κέρδισες στὸν δρόμο,
μὴ προσδοκῶντας πλούτη νὰ σὲ δώσει ἡ Ἰθάκη.

ITHACA

As you set out on your passage to Ithaca,
pray that the road be a long one,
full of adventure, full of learning.
Those Laestrygonians and the Cyclops,
angry Poseidon—be not afraid of them,
you'll never find them crossing your path,
as long as you're made of loftier thoughts, as long as an exquisite
passion stirs your spirit and your body.
Those Laestrygonians and the Cyclops,
wild Poseidon—you'll never meet with them,
unless you carry them deep inside you,
unless your soul erects them before you.

Pray your journey be a long one;
that there be many a summer's morning
when, with what pleasure, what joy,
you come to ports espied for the first time;
that you stop at Phoenician trading posts,
revelling in their goodly wares,
mother of pearl and coral, amber and ebony,
myriad perfumes of every sensual abandon;
and that you visit hosts of Egyptian cities,
to learn and learn from those schooled in wisdom.

Keep Ithaca always in view.
Getting there is your final purpose.
But never speed up your journey, no.
Better to let it last for many years;
and anchor on the island when you're old;
rich with what you gained on the road,
never expect Ithaca to give you riches.

Ἡ Ἰθάκη σ᾽ ἔδωσε τ᾽ ὡραῖο ταξεῖδι.
Χωρὶς αὐτὴν δὲν θά ᾽βγαινες στὸν δρόμο.
Ἄλλα δὲν ἔχει νὰ σὲ δώσει πιά.

Κι ἂν πτωχικὴ τὴν βρεῖς, ἡ Ἰθάκη δὲν σὲ γέλασε.
Ἔτσι σοφὸς ποὺ ἔγινες, μὲ τόση πεῖρα,
ἤδη θὰ τὸ κατάλαβες ἡ Ἰθάκες τί σημαίνουν.

Ithaca granted you the beautiful journey.
Without her you'd never have taken to the road.
She has nothing left to give you.

And if you find her poor, Ithaca will not have fooled you.
Wise as you've now become, rich with experience,
you'll have already understood what these Ithacas mean.

ΟΣΟ ΜΠΟΡΕΙΣ

Κι ἂν δὲν μπορεῖς νὰ κάμεις τὴν ζωή σου ὅπως τὴν θέλεις,
τοῦτο προσπάθησε τουλάχιστον
ὅσο μπορεῖς: μὴν τὴν ἐξευτελίζεις
μὲς στὴν πολλὴ συνάφεια τοῦ κόσμου,
μὲς στὲς πολλὲς κινήσεις κι ὁμιλίες.

Μὴν τὴν ἐξευτελίζεις πηαίνοντάς την,
γυρίζοντας συχνὰ κ' ἐκθέτοντάς την
στῶν σχέσεων καὶ τῶν συναναστροφῶν
τὴν καθημερινὴν ἀνοησία,
ὣς ποὺ νὰ γίνει σὰ μιὰ ξένη φορτική.

22

AS MUCH AS YOU CAN

And if you cannot make your life the way you want it,
try this at least,
as much as you can: do not debase it
amid the company this world offers,
amid the wandering and idle talk.

Do not debase it by dragging it along,
here and there, exposing it so often
to your affairs, to various encounters,
the foolish daily socials,
until it becomes the stranger who bores you.

ΤΡΩΕΣ

Εἶν' ἡ προσπάθειές μας, τῶν συφοριασμένων·
εἶν' ἡ προσπάθειές μας σὰν τῶν Τρώων.
Κομμάτι κατορθώνουμε· κομμάτι
παίρνουμ' ἐπάνω μας· κι ἀρχίζουμε
νά 'χουμε θάρρος καὶ καλὲς ἐλπίδες.

Μὰ πάντα κάτι βγαίνει καὶ μᾶς σταματᾶ.
Ὁ Ἀχιλλεὺς στὴν τάφρον ἐμπροστά μας
βγαίνει καὶ μὲ φωνὲς μεγάλες μᾶς τρομάζει.—

Εἶν' ἡ προσπάθειές μας σὰν τῶν Τρώων.
Θαρροῦμε πὼς μὲ ἀπόφασι καὶ τόλμη
θ' ἀλλάξουμε τῆς τύχης τὴν καταφορά,
κ' ἔξω στεκόμεθα ν' ἀγωνισθοῦμε.

Ἀλλ' ὅταν ἡ μεγάλη κρίσις ἔλθει,
ἡ τόλμη κ' ἡ ἀπόφασίς μας χάνονται·
ταράττεται ἡ ψυχή μας, παραλύει·
κι ὁλόγυρα ἀπ' τὰ τείχη τρέχουμε
ζητῶντας νὰ γλυτώσουμε μὲ τὴν φυγή.

Ὅμως ἡ πτῶσις μας εἶναι βεβαία. Ἐπάνω,
στὰ τείχη, ἄρχισεν ἤδη ὁ θρῆνος.
Τῶν ἡμερῶν μας ἀναμνήσεις κλαῖν κ' αἰσθήματα.
Πικρὰ γιὰ μᾶς ὁ Πρίαμος κ' ἡ Ἑκάβη κλαῖνε.

TROJANS

Our efforts are those of the fated, the ill-marked men;
our efforts are like those of the Trojans.
For a while, we win out; for a while,
we forge ahead; and we begin
to take courage and have high hopes.

But always something blocks our path to stop us.
Achilles appears before us atop the trenches
and his loud shouts terrify us.—

They are—all our efforts are those of the Trojans.
We believe by being decisive and daring
we'll change our run of bad luck,
and we stand outside ready for battle.

But when the final crisis comes,
our daring and resolve vanish;
our soul is fearful, paralyzed;
and we run in circles round the walls
seeking to escape and save ourselves.

Yet our fall is certain now. Atop
the walls the dirge has already begun.
They're lamenting the memories, the aura of our days.
Bitter for us now—that Priam and Hecuba weep.

Ο ΒΑΣΙΛΕΥΣ ΔΗΜΗΤΡΙΟΣ

Ὥσπερ οὐ βασιλεύς, ἀλλ᾽ ὑποκριτής, μεταμφιέννυται
χλαμύδα φαιὰν ἀντὶ τῆς τραγικῆς ἐκείνης, καὶ διαλαθὼν
ὑπεχώρησεν.

Πλούταρχος, *Βίος Δημητρίου*

Σὰν τὸν παραίτησαν οἱ Μακεδόνες
κι ἀπέδειξαν πὼς προτιμοῦν τὸν Πύρρο
ὁ βασιλεὺς Δημήτριος (μεγάλην
εἶχε ψυχή) καθόλου—ἔτσι εἶπαν—
δὲν φέρθηκε σὰν βασιλεύς. Ἐπῆγε
κ᾽ ἔβγαλε τὰ χρυσὰ φορέματά του,
καὶ τὰ ποδήματά του πέταξε
τὰ ὁλοπόρφυρα. Μὲ ροῦχ᾽ ἁπλὰ
ντύθηκε γρήγορα καὶ ξέφυγε.
Κάμνοντας ὅμοια σὰν ἠθοποιὸς
ποὺ ὅταν ἡ παράστασις τελειώσει,
ἀλλάζει φορεσιὰ κι ἀπέρχεται.

KING DEMETRIOS

> Not like a king, but an actor, he donned a gray cloak
> instead of his tragic one and quietly stole away.
>
> Plutarch, *Life of Demetrios*

As the Makedonians gave up on him
and made clear their preference for Pyrrhos,
King Demetrios (a goodly noble soul)
did not behave—so they said—
at all like a king. He went ahead,
shed his golden robes,
discarded his purple glittering
footwear. And now, clothed
in simple garments, he slipped away;
behaving just like an actor,
who, when the performance is over,
changes into his own clothes and leaves.

Η ΔΟΞΑ ΤΩΝ ΠΤΟΛΕΜΑΙΩΝ

Εἴμ' ὁ Λαγίδης, βασιλεύς. Ὁ κάτοχος τελείως
(μὲ τὴν ἰσχύ μου καὶ τὸν πλοῦτο μου) τῆς ἡδονῆς.
Ἢ Μακεδών, ἢ βάρβαρος δὲν βρίσκεται κανεὶς
ἴσος μου, ἢ νὰ μὲ πλησιάζει κάν. Εἶναι γελοῖος
ὁ Σελευκίδης μὲ τὴν ἀγοραία του τρυφή.
Ἂν ὅμως σεῖς ἄλλα ζητεῖτε, ἰδοὺ κι αὐτὰ σαφῆ.
Ἡ πόλις ἡ διδάσκαλος, ἡ πανελλήνια κορυφή,
εἰς κάθε λόγο, εἰς κάθε τέχνη ἡ πιὸ σοφή.

THE GLORY OF THE PTOLEMIES

I'm the king here, king Lagides. In perfect knowledge
(with all my power and wealth), the possessor of sensual pleasure.
You'll not find a single Makedonian or Barbarian
my equal, not even near my equal. Seleukides
is a laughing stock, a vulgar voluptuary.
But if you're looking for the other, it's here and yours to take.
This teacher-city, this panhellenic crown,
it's the latest word, in every art most wise.

Η ΣΥΝΟΔΕΙΑ ΤΟΥ ΔΙΟΝΥΣΟΥ

Ὁ Δάμων ὁ τεχνίτης (ἄλλον πιὸ ἱκανὸ
στὴν Πελοπόννησο δὲν ἔχει) εἰς παριανὸ
μάρμαρο ἐπεξεργάζεται τὴν συνοδεία
τοῦ Διονύσου. Ὁ θεὸς μὲ θεσπεσία
δόξαν ἐμπρός, μὲ δύναμι στὸ βάδισμά του.
Ὁ Ἄκρατος πίσω. Στὸ πλάγι τοῦ Ἀκράτου
ἡ Μέθη χύνει στοὺς Σατύρους τὸ κρασὶ
ἀπὸ ἀμφορέα ποὺ τὸν στέφουνε κισσοί.
Κοντά των ὁ Ἡδύοινος ὁ μαλθακός,
τὰ μάτια του μισοκλειστά, ὑπνωτικός.
Καὶ παρακάτω ἔρχοντ' οἱ τραγουδισταὶ
Μόλπος κ' Ἡδυμελής, κι ὁ Κῶμος ποὺ ποτὲ
νὰ σβύσει δὲν ἀφίνει τῆς πορείας τὴν σεπτὴ
λαμπάδα ποὺ βαστᾶ· καί, σεμνοτάτη, ἡ Τελετή.—
Αὐτὰ ὁ Δάμων κάμνει. Καὶ κοντὰ σ' αὐτὰ
ὁ λογισμός του κάθε τόσο μελετᾶ
τὴν ἀμοιβή του ἀπὸ τῶν Συρακουσῶν
τὸν βασιλέα, τρία τάλαντα, πολὺ ποσόν.
Μὲ τ' ἄλλα του τὰ χρήματα κι αὐτὰ μαζὺ
σὰν μποῦν, ὡς εὔπορος σπουδαῖα πιὰ θὰ ζεῖ,
καὶ θὰ μπορεῖ νὰ πολιτεύεται—χαρά!—
κι αὐτὸς μὲς στὴν βουλή, κι αὐτὸς στὴν ἀγορά.

THE FOLLOWERS OF DIONYSOS

Damon the master artisan (none better in
the Peloponnese) puts the final touches to his
"Followers of Dionysos" on Parian marble:
the god in front, leading them in divine
glory, all powerful in his stride. After him
follows Intemperance. Next to Intemperance,
Drunkenness, who spills out the wine for the Satyrs
from an amphora wreathed in ivy.
Nearby, Hedyoinos of the soft and sweet manners,
heavy eyes, half-closed, soporific.
Then the singers bring up the rear,
Molpos, Hedymeles, and Komos: tune, melody,
and reveler, who never lets his honorific torch go out
—and modest Telete, true Ceremony.
Here Damon shapes them all. And along with these
his thoughts turn now and again to the reward,
the fee he will be paid by the Syracusan
King, three talents, a fairly large sum.
This, added to the money he already has,
will make him a rich man; he'll live in grand style
hereafter; he'll be able to enter politics—o happy turn—
he too may be in the Senate, he too in the Agora.

Η ΜΑΧΗ ΤΗΣ ΜΑΓΝΗΣΙΑΣ

Ἔχασε τὴν παληά του ὁρμή, τὸ θάρρος του.
Τοῦ κουρασμένου σώματός του, τοῦ ἄρρωστου

σχεδόν, θά 'χει κυρίως τὴν φροντίδα. Κι ὁ ἐπίλοιπος
βίος του θὰ διέλθει ἀμέριμνος. Αὐτὰ ὁ Φίλιππος

τουλάχιστον διατείνεται. Ἀπόψι κύβους παίζει·
ἔχει ὄρεξι νὰ διασκεδάσει. Στὸ τραπέζι

βάλτε πολλὰ τριαντάφυλλα. Τί ἂν στὴν Μαγνησία
ὁ Ἀντίοχος κατεστράφηκε. Λένε πανωλεθρία

ἔπεσ' ἐπάνω στοῦ λαμπροῦ στρατεύματος τὰ πλήθια.
Μπορεῖ νὰ τὰ μεγάλωσαν· ὅλα δὲν θά 'ναι ἀλήθεια.

Εἴθε. Γιατὶ ἀγκαλὰ κ' ἐχθρός, ἤσανε μιὰ φυλή.
Ὅμως ἕνα «εἴθε» εἶν' ἀρκετό. Ἴσως κιόλας πολύ.

Ὁ Φίλιππος τὴν ἑορτὴ βέβαια δὲν θ' ἀναβάλει.
Ὅσο κι ἂν στάθηκε τοῦ βίου του ἡ κόπωσις μεγάλη,

ἕνα καλὸ διατήρησεν, ἡ μνήμη διόλου δὲν τοῦ λείπει.
Θυμᾶται πόσο στὴν Συρία θρήνησαν, τί εἶδος λύπη

εἶχαν, σὰν ἔγινε σκουπίδι ἡ μάνα των Μακεδονία.—
Ν' ἀρχίσει τὸ τραπέζι. Δοῦλοι· τοὺς αὐλούς, τὴ φωταψία.

THE BATTLE OF MAGNESIA

He's lost his old nerve, his daring.
To his worn-out body, almost sick,

he'll give his full attention. And he'll spend the rest
of his days without care or worry. So Philip seems

to think, at least. Tonight he plays a game of dice;
he's in the mood to entertain himself. Fill up the table

with roses everywhere. And what if Antiochos was wholly
ruined in Magnesia? They say complete disaster

befell his brilliant multitude of soldiers.
Maybe they told tales; it can't all be true.

We may hope; for, though our enemy, they were of our race.
Let one "we may hope" suffice. That may be even too much.

Of course Philip will not postpone the feast.
However much his life has left him a wreck,

he has held on to one good thing: his memory never left him.
He recalls how they mourned in Syria, their kind of sorrow,

when their mother Makedonia was turned to shameful waste.—
Let the banquet begin. Slaves! The flutes! The lights!

Η ΔΥΣΑΡΕΣΚΕΙΑ ΤΟΥ ΣΕΛΕΥΚΙΔΟΥ

Δυσαρεστήθηκεν ὁ Σελευκίδης
Δημήτριος νὰ μάθει ποὺ στὴν Ἰταλία
ἔφθασεν ἕνας Πτολεμαῖος σὲ τέτοιο χάλι.
Μὲ τρεῖς ἢ τέσσαρες δούλους μονάχα·
πτωχοντυμένος καὶ πεζός. Ἔτσι μιὰ εἰρωνία
θὰ καταντήσουν πιά, καὶ παίγνιο μὲς στὴν Ρώμη
τὰ γένη των. Ποὺ κατὰ βάθος ἔγιναν
σὰν ἕνα εἶδος ὑπηρέται τῶν Ρωμαίων
τὸ ξέρει ὁ Σελευκίδης, ποὺ αὐτοὶ τοὺς δίδουν
κι αὐτοὶ τοὺς παίρνουνε τοὺς θρόνους των
αὐθαίρετα, ὡς ἐπιθυμοῦν, τὸ ξέρει.
Ἀλλὰ τουλάχιστον στὸ παρουσιαστικό των
ἂς διατηροῦν κάποια μεγαλοπρέπεια·
νὰ μὴ ξεχνοῦν ποὺ εἶναι βασιλεῖς ἀκόμη,
ποὺ λέγονται (ἀλλοίμονον!) ἀκόμη βασιλεῖς.

Γι' αὐτὸ συγχίσθηκεν ὁ Σελευκίδης
Δημήτριος· κι ἀμέσως πρόσφερε στὸν Πτολεμαῖο
ἐνδύματα ὁλοπόρφυρα, διάδημα λαμπρό,
βαρύτιμα διαμαντικά, πολλοὺς
θεράποντας καὶ συνοδούς, τὰ πιὸ ἀκριβά του ἄλογα,
γιὰ νὰ παρουσιασθεῖ στὴν Ρώμη καθὼς πρέπει,
σὰν Ἀλεξανδρινὸς Γραικὸς μονάρχης.

Ἀλλ' ὁ Λαγίδης, ποὺ ἦλθε γιὰ τὴν ἐπαιτεία,
ἤξερε τὴν δουλειά του καὶ τ' ἀρνήθηκε ὅλα·
διόλου δὲν τοῦ χρειάζονταν αὐτὲς ἡ πολυτέλειες.
Παληοντυμένος, ταπεινὸς μπῆκε στὴν Ρώμη,
καὶ κόνεψε σ' ἑνὸς μικροῦ τεχνίτου σπίτι.
Κ' ἔπειτα παρουσιάσθηκε σὰν κακομοίρης
καὶ σὰν πτωχάνθρωπος στὴν Σύγκλητο,
ἔτσι μὲ πιὸ ἀποτέλεσμα νὰ ζητιανέψει.

34

THE DISPLEASURE OF SELEUKIDES

Displeased, to be sure, was Demetrios
Seleukides, when he learned that from Italy
a Ptolemy had just arrived in a sorry state.
Having only three or four slaves;
miserably dressed and on foot. In this way
their dynasty will become the laughing-stock
of Rome. Of course, deep down Seleukides
knows they've become a sort of servant
to the Romans—the very same Romans, those who give
and those who take away their thrones
at will, as they please; this he knows.
But they should hold onto some stateliness,
at least for appearances' sake;
and not forget they are still kings,
are still (alas!) called kings.

This was the reason for the displeasure
of Demetrios Seleukides; and at once he offered
to Ptolemy royal purple robes, a brilliant diadem,
precious jewels, many
servants and attendants, his most expensive horses,
to make his appearance in Rome as he should,
as an Alexandrian Greek monarch.

But Ptolemy, the Lagid, who had come to beg,
knew well his business and refused everything;
he had no use at all for such luxuries.
Dismally dressed and meek, he entered Rome,
and put himself up in a minor artist's home.
And later, he made his appearance before the Senate,
looking a miserable wretch and a pauper,
so to be most effective in his begging.

ΟΡΟΦΕΡΝΗΣ

Αὐτὸς ποὺ εἰς τὸ τετράδραχμον ἐπάνω
μοιάζει σὰν νὰ χαμογελᾶ τὸ πρόσωπό του,
τὸ ἔμορφο, λεπτό του πρόσωπο,
αὐτὸς εἶν' ὁ Ὀροφέρνης Ἀριαράθου.

Παιδὶ τὸν ἔδιωξαν ἀπ' τὴν Καππαδοκία,
ἀπ' τὸ μεγάλο πατρικὸ παλάτι,
καὶ τὸν ἐστείλανε νὰ μεγαλώσει
στὴν Ἰωνία, καὶ νὰ ξεχασθεῖ στοὺς ξένους.

Ἀ ἐξαίσιες τῆς Ἰωνίας νύχτες
ποὺ ἄφοβα, κ' ἑλληνικὰ ὅλως διόλου
ἐγνώρισε πλήρη τὴν ἡδονή.
Μὲς στὴν καρδιά του, πάντοτε Ἀσιανός·
ἀλλὰ στοὺς τρόπους του καὶ στὴν λαλιά του Ἕλλην,
μὲ περουζέδες στολισμένος, ἑλληνοντυμένος,
τὸ σῶμα του μὲ μύρον ἰασεμιοῦ εὐωδιασμένο,
κι ἀπ' τοὺς ὡραίους τῆς Ἰωνίας νέους,
ὁ πιὸ ὡραῖος αὐτός, ὁ πιὸ ἰδανικός.

Κατόπι σὰν οἱ Σύροι στὴν Καππαδοκία
μπῆκαν, καὶ τὸν ἐκάμαν βασιλέα,
στὴν βασιλεία χύθηκεν ἐπάνω
γιὰ νὰ χαρεῖ μὲ νέον τρόπο κάθε μέρα,
γιὰ νὰ μαζεύει ἁρπαχτικὰ χρυσὸ κι ἀσῆμι,
καὶ γιὰ νὰ εὐφραίνεται, καὶ νὰ κομπάζει,
βλέποντας πλούτη στοιβαγμένα νὰ γυαλίζουν.
Ὅσο γιὰ μέριμνα τοῦ τόπου, γιὰ διοίκησι—
οὔτ' ἤξερε τί γένονταν τριγύρω του.

Οἱ Καππαδόκες γρήγορα τὸν βγάλαν·
καὶ στὴν Συρία ξέπεσε, μὲς στὸ παλάτι
τοῦ Δημητρίου νὰ διασκεδάζει καὶ νὰ ὀκνεύει.

OROPHERNES

The one who appears on the four-drachma coin
and seems to have a smile on his face—
his beautiful, delicate face—
this is the one, Orophernes, son of Ariarathes.

A child, they drove him out of Kappadokia,
away from his great ancestral palace,
they sent him to be brought up
in Ionia, and be forgotten there among strangers.

Yes, those exquisite Ionian nights,
when fearless, and in a fully Greek way,
he came to know fulfilling sensual pleasure.
In his heart, an Asian always;
but in his manner and his speech, a Greek,
with turquoise adornments and Greek dress,
his body fragrant with jasmine oil,
and among the beautiful Ionian youths,
he was the most beautiful, the most ideal.

Later, when the Syrians entered Kappadokia,
and made him king,
he immersed himself into the kingship
to take pleasure in new ways each day,
voraciously hoarding gold and silver,
gleefully boasting,
seeing the heaps of his riches glitter.
As for any care of the country, of running it—
he had no clue of what went on around him.

Soon enough the Kappadocians had him ousted;
he ended up in Syria, at the palace of Demetrios,
entertaining himself and basking in leisure.

Μιὰ μέρα ὡστόσο τὴν πολλὴν ἀργία του
συλλογισμοὶ ἀσυνείθιστοι διεκόψαν·
θυμήθηκε ποὺ ἀπ' τὴν μητέρα του Ἀντιοχίδα,
κι ἀπ' τὴν παληὰν ἐκείνη Στρατονίκη,
κι αὐτὸς βαστοῦσε ἀπ' τὴν κορώνα τῆς Συρίας,
καὶ Σελευκίδης ἤτανε σχεδόν.
Γιὰ λίγο βγῆκε ἀπ' τὴν λαγνεία κι ἀπ' τὴν μέθη,
κι ἀνίκανα, καὶ μισοζαλισμένος
κάτι ἐζήτησε νὰ ραδιουργήσει,
κάτι νὰ κάμει, κάτι νὰ σχεδιάσει,
κι ἀπέτυχεν οἰκτρὰ κ' ἐξουδενώθη.

Τὸ τέλος του κάπου θὰ γράφηκε κ' ἐχάθη·
ἢ ἴσως ἡ ἱστορία νὰ τὸ πέρασε,
καί, μὲ τὸ δίκιο της, τέτοιο ἀσήμαντο
πρᾶγμα δὲν καταδέχθηκε νὰ τὸ σημειώσει.

Αὐτὸς ποὺ εἰς τὸ τετράδραχμον ἐπάνω
μιὰ χάρι ἀφῆκε ἀπ' τὰ ὡραῖα του νειάτα,
ἀπ' τὴν ποιητικὴ ἐμορφιά του ἕνα φῶς,
μιὰ μνήμη αἰσθητικὴ ἀγοριοῦ τῆς Ἰωνίας,
αὐτὸς εἶν' ὁ Ὀροφέρνης Ἀριαράθου.

But one day his usual sloth
was interrupted by unfamiliar thoughts.
He remembered how, through his mother Antiochis
and through his old grandmother Stratonike,
he too was an offshoot of the Syrian crown,
he too a Seleukid, almost.
For a while he snapped out of his lechery and drink,
and inept and half dazed,
he took it in his head to start an intrigue,
that he should do something, have a plan,
but he failed miserably and was reduced to rubble.

His end must have been written down somewhere,
but was lost; or perhaps History passed it by,
and rightly so, such a trivial
thing, she wouldn't stoop to mention it.

The one who on the four-drachma coin
left us that certain charm of his lovely youth,
a shining light of his poetic beauty,
this emotional memory of an Ionian boy;
this is the one, Orophernes, son of Ariarathes.

ΑΛΕΞΑΝΔΡΙΝΟΙ ΒΑΣΙΛΕΙΣ

Μαζεύθηκαν οἱ Ἀλεξανδρινοὶ
νὰ δοῦν τῆς Κλεοπάτρας τὰ παιδιά,
τὸν Καισαρίωνα, καὶ τὰ μικρά του ἀδέρφια,
Ἀλέξανδρο καὶ Πτολεμαῖο, ποὺ πρώτη
φορὰ τὰ βγάζαν ἔξω στὸ Γυμνάσιο,
ἐκεῖ νὰ τὰ κηρύξουν βασιλεῖς,
μὲς στὴ λαμπρὴ παράταξι τῶν στρατιωτῶν.

Ὁ Ἀλέξανδρος—τὸν εἶπαν βασιλέα
τῆς Ἀρμενίας, τῆς Μηδίας, καὶ τῶν Πάρθων.
Ὁ Πτολεμαῖος—τὸν εἶπαν βασιλέα
τῆς Κιλικίας, τῆς Συρίας, καὶ τῆς Φοινίκης.
Ὁ Καισαρίων στέκονταν πιὸ ἐμπροστά,
ντυμένος σὲ μετάξι τριανταφυλλί,
στὸ στῆθος του ἀνθοδέσμη ἀπὸ ὑακίνθους,
ἡ ζώνη του διπλὴ σειρὰ σαπφείρων κι ἀμεθύστων,
δεμένα τὰ ποδήματά του μ' ἄσπρες
κορδέλλες κεντημένες μὲ ροδόχροα μαργαριτάρια.
Αὐτὸν τὸν εἶπαν πιότερο ἀπὸ τοὺς μικρούς,
αὐτὸν τὸν εἶπαν Βασιλέα τῶν Βασιλέων.

Οἱ Ἀλεξανδρινοὶ ἔνοιωθαν βέβαια
ποὺ ἦσαν λόγια αὐτὰ καὶ θεατρικά.

Ἀλλὰ ἡ μέρα ἤτανε ζεστὴ καὶ ποιητική,
ὁ οὐρανὸς ἕνα γαλάζιο ἀνοιχτό,
τὸ Ἀλεξανδρινὸ Γυμνάσιον ἕνα
θριαμβικὸ κατόρθωμα τῆς τέχνης,
τῶν αὐλικῶν ἡ πολυτέλεια ἔκτακτη,
ὁ Καισαρίων ὅλο χάρις κ' ἐμορφιὰ
(τῆς Κλεοπάτρας υἱός, αἷμα τῶν Λαγιδῶν)·
κ' οἱ Ἀλεξανδρινοὶ ἔτρεχαν πιὰ στὴν ἑορτή,

ALEXANDRIAN KINGS

The Alexandrians came out in hordes
to see Kleopatra's children,
Kaisarion and his younger brothers,
Alexander and Ptolemy, who for the first
time were brought out to the Gymnasium,
where they're to be proclaimed kings,
amid the brilliant array of soldiers.

Alexander—they proclaimed him king
of Armenia, of Media, and of the Parthians.
Ptolemy—they proclaimed him king
of Kilikia, Syria, and Phoenicia.
Kaisarion stood more forward than the others,
dressed in rose-colored silk,
a spray of hyacinths on his chest,
his belt a double row of amethysts and sapphires,
his shoes sewn with white ribbons
and rose-colored pearls.
Him they declared above his younger brothers,
him they declared King of Kings.

The Alexandrians of course knew well
these were only words—and a bit of theatre.

But the day was warm and a little poetic,
the sky a pale blue,
the Alexandrian Gymnasium
a thorough triumph of true art,
the lavishness of the courtiers superb,
Kaisarion, warm grace and beauty
(Kleopatra's son, blood of the Lagids, after all);
so the Alexandrians crowded to the festivities,

κ' ἐνθουσιάζονταν, κ' ἐπευφημοῦσαν
ἑλληνικά, κ' αἰγυπτιακά, καὶ ποιοὶ ἑβραίικα,
γοητευμένοι μὲ τ' ὡραῖο θέαμα—
μ' ὅλο ποὺ βέβαια ἤξευραν τί ἄξιζαν αὐτά,
τί κούφια λόγια ἤσανε αὐτὲς ἡ βασιλεῖες.

and grew enthusiastic, and shouted their cheers
in Greek, in Egyptian, and some in Hebrew,
spellbound by the lovely spectacle—
though, of course, they knew well the worth of it all,
what empty words were all these kingly titles.

ΦΙΛΕΛΛΗΝ

Τὴν χάραξι φρόντισε τεχνικὰ νὰ γίνει.
Ἔκφρασις σοβαρὴ καὶ μεγαλοπρεπής.
Τὸ διάδημα καλλίτερα μᾶλλον στενό·
ἐκεῖνα τὰ φαρδιὰ τῶν Πάρθων δὲν μὲ ἀρέσουν.
Ἡ ἐπιγραφή, ὡς σύνηθες, ἑλληνικά·
ὄχ' ὑπερβολική, ὄχι πομπώδης—
μὴν τὰ παρεξηγήσει ὁ ἀνθύπατος
ποὺ ὅλο σκαλίζει καὶ μηνᾶ στὴν Ρώμη—
ἀλλ' ὅμως βέβαια τιμητική.
Κάτι πολὺ ἐκλεκτὸ ἀπ' τὸ ἄλλο μέρος·
κανένας δισκοβόλος ἔφηβος ὡραῖος.
Πρὸ πάντων σὲ συστήνω νὰ κυττάξεις
(Σιθάσπη, πρὸς θεοῦ, νὰ μὴ λησμονηθεῖ)
μετὰ τὸ Βασιλεὺς καὶ τὸ Σωτήρ,
νὰ χαραχθεῖ μὲ γράμματα κομψά, Φιλέλλην.
Καὶ τώρα μὴ μὲ ἀρχίζεις εὐφυολογίες,
τὰ «Ποῦ οἱ Ἕλληνες;» καὶ «Ποῦ τὰ Ἑλληνικὰ
πίσω ἀπ' τὸν Ζάγρο ἐδῶ, ἀπὸ τὰ Φράατα πέρα».
Τόσοι καὶ τόσοι βαρβαρότεροί μας ἄλλοι
ἀφοῦ τὸ γράφουν, θὰ τὸ γράψουμε κ' ἐμεῖς.
Καὶ τέλος μὴ ξεχνᾶς ποὺ ἐνίοτε
μᾶς ἔρχοντ' ἀπὸ τὴν Συρία σοφισταί,
καὶ στιχοπλόκοι, κι ἄλλοι ματαιόσπουδοι.
Ὥστε ἀνελλήνιστοι δὲν εἴμεθα, θαρρῶ.

PHILHELLENE

Take care the engraving is done with skill.
The expression serious and properly elevated.
And better make the diadem somewhat narrow;
I don't like those broad Parthian ones.
The inscription, as usual, in Greek;
nothing excessive, or pompous—we don't need
the proconsul ferreting out news, taking it
the wrong way, and reporting back to Rome—
but of course with due honor to me.
On the opposite side something well chosen;
perhaps a discus-thrower, young, beautiful.
Above all I insist you see to it
(Sithaspes, in God's name don't let them forget)
that after "King" and "Savior"
they engrave in elegant letters: "Philhellene."
And don't start your clever comments with me,
like "are there Greeks here?" and "is Greek spoken
this side of Zagros and beyond Fraata?"
Since so many, more barbarian than ourselves,
choose to inscribe it, we will do so too.
And further, don't forget that oftentimes
Sophists do come to us from Syria,
to say nothing of versifiers and pretentious scholars.
So we are not, I think, lacking in Greek.

ΤΑ ΒΗΜΑΤΑ

Σ' ἐβένινο κρεββάτι στολισμένο
μὲ κοραλλένιους ἀετούς, βαθυὰ κοιμᾶται
ὁ Νέρων—ἀσυνείδητος, ἥσυχος, κ' εὐτυχής·
ἀκμαῖος μὲς στὴν εὐρωστία τῆς σαρκός,
καὶ στῆς νεότητος τ' ὡραῖο σφρῖγος.

Ἀλλὰ στὴν αἴθουσα τὴν ἀλαβάστρινη ποὺ κλείνει
τῶν Ἀηνοβάρβων τὸ ἀρχαῖο λαράριο
τί ἀνήσυχοι ποὺ εἶν' οἱ Λάρητές του.
Τρέμουν οἱ σπιτικοὶ μικροὶ θεοί,
καὶ προσπαθοῦν τ' ἀσήμαντά των σώματα νὰ κρύψουν.
Γιατὶ ἄκουσαν μιὰ ἀπαίσια βοή,
θανάσιμη βοὴ τὴν σκάλα ν' ἀνεβαίνει,
βήματα σιδερένια ποὺ τραντάζουν τὰ σκαλιά.
Καὶ λιγοθυμισμένοι τώρα οἱ ἄθλιοι Λάρητες,
μέσα στὸ βάθος τοῦ λαράριου χώνονται,
ὁ ἕνας τὸν ἄλλονα σκουντᾶ καὶ σκουντουφλᾶ,
ὁ ἕνας μικρὸς θεὸς πάνω στὸν ἄλλον πέφτει
γιατὶ κατάλαβαν τί εἶδος βοὴ εἶναι τούτη,
τά 'νοιωσαν πιὰ τὰ βήματα τῶν Ἐρινννύων.

THE FOOTSTEPS

On a bed of ebony, adorned
with coral eagles, Nero lies
in deep sleep—thick-skinned, peaceful, and happy;
potent in the power of his flesh,
pounding with all his youth and beauty.

But in the sheltering hall of alabaster,
inside the ancient shrine of the Aenobarbi,
how restless are their gods, the Lares.
These little homebody gods do tremble,
and try to hide their meagre bodies.
For they have heard an awful sound,
a sound of death coming up the stairs,
iron footsteps that shake the staircase.
And now, fainting and fearful, the miserable Lares
scramble inside the depths of the shrine,
shoving each other and stumbling,
one little god tripping over another,
for they know now what kind of sound that is,
they know well the footsteps of the Furies.

ΗΡΩΔΗΣ ΑΤΤΙΚΟΣ

Ἀ τοῦ Ἡρώδη τοῦ Ἀττικοῦ τί δόξα εἶν' αὐτή.

Ὁ Ἀλέξανδρος τῆς Σελευκείας, ἀπ' τοὺς καλούς μας σοφιστάς,
φθάνοντας στὰς Ἀθήνας νὰ ὁμιλήσει,
βρίσκει τὴν πόλιν ἄδεια, ἐπειδὴ ὁ Ἡρώδης
ἦταν στὴν ἐξοχή. Κ' ἡ νεολαία
ὅλη τὸν ἀκολούθησεν ἐκεῖ νὰ τὸν ἀκούει.
Ὁ σοφιστὴς Ἀλέξανδρος λοιπὸν
γράφει πρὸς τὸν Ἡρώδη ἐπιστολή,
καὶ τὸν παρακαλεῖ τοὺς Ἕλληνας νὰ στείλει.
Ὁ δὲ λεπτὸς Ἡρώδης ἀπαντᾶ εὐθύς,
«Ἔρχομαι μὲ τοὺς Ἕλληνας μαζὺ κ' ἐγώ».—

Πόσα παιδιὰ στὴν Ἀλεξάνδρεια τώρα,
στὴν Ἀντιόχεια, ἢ στὴν Βηρυτὸ
(οἱ ρήτορές του οἱ αὐριανοὶ ποὺ ἑτοιμάζει ὁ ἑλληνισμός),
ὅταν μαζεύονται στὰ ἐκλεκτὰ τραπέζια
ποὺ πότε ἡ ὁμιλία εἶναι γιὰ τὰ ὡραῖα σοφιστικά,
καὶ πότε γιὰ τὰ ἐρωτικά των τὰ ἐξαίσια,
ἔξαφν' ἀφηρημένα σιωποῦν.
Ἄγγιχτα τὰ ποτήρια ἀφίνουνε κοντά των,
καὶ συλλογίζονται τὴν τύχη τοῦ Ἡρώδη—
ποιὸς ἄλλος σοφιστὴς τ' ἀξιώθηκεν αὐτά;—
κατὰ ποῦ θέλει καὶ κατὰ ποῦ κάμνει
οἱ Ἕλληνες (οἱ Ἕλληνες!) νὰ τὸν ἀκολουθοῦν,
μήτε νὰ κρίνουν ἢ νὰ συζητοῦν,
μήτε νὰ ἐκλέγουν πιά, ν' ἀκολουθοῦνε μόνο.

HERODES ATTIKOS

What great glory, this glory of Herodes Attikos!

Alexander of Seleukeia, one of our better sophists,
arriving in Athens to give a lecture,
finds the city abandoned because Herodes
took a trip to the country. And every youth
followed him there to listen to his every word.
And so the sophist Alexander
writes Herodes a letter,
begging him to send the Greeks back.
And the tactful Herodes responds at once:
"Along with the Greeks, I'm coming as well."—

How many youths in Alexandria nowadays,
in Antioch or in Beirut
(tomorrow's orators that Hellenism is preparing),
as they gather at select banquets where,
at times, the discussions are about fine sophistry,
and at times about their exquisite love intrigues,
here, suddenly distracted, they fall silent.
Their glasses they leave to the side, untouched,
and contemplate the good fortune of Herodes—
what other sophist has had such honors?—
Whatever he wishes, and in whatever he does
the Greeks (the Greeks!) follow him,
no judgment from them or debate,
no choice, they want only to follow.

ΤΥΑΝΕΥΣ ΓΛΥΠΤΗΣ

Καθὼς ποὺ θὰ τὸ ἀκούσατε, δὲν εἶμ' ἀρχάριος.
Κάμποση πέτρα ἀπὸ τὰ χέρια μου περνᾶ.
Καὶ στὴν πατρίδα μου, τὰ Τύανα, καλὰ
μὲ ξέρουνε· κ' ἐδῶ ἀγάλματα πολλὰ
μὲ παραγγείλανε συγκλητικοί.

                    Καὶ νὰ σᾶς δείξω
ἀμέσως μερικά. Παρατηρεῖστ' αὐτὴν τὴν Ρέα·
σεβάσμια, γεμάτη καρτερία, παναρχαία.
Παρατηρεῖστε τὸν Πομπήϊον. Ὁ Μάριος,
ὁ Αἰμίλιος Παῦλος, ὁ Ἀφρικανὸς Σκιπίων.
Ὁμοιώματα, ὅσο ποὺ μπόρεσα, πιστά.
Ὁ Πάτροκλος (ὀλίγο θὰ τὸν ξαναγγίξω).
Πλησίον στοῦ μαρμάρου τοῦ κιτρινωποῦ
ἐκεῖνα τὰ κομμάτια, εἶν' ὁ Καισαρίων.

Καὶ τώρα καταγίνομαι ἀπὸ καιρὸ ἀρκετὸ
νὰ κάμω ἔναν Ποσειδῶνα. Μελετῶ
κυρίως γιὰ τ' ἄλογά του, πῶς νὰ πλάσω αὐτά.
Πρέπει ἐλαφρὰ ἔτσι νὰ γίνουν ποὺ
τὰ σώματα, τὰ πόδια των νὰ δείχνουν φανερὰ
ποὺ δὲν πατοῦν τὴν γῆ, μόν' τρέχουν στὰ νερά.

Μὰ νά τὸ ἔργον μου τὸ πιὸ ἀγαπητὸ
ποὺ δούλεψα συγκινημένα καὶ τὸ πιὸ προσεκτικά·
αὐτόν, μιὰ μέρα τοῦ καλοκαιριοῦ θερμὴ
ποὺ ὁ νοῦς μου ἀνέβαινε στὰ ἰδανικά,
αὐτὸν ἐδῶ ὀνειρεύομουν τὸν νέον Ἑρμῆ.

SCULPTOR OF TYANA

As you no doubt heard about me, I'm not a novice.
A good deal of stone passes through my hands.
And in my country, in Tyana, everyone knows me
pretty well; and even here, senators often
commission many a statue from me.

                Now, let me show you
a few of them. Observe this Rhea here:
reverent, all-merciful, archaic.
Note Pompey over here. And Marius,
and Aemilius Paulus, and Scipio Africanus.
A likeness as faithful as I could make it.
Patroklos here (I will need to retouch him a bit).
Nearby, the yellowish marble lying there,
is my Kaisarion, those strewn shards.

At the moment I'm preoccupied with
the making of a Poseidon. I study
with care his horses, how to shape them.
They must be created to seem so light
that their bodies, their legs, do not touch ground,
they run instead only over water.

But here's the one work, the one I love,
the one that moved me most; I fashioned it with
the greatest care; this here—on a hot summer's day,
my mind soaring into the sublime—
it was him I dreamt of, this young Hermes.

51

ΛΥΣΙΟΥ ΓΡΑΜΜΑΤΙΚΟΥ ΤΑΦΟΣ

Πλησιέστατα, δεξιὰ ποὺ μπαίνεις, στὴν βιβλιοθήκη
τῆς Βηρυτοῦ θάψαμε τὸν σοφὸ Λυσία,
γραμματικόν. Ὁ χῶρος κάλλιστα προσήκει.
Τὸν θέσαμε κοντὰ σ' αὐτά του ποὺ θυμᾶται
ἴσως κ' ἐκεῖ—σχόλια, κείμενα, τεχνολογία,
γραφές, εἰς τεύχη ἑλληνισμῶν πολλὴ ἑρμηνεία.
Κ' ἐπίσης ἔτσι ἀπὸ μᾶς θὰ βλέπεται καὶ θὰ τιμᾶται
ὁ τάφος του, ὅταν ποὺ περνοῦμε στὰ βιβλία.

TOMB OF THE GRAMMARIAN LYSIAS

Very near here, just to the right as you enter
the library of Beirut, we buried wise Lysias,
the grammarian. The place is beautifully fitting.
We put him near those things of his he would remember
even there—commentaries, texts, technical grammars,
much writing, and volumes, interpreting Greek idioms.
In this spot, too, his tomb graces our path
and is honored each time we pass to see the books.

ΕΥΡΙΩΝΟΣ ΤΑΦΟΣ

Εἰς τὸ περίτεχνον αὐτὸ μνημεῖον,
ὁλόκληρον ἐκ λίθου συηνίτου,
ποὺ τὸ σκεπάζουν τόσοι μενεξέδες, τόσοι κρίνοι,
εἶναι θαμένος ὁ ὡραῖος Εὐρίων.
Παιδὶ ἀλεξανδρινό, εἴκοσι πέντε χρόνων.
Ἀπ᾽ τὸν πατέρα του, γενιὰ παλῃὰ τῶν Μακεδόνων·
ἀπὸ ἀλαβάρχας τῆς μητέρας του ἡ σειρά.
Ἔκαμε μαθητὴς τοῦ Ἀριστοκλείτου στὴν φιλοσοφία,
τοῦ Πάρου στὰ ῥητορικά. Στὰς Θήβας τὰ ἱερὰ
γράμματα σπούδασε. Τοῦ Ἀρσινοΐτου
νομοῦ συνέγραψε ἱστορίαν. Αὐτὸ τουλάχιστον θὰ μείνει.
Χάσαμεν ὅμως τὸ πιὸ τίμιο—τὴν μορφή του,
ποὺ ἤτανε σὰν μιὰ ἀπολλώνια ὀπτασία.

TOMB OF EURION

Here, this artful, ornate memorial,
the whole built of syenite stone,
covered with so many violets, so many lilies—
here the beauty of Eurion is laid to rest,
an Alexandrian boy, a twenty-five year old.
On his father's side, of old Makedonian stock;
of Jewish magistrates, his mother's line.
He was an Aristokleitos's student in philosophy,
and one of Paros's in rhetoric. At Thebes he studied
the sacred scriptures. And he wrote a history
of the Arsinoites province. That, at least, will survive.
Though what was most precious about him we lost—
his lovely form, like a living vision of Apollo.

ΟΥΤΟΣ ΕΚΕΙΝΟΣ

Ἄγνωστος—ξένος μὲς στὴν Ἀντιόχεια—Ἐδεσσηνὸς
γράφει πολλά. Καὶ τέλος πάντων, νά, ὁ λίνος
ὁ τελευταῖος ἔγινε. Μὲ αὐτὸν ὀγδόντα τρία

ποιήματα ἐν ὅλῳ. Πλὴν τὸν ποιητὴ
κούρασε τόσο γράψιμο, τόση στιχοποιΐα,
καὶ τόση ἔντασις σ' ἑλληνικὴ φρασιολογία,
καὶ τώρα τὸν βαραίνει πιὰ τὸ κάθε τί.—

Μιὰ σκέψις ὅμως παρευθὺς ἀπὸ τὴν ἀθυμία
τὸν βγάζει, τὸ ἐξαίσιον «Οὗτος Ἐκεῖνος»,
ποὺ ἄλλοτε στὸν ὕπνο του ἄκουσε ὁ Λουκιανός.

THAT WOULD BE THE MAN

Unknown—a stranger in Antioch—from Edessa,
he writes without end. Now, at last, here,
the final canto is done. That makes

eighty-three poems in all. Only the poet
is tired of writing: so much versifying,
so much strain with phrasing in Greek,
that now every little thing weighs him down.

But all at once a thought brings him out of his
depressed state: the sublime "That would be the Man"
—Lucian heard it once in his sleep.

ΤΑ ΕΠΙΚΙΝΔΥΝΑ

Εἶπε ὁ Μυρτίας (Σύρος σπουδαστὴς
στὴν Ἀλεξάνδρεια· ἐπὶ βασιλείας
αὐγούστου Κώνσταντος καὶ αὐγούστου Κωνσταντίου·
ἐν μέρει ἐθνικός, κ' ἐν μέρει χριστιανίζων)·
«Δυναμωμένος μὲ θεωρία καὶ μελέτη,
ἐγὼ τὰ πάθη μου δὲν θὰ φοβοῦμαι σὰ δειλός.
Τὸ σῶμα μου στὲς ἡδονὲς θὰ δώσω,
στὲς ἀπολαύσεις τὲς ὀνειρεμένες,
στὲς τολμηρότερες ἐρωτικὲς ἐπιθυμίες,
στὲς λάγνες τοῦ αἵματός μου ὁρμές, χωρὶς
κανέναν φόβο, γιατὶ ὅταν θέλω—
καὶ θά 'χω θέλησι, δυναμωμένος
ὡς θά 'μαι μὲ θεωρία καὶ μελέτη—
στὲς κρίσιμες στιγμὲς θὰ ξαναβρίσκω
τὸ πνεῦμα μου, σὰν πρίν, ἀσκητικό.»

FRAUGHT WITH DANGER

Myrtias let it be known (he was a Syrian student
in Alexandria during the reign
of Augustus Constans and Augustus Constantios;
in part pagan, in part Christianized):
"Gaining my strength with the study of theory, and reflection,
I will not fear my passions like a coward.
I intend to give my body over to sexual pleasures,
to all those pleasures I have dreamed of,
and to every unspeakable erotic desire,
to the lustful drives in my blood,
without fear, for when I have a mind to—
and the desire, having gained my strength,
as I will have, with study and reflection—
during the critical moments, I will again find
my ascetic spirit as before."

ΜΑΝΟΥΗΛ ΚΟΜΝΗΝΟΣ

Ὁ βασιλεὺς κὺρ Μανουὴλ ὁ Κομνηνὸς
μιὰ μέρα μελαγχολικὴ τοῦ Σεπτεμβρίου
αἰσθάνθηκε τὸν θάνατο κοντά. Οἱ ἀστρολόγοι
(οἱ πληρωμένοι) τῆς αὐλῆς ἐφλυαροῦσαν
ποὺ ἄλλα πολλὰ χρόνια θὰ ζήσει ἀκόμη.
Ἐνῶ ὅμως ἔλεγαν αὐτοί, ἐκεῖνος
παληὲς συνήθειες εὐλαβεῖς θυμᾶται,
κι ἀπ' τὰ κελλιὰ τῶν μοναχῶν προστάζει
ἐνδύματα ἐκκλησιαστικὰ νὰ φέρουν,
καὶ τὰ φορεῖ, κ' εὐφραίνεται ποὺ δείχνει
ὄψι σεμνὴν ἱερέως ἢ καλογήρου.

Εὐτυχισμένοι ὅλοι ποὺ πιστεύουν,
καὶ σὰν τὸν βασιλέα κὺρ Μανουὴλ τελειώνουν
ντυμένοι μὲς στὴν πίστι των σεμνότατα.

MANUEL KOMNENOS

The Emperor Manuel Komnenos
on one melancholy September day
felt death to be near. The court astrologers
(the well-paid ones) went on babbling
that he would live for many more years.
As they were having their say, he recalls
old habits, devout customs of times past,
and from the cells of monks orders
ecclesiastical vestments be brought to him
and puts them on, happy to assume
the modest aspect of a priest or monk.

Fortunate all those who believe,
and like Emperor Manuel end their days
dressed most modestly in their faith.

ΣΤΗΝ ΕΚΚΛΗΣΙΑ

Τὴν ἐκκλησίαν ἀγαπῶ—τὰ ἑξαπτέρυγά της,
τ᾽ ἀσήμια τῶν σκευῶν, τὰ κηροπήγιά της,
τὰ φῶτα, τὲς εἰκόνες της, τὸν ἄμβωνά της.

Ἐκεῖ σὰν μπῶ, μὲς σ᾽ ἐκκλησία τῶν Γραικῶν·
μὲ τῶν θυμιαμάτων της τὲς εὐωδίες,
μὲ τὲς λειτουργικὲς φωνὲς καὶ συμφωνίες,
τὲς μεγαλοπρεπεῖς τῶν ἱερέων παρουσίες
καὶ κάθε των κινήσεως τὸν σοβαρὸ ρυθμό—
λαμπρότατοι μὲς στῶν ἀμφίων τὸν στολισμό—
ὁ νοῦς μου πηαίνει σὲ τιμὲς μεγάλες τῆς φυλῆς μας,
στὸν ἔνδοξό μας Βυζαντινισμό.

IN CHURCH

I do love the church: the labara,
the silver of the sacred utensils, the candlesticks,
the lights, the icons, the pulpit.

When I enter there, into the church of the Greeks,
with its perfume of incense,
with the liturgical voices and harmonies,
the majestic presence of the priests,
and the grand rhythm of their every move—
all aglitter in their elaborate vestments—
my mind turns to the great glories of our race,
to the grandeur of our Byzantine past.

ΠΟΛΥ ΣΠΑΝΙΩΣ

Εἶν' ἕνας γέροντας. Ἐξηντλημένος καὶ κυρτός,
σακατεμένος ἀπ' τὰ χρόνια, κι ἀπὸ καταχρήσεις,
σιγὰ βαδίζοντας διαβαίνει τὸ σοκάκι.
Κι ὅμως σὰν μπεῖ στὸ σπίτι του νὰ κρύψει
τὰ χάλια καὶ τὰ γηρατειά του, μελετᾶ
τὸ μερτικὸ ποὺ ἔχει ἀκόμη αὐτὸς στὰ νειάτα.

Ἔφηβοι τώρα τοὺς δικούς του στίχους λένε.
Στὰ μάτια των τὰ ζωηρὰ περνοῦν ἡ ὀπτασίες του.
Τὸ ὑγιές, ἡδονικὸ μυαλό των,
ἡ εὔγραμμη, σφιχτοδεμένη σάρκα των,
μὲ τὴν δική του ἔκφανσι τοῦ ὡραίου συγκινοῦνται.

VERY SELDOM

He's but an old man. Worn to the bone and bent,
fallen by the wayside, crippled by time,
slowly he walks to cross the narrow pathway.
Still, when he goes inside his home to hide
the chaos of his old age, his thoughts turn
to the share in youth that is still his.

Young men nowadays recite his verses.
His visions pass before their lively eyes.
Their healthy, sensual minds,
their well-formed, taut bodies
are moved at his perception of beauty.

ΤΟΥ ΜΑΓΑΖΙΟΥ

Τὰ ντύλιξε προσεκτικά, μὲ τάξι
σὲ πράσινο πολύτιμο μετάξι.

Ἀπὸ ρουμπίνια ρόδα, ἀπὸ μαργαριτάρια κρίνοι,
ἀπὸ ἀμεθύστους μενεξέδες. Ὡς αὐτὸς τὰ κρίνει,

τὰ θέλησε, τὰ βλέπει ὡραῖα· ὄχι ὅπως στὴν φύσι
τὰ εἶδεν ἢ τὰ σπούδασε. Μὲς στὸ ταμεῖον θὰ τ' ἀφίσει,

δεῖγμα τῆς τολμηρῆς δουλειᾶς του καὶ ἱκανῆς.
Στὸ μαγαζὶ σὰν μπεῖ ἀγοραστὴς κανεὶς

βγάζει ἀπ' τὲς θῆκες ἄλλα καὶ πουλεῖ—περίφημα στολίδια—
βραχιόλια, ἀλυσίδες, περιδέραια, καὶ δαχτυλίδια.

FOR THE SHOP

He wrapped them up with care, neatly,
in precious cloth of green silk.

Roses of rubies, lilies of pearls,
violets of amethyst. To his taste: just what he wanted,

he deems them beautiful, not as he saw
or studied them in nature. He'll keep them in the safe;

samples of his more bold and skillful work.
And when a customer comes into the shop,

he shows them many things in his cases to buy—fine
ornaments—bracelets, chains, necklaces, and rings.

ΖΩΓΡΑΦΙΣΜΕΝΑ

Τὴν ἐργασία μου τὴν προσέχω καὶ τὴν ἀγαπῶ.
Μὰ τῆς συνθέσεως μ' ἀποθαρρύνει σήμερα ἡ βραδύτης.
Ἡ μέρα μ' ἐπηρέασε. Ἡ μορφή της
ὅλο καὶ σκοτεινιάζει. Ὅλο φυσᾶ καὶ βρέχει.
Πιότερο ἐπιθυμῶ νὰ δῶ παρὰ νὰ πῶ.
Στὴ ζωγραφιὰν αὐτὴ κυττάζω τώρα
ἕνα ὡραῖο ἀγόρι ποὺ σιμὰ στὴ βρύσι
ἐπλάγιασεν, ἀφοῦ θ' ἀπέκαμε νὰ τρέχει.
Τί ὡραῖο παιδί· τί θεῖο μεσημέρι τὸ ἔχει
παρμένο πιὰ γιὰ νὰ τὸ ἀποκοιμίσει.—
Κάθομαι καὶ κυττάζω ἔτσι πολλὴν ὥρα.
Καὶ μὲς στὴν τέχνη πάλι, ξεκουράζομαι ἀπ' τὴν δούλεψή της.

PAINTED

I do my work with great care, and I love it.
But today's composition went too slowly, I was dismayed.
This day has affected me. Its mood keeps
growing darker all the time. Great wind and rain.
I have a desire to look at things rather than speak of them.
In this painting, I now gaze
at a lovely boy who lay down to sleep
near the fountain, having tired himself running.
What a lovely boy! What a heavenly noontime
has taken him and put him gently to sleep—
I sit and gaze all this for a long time.
Now, inside art this way, I take a rest from creating it.

ΘΑΛΑΣΣΑ ΤΟΥ ΠΡΩΪΟΥ

Ἐδῶ ἂς σταθῶ. Κι ἂς δῶ κ' ἐγὼ τὴν φύσι λίγο.
Θάλασσας τοῦ πρωϊοῦ κι ἀνέφελου οὐρανοῦ
λαμπρὰ μαβιά, καὶ κίτρινη ὄχθη· ὅλα
ὡραῖα καὶ μεγάλα φωτισμένα.

Ἐδῶ ἂς σταθῶ. Κι ἂς γελασθῶ πὼς βλέπω αὐτὰ
(τὰ εἶδ' ἀλήθεια μιὰ στιγμὴ σὰν πρωτοστάθηκα)·
κι ὄχι κ' ἐδῶ τὲς φαντασίες μου,
τὲς ἀναμνήσεις μου, τὰ ἰνδάλματα τῆς ἡδονῆς.

MORNING SEA

Let me linger here a bit. And let me gaze at nature a while.
Morning sea of the cloudless sky
shining dark blue, and yellow shore; all
gorgeous and grand and swimming in light.

Let me linger a bit. Let me deceive myself I see all this
(and truly, I did see it for a moment when I first stopped),
let me not think them fantasies,
just my memories, the visions of sexual desire.

ΙΩΝΙΚΟΝ

Γιατὶ τὰ σπάσαμε τ' ἀγάλματά των,
γιατὶ τοὺς διώξαμεν ἀπ' τοὺς ναούς των,
διόλου δὲν πέθαναν γι' αὐτὸ οἱ θεοί.
Ὦ γῆ τῆς Ἰωνίας, σένα ἀγαποῦν ἀκόμη,
σένα ἡ ψυχές των ἐνθυμοῦνται ἀκόμη.
Σὰν ξημερώνει ἐπάνω σου πρωῖ αὐγουστιάτικο
τὴν ἀτμοσφαίρα σου περνᾶ σφρῖγος ἀπ' τὴν ζωή των·
καὶ κάποτ' αἰθερία ἐφηβικὴ μορφή,
ἀόριστη, μὲ διάβα γρήγορο,
ἐπάνω ἀπὸ τοὺς λόφους σου περνᾶ.

72

IONIC

Though we busted their statues,
though we drove them from their temples,
it was no reason for the gods to be dead.
O earth of Ionia, it is you they still love,
it is you their souls still remember.
When an August dawn awakens over you,
your atmosphere is lush with their life;
and sometimes the lithe form of an ephebe,
ethereal, indistinct, passes swiftly
across your hills, in flight.

ΣΤΟΥ ΚΑΦΕΝΕΙΟΥ ΤΗΝ ΕΙΣΟΔΟ

Τὴν προσοχή μου κάτι ποὺ εἶπαν πλάγι μου
διεύθυνε στοῦ καφενείου τὴν εἴσοδο.
Κ' εἶδα τ' ὡραῖο σῶμα ποὺ ἔμοιαζε
σὰν ἀπ' τὴν ἄκρα πεῖρα του νὰ τό 'καμεν ὁ Ἔρως—
πλάττοντας τὰ συμμετρικά του μέλη μὲ χαρά·
ὑψώνοντας γλυπτὸ τὸ ἀνάστημα·
πλάττοντας μὲ συγκίνησι τὸ πρόσωπο
κι ἀφίνοντας ἀπ' τῶν χεριῶν του τὸ ἄγγιγμα
ἕνα αἴσθημα στὸ μέτωπο, στὰ μάτια, καὶ στὰ χείλη.

AT THE CAFÉ ENTRANCE

Something I heard said beside me
drew my attention toward the café entrance.
There I saw the beautiful body that looked
as if Eros in his endless wisdom had shaped it—
those symmetrical limbs, molded in utter joy;
sculpting its stature tall,
shaping the face filled with passion,
and, from the touch of his fingers, Eros is brushing in
a sentiment on the brow, the eyes, the lips.

ΜΙΑ ΝΥΧΤΑ

Ἡ κάμαρα ἦταν πτωχικὴ καὶ πρόστυχη,
κρυμένη ἐπάνω ἀπὸ τὴν ὕποπτη ταβέρνα.
Ἀπ' τὸ παράθυρο φαίνονταν τὸ σοκάκι,
τὸ ἀκάθαρτο καὶ τὸ στενό. Ἀπὸ κάτω
ἤρχονταν ἡ φωνὲς κάτι ἐργατῶν
ποὺ ἔπαιζαν χαρτιὰ καὶ ποὺ γλεντοῦσαν.

Κ' ἐκεῖ στὸ λαϊκό, τὸ ταπεινὸ κρεββάτι
εἶχα τὸ σῶμα τοῦ ἔρωτος, εἶχα τὰ χείλη
τὰ ἡδονικὰ καὶ ρόδινα τῆς μέθης—
τὰ ρόδινα μιᾶς τέτοιας μέθης, ποὺ καὶ τώρα
ποὺ γράφω, ἔπειτ' ἀπὸ τόσα χρόνια!,
μὲς στὸ μονῆρες σπίτι μου, μεθῶ ξανά.

ONE NIGHT

The room was poor and profligate,
hidden above that suspect bar.
Out of the window you saw the alley,
dirty and narrow. From below
you heard the voices of workmen,
playing cards and carousing.

And there, on that common, that plain bed
I had the body of love, I had the lips,
the same sensual, rosy-red ecstasy—
rosy-red lips of such ecstasy, that even now
as I write after so many years,
in my solitary home, I am drunk again.

ΕΠΕΣΤΡΕΦΕ

Ἐπέστρεφε συχνὰ καὶ παῖρνε με,
ἀγαπημένη αἴσθησις ἐπέστρεφε καὶ παῖρνε με—
ὅταν ξυπνᾶ τοῦ σώματος ἡ μνήμη,
κ' ἐπιθυμία παληὰ ξαναπερνᾶ στὸ αἷμα·
ὅταν τὰ χείλη καὶ τὸ δέρμα ἐνθυμοῦνται,
κ' αἰσθάνονται τὰ χέρια σὰν ν' ἀγγίζουν πάλι.

Ἐπέστρεφε συχνὰ καὶ παῖρνε με τὴν νύχτα,
ὅταν τὰ χείλη καὶ τὸ δέρμα ἐνθυμοῦνται …

REAPPEAR

Reappear often and take me,
dearest feeling, reappear and take me—
when the body's memory stirs,
and some old desire lashes the blood;
the time lips and flesh touched—remember,
as the hands now once more feel the hold.

Reappear often and take me in the night,
when lips and skin touched, remember …

ΜΑΚΡΥΑ

Θά 'θελα αὐτὴν τὴν μνήμη νὰ τὴν πῶ ...
Μὰ ἔτσι ἐσβύσθη πιά ... σὰν τίποτε δὲν ἀπομένει—
γιατὶ μακρυά, στὰ πρῶτα ἐφηβικά μου χρόνια κεῖται.

Δέρμα σὰν καμωμένο ἀπὸ ἰασεμί ...
Ἐκείνη τοῦ Αὐγούστου—Αὔγουστος ἦταν;—ἡ βραδυά ...
Μόλις θυμοῦμαι πιὰ τὰ μάτια· ἦσαν, θαρρῶ, μαβιά ...
Ἀ ναί, μαβιά· ἕνα σαπφείρινο μαβί.

LONG AGO

This memory, I want to speak of it now …
So distant, so faded … as if nothing of it remained—
it lingers on from my first adolescent years.

A skin as if of jasmine …
that August evening—was it August? …
I can barely recall the eyes now; they were, I think, blue …
Ah yes, blue: a sapphire blue.

OMNYEI

Ὀμνύει κάθε τόσο   ν' ἀρχίσει πιὸ καλὴ ζωή.
Ἀλλ' ὅταν ἔλθ' ἡ νύχτα   μὲ τὲς δικές της συμβουλές,
μὲ τοὺς συμβιβασμούς της,   καὶ μὲ τὲς ὑποσχέσεις της·
ἀλλ' ὅταν ἔλθ' ἡ νύχτα   μὲ τὴν δική της δύναμι
τοῦ σώματος ποὺ θέλει καὶ ζητεῖ, στὴν ἴδια
μοιραία χαρά, χαμένος, ξαναπηαίνει.

HE SWEARS

He swears every so often   to start a better life.
Ah, when night comes   with its own advice,
its own compromises,   its own promises;
ah, when night comes   with its own swaying power
of the body that desires and begs for it—that same
fateful joy, where he loses himself yet one more time.

ΕΠΗΓΑ

Δὲν ἐδεσμεύθηκα. Τελείως ἀφέθηκα κ' ἐπῆγα.
Στὲς ἀπολαύσεις, ποὺ μισὸ πραγματικές,
μισὸ γυρνάμενες μὲς στὸ μυαλό μου ἦσαν,
ἐπῆγα μὲς στὴν φωτισμένη νύχτα.
Κ' ἤπια ἀπὸ δυνατὰ κρασιά, καθὼς
ποὺ πίνουν οἱ ἀνδρεῖοι τῆς ἡδονῆς.

I WENT

I did not hold back. I let go completely and went.
I took in those savoring pleasures, the half-real,
half-shaped in my own mind they were;
I went into the brilliant night.
And I drank of potent wines, such as
the bold in their sensual pleasure drink.

ΠΟΛΥΕΛΑΙΟΣ

Σὲ κάμαρη ἄδεια καὶ μικρή, τέσσαρες τοῖχοι μόνοι,
καὶ σκεπασμένοι μὲ ὁλοπράσινα πανιά,
καίει ἕνας πολυέλαιος ὡραῖος καὶ κορώνει·
καὶ μὲς στὴ φλόγα του τὴν καθεμιὰ πυρώνει
μιὰ λάγνη πάθησις, μιὰ λάγνη ὁρμή.

Μὲς στὴν μικρὴ τὴν κάμαρη, ποὺ λάμπει ἀναμένη
ἀπὸ τοῦ πολυελαίου τὴν δυνατὴ φωτιά,
διόλου συνειθισμένο φῶς δὲν εἶν' αὐτὸ ποὺ βγαίνει.
Γι' ἄτολμα σώματα δὲν εἶναι καμωμένη
αὐτῆς τῆς ζέστης ἡ ἡδονή.

CHANDELIER

The chamber, empty and small, four lonely walls,
strewn with bright green rags of linen:
a beautiful chandelier burns its heavy glow
and in each of its flames blazes
a lusty passion, a lusty drive.

Inside the small chamber, all radiant and aflame
by the chandelier's powerful fire,
no ordinary flame emerges from it.
No glow for timid flesh, this sensual heat,
it is only made for bodies on fire.

ΑΠ' ΤΕΣ ΕΝΝΙΑ—

Δώδεκα καὶ μισή. Γρήγορα πέρασεν ἡ ὥρα
ἀπ' τὲς ἐννιὰ ποὺ ἄναψα τὴν λάμπα,
καὶ κάθισα ἐδῶ. Κάθουμουν χωρὶς νὰ διαβάζω,
καὶ χωρὶς νὰ μιλῶ. Μὲ ποιόνα νὰ μιλήσω
κατάμονος μέσα στὸ σπίτι αὐτό.

Τὸ εἴδωλον τοῦ νέου σώματός μου,
ἀπ' τὲς ἐννιὰ ποὺ ἄναψα τὴν λάμπα,
ἦλθε καὶ μὲ ηὗρε καὶ μὲ θύμισε
κλειστὲς κάμαρες ἀρωματισμένες,
καὶ περασμένην ἡδονή—τί τολμηρὴ ἡδονή!
Κ' ἐπίσης μ' ἔφερε στὰ μάτια ἐμπρός,
δρόμους ποὺ τώρα ἔγιναν ἀγνώριστοι,
κέντρα γεμάτα κίνησι ποὺ τέλεψαν,
καὶ θέατρα καὶ καφενεῖα ποὺ ἦσαν μιὰ φορά.

Τὸ εἴδωλον τοῦ νέου σώματός μου
ἦλθε καὶ μ' ἔφερε καὶ τὰ λυπητερά·
πένθη τῆς οἰκογένειας, χωρισμοί,
αἰσθήματα δικῶν μου, αἰσθήματα
τῶν πεθαμένων τόσο λίγο ἐκτιμηθέντα.

Δώδεκα καὶ μισή. Πῶς πέρασεν ἡ ὥρα.
Δώδεκα καὶ μισή. Πῶς πέρασαν τὰ χρόνια.

SINCE NINE O'CLOCK—

Half past twelve. Time has passed so quickly
since nine o'clock when I lit the lamp
and sat down here. I've been sitting without a book,
without speaking to anyone. Then again, who
could I speak with, all alone in this house?

The vision of my youthful body,
since nine o'clock when I lit the lamp,
has come to me, come to remind me
of perfumed bedrooms shut tight,
of sensual abandon long gone—what daring abandon!
And it brought before my eyes streets
that have become altered beyond recognition,
clubs buzzing, full with people that are no more,
theatres and cafés that once were here.

The vision of my youthful body
has also come to bring me these sad things:
family grievings, separations,
feelings for those near to me, feelings
for those already dead and little honored.

Half past twelve. How time has passed.
Half past twelve. How the years have passed.

ΝΟΗΣΙΣ

Τὰ χρόνια τῆς νεότητός μου, ὁ ἡδονικός μου βίος—
πῶς βλέπω τώρα καθαρὰ τὸ νόημά των.

Τί μεταμέλειες περιττές, τί μάταιες …

Ἀλλὰ δὲν ἔβλεπα τὸ νόημα τότε.

Μέσα στὸν ἔκλυτο τῆς νεότητός μου βίο
μορφώνονταν βουλὲς τῆς ποιήσεώς μου,
σχεδιάζονταν τῆς τέχνης μου ἡ περιοχή.

Γι' αὐτὸ κ' ἡ μεταμέλειες σταθερὲς ποτὲ δὲν ἦσαν.
Κ' ἡ ἀποφάσεις μου νὰ κρατηθῶ, ν' ἀλλάξω
διαρκοῦσαν δυὸ ἑβδομάδες τὸ πολύ.

UNDERSTANDING

The years of my youth, my hedonistic days—
I see clearly what they meant to me.

How useless repenting, how futile now …

But I couldn't see what it all meant then.

In the profligate years of my youth
the motive for this poetry was shaped,
the ground for my art was hammered out.

That's why repentance was never firm enough.
And my resolve to hold back, to change my ways,
would only last some two weeks at most.

ΕΝΩΠΙΟΝ ΤΟΥ ΑΓΑΛΜΑΤΟΣ ΤΟΥ ΕΝΔΥΜΙΩΝΟΣ

Ἐπὶ ἅρματος λευκοῦ ποὺ τέσσαρες ἡμίονοι
πάλλευκοι σύρουν, μὲ κοσμήματ' ἀργυρᾶ,
φθάνω ἐκ Μιλήτου εἰς τὸν Λάτμον. Ἱερὰ
τελῶν—θυσίας καὶ σπονδάς—τῷ Ἐνδυμίωνι,
ἀπὸ τὴν Ἀλεξάνδρειαν ἔπλευσα ἐν τριήρει πορφυρᾷ.—
Ἰδοὺ τὸ ἄγαλμα. Ἐν ἐκστάσει βλέπω νῦν
τοῦ Ἐνδυμίωνος τὴν φημισμένην καλλονήν.
Ἰάσμων κάνιστρα κενοῦν οἱ δοῦλοι μου· κ' εὐοίωνοι
ἐπευφημίαι ἐξύπνησαν ἀρχαίων χρόνων ἡδονήν.

BEFORE THE STATUE OF ENDYMION

I arrived upon a white chariot, all-silver
ornaments, drawn by four snow-white mules,
traveling from Miletos to Latmos. I sailed
out of Alexandria in a purple trireme to perform
sacred rites—sacrifices and libations—to honor Endymion.
Behold this statue. I now look in ecstasy
at Endymion's timeless beauty.
My servants have strewn baskets of jasmine; favorable
tribute awakens the pleasures of ancient days.

ΠΡΕΣΒΕΙΣ ΑΠ' ΤΗΝ ΑΛΕΞΑΝΔΡΕΙΑ

Δὲν εἶδαν, ἐπὶ αἰῶνας, τέτοια ὡραῖα δῶρα στοὺς Δελφοὺς
σὰν τοῦτα ποὺ ἐστάλθηκαν ἀπὸ τοὺς δυὸ τοὺς ἀδελφούς,
τοὺς ἀντιζήλους Πτολεμαίους βασιλεῖς. Ἀφοῦ τὰ πῆραν
ὅμως, ἀνησυχῆσαν οἱ ἱερεῖς γιὰ τὸν χρησμό. Τὴν πεῖραν
ὅλην των θὰ χρειασθοῦν τὸ πῶς μὲ ὀξύνοιαν νὰ συνταχθεῖ,
ποιὸς ἀπ' τοὺς δυό, ποιὸς ἀπὸ τέτοιους δυὸ νὰ δυσαρεστηθεῖ.
Καὶ συνεδριάζουνε τὴν νύχτα μυστικὰ
καὶ συζητοῦν τῶν Λαγιδῶν τὰ οἰκογενειακά.

Ἀλλὰ ἰδοὺ οἱ πρέσβεις ἐπανῆλθαν. Χαιρετοῦν.
Στὴν Ἀλεξάνδρεια ἐπιστρέφουν, λέν. Καὶ δὲν ζητοῦν
χρησμὸ κανένα. Κ' οἱ ἱερεῖς τ' ἀκοῦνε μὲ χαρὰ
(ἐννοεῖται, ποὺ κρατοῦν τὰ δῶρα τὰ λαμπρά),
ἀλλ' εἶναι καὶ στὸ ἔπακρον ἀπορημένοι,
μὴ νοιώθοντας τί ἡ ἐξαφνικὴ ἀδιαφορία αὐτὴ σημαίνει.
Γιατὶ ἀγνοοῦν ποὺ χθὲς στοὺς πρέσβεις ἦλθαν νέα βαρυά.
Στὴν Ρώμη δόθηκε ὁ χρησμός· ἔγιν' ἐκεῖ ἡ μοιρασιά.

ENVOYS FROM ALEXANDRIA

They haven't seen for centuries such beautiful gifts
at Delphi as these sent to them by the two brothers,
the rival Ptolemaic Kings. But as they received them,
the priests began to worry as to the oracle. They'll need
to call up all their experience, how to compose it discreetly,
worrying which of the two, which of these two would take offense.
So they decide to meet in secret, at night,
to talk of family matters of the Lagids.

But see now, the envoys are back. They take their leave.
Returning to Alexandria, they say. And they do not ask for
an oracle at all. The priests hear them with pleasure
(it's understood they should keep the brilliant gifts),
but they're completely bewildered as well,
unable to fathom what this abrupt indifference means.
For they could not know that yesterday the envoys heard vital news.
The oracle was issued in Rome; there the partition was decided already.

ΑΡΙΣΤΟΒΟΥΛΟΣ

Κλαίει τὸ παλάτι, κλαίει ὁ βασιλεύς,
ἀπαρηγόρητος θρηνεῖ ὁ βασιλεὺς Ἡρώδης,
ἡ πολιτεία ὁλόκληρη κλαίει γιὰ τὸν Ἀριστόβουλο
ποὺ ἔτσι ἄδικα, τυχαίως πνίχθηκε
παίζοντας μὲ τοὺς φίλους του μὲς στὸ νερό.

Κι ὅταν τὸ μάθουνε καὶ στ' ἄλλα μέρη,
ὅταν ἐπάνω στὴν Συρία διαδοθεῖ,
κι ἀπὸ τοὺς Ἕλληνας πολλοὶ θὰ λυπηθοῦν·
ὅσοι ποιηταὶ καὶ γλύπται θὰ πενθήσουν,
γιατ' εἶχεν ἀκουσθεῖ σ' αὐτοὺς ὁ Ἀριστόβουλος,
καὶ ποιά τους φαντασία γιὰ ἔφηβο ποτὲ
ἔφθασε τέτοιαν ἐμορφιὰ σὰν τοῦ παιδιοῦ αὐτοῦ·
ποιὸ ἄγαλμα θεοῦ ἀξιώθηκεν ἡ Ἀντιόχεια
σὰν τὸ παιδὶ αὐτὸ τοῦ Ἰσραήλ.

Ὀδύρεται καὶ κλαίει ἡ Πρώτη Πριγκηπέσσα·
ἡ μάνα του ἡ πιὸ μεγάλη Ἑβρέσσα.
Ὀδύρεται καὶ κλαίει ἡ Ἀλεξάνδρα γιὰ τὴν συμφορά.—
Μὰ σὰν βρεθεῖ μονάχη της ἀλλάζει ὁ καϋμός της.
Βογγᾶ· φρενιάζει· βρίζει· καταριέται.
Πῶς τὴν ἐγέλασαν! Πῶς τὴν φενάκισαν!
Πῶς ἐπὶ τέλους ἔ γ ι ν ε ὁ σκοπός των!
Τὸ ρήμαξαν τὸ σπίτι τῶν Ἀσαμωναίων.
Πῶς τὸ κατόρθωσε ὁ κακοῦργος βασιλεύς·
ὁ δόλιος, ὁ φαῦλος, ὁ ἀλιτήριος.
Πῶς τὸ κατόρθωσε. Τί καταχθόνιο σχέδιο
ποὺ νὰ μὴ νοιώσει κ' ἡ Μαριάμμη τίποτε.
Ἂν ἔνοιωθε ἡ Μαριάμμη, ἂν ὑποπτεύονταν,
θὰ 'βρισκε τρόπο τὸ ἀδέρφι της νὰ σώσει·
βασίλισσα εἶναι τέλος, θὰ μποροῦσε κάτι.
Πῶς θὰ θριαμβεύουν τώρα καὶ θὰ χαίρονται κρυφὰ

ARISTOBOULOS

The palace weeps, the king weeps,
King Herodes mourns, grief-stricken,
the whole province weeps for Aristoboulos
drowned unjustly, by accident,
while playing with his friends in the water.

And when they learn of it abroad,
when the news reaches as far as Syria,
even the Greeks there, many of them will be sad;
the poets and sculptors too will mourn,
for they had heard of Aristoboulos,
even if their art could never imagine
a youth with the beauty of this boy—
what statue of a god can Antioch show
to be the equal of this child of Israel!

The First Princess, his mother, weeps,
his mother, the great Hebrew lady.
Alexandra laments and weeps over the tragedy.
But when she is alone, her grief undergoes a change.
She groans, rails, swears, she brings down curses.
How they've fooled her! How they've duped her!
How they've finally *had their way*—for they have
devastated the house of the Asamonaeans!
How did he manage it, this murdering king?
This treacherous, vicious, scheming man.
How did he do it? An infernal scheme
that not even Mariamme could see coming.
If Mariamme had foreseen it, or suspected it,
she'd have found a way to save her brother;
she is a queen after all, she could have done something.
How they will triumph and gloat in secret,

97

ἡ μοχθηρὲς ἐκεῖνες, Κύπρος καὶ Σαλώμη·
ἡ πρόστυχες γυναῖκες, Κύπρος καὶ Σαλώμη.—
Καὶ νά 'ναι ἀνίσχυρη, κι ἀναγκασμένη
νὰ κάνει ποὺ πιστεύει τὲς ψευτιές των·
νὰ μὴ μπορεῖ πρὸς τὸν λαὸ νὰ πάγει,
νὰ βγεῖ καὶ νὰ φωνάξει στοὺς Ἑβραίους,
νὰ πεῖ, νὰ πεῖ πῶς ἔγινε τὸ φονικό.

those sinister women, Kypris and Salome;
those cheap sluts, Kypris and Salome.
And for her to be powerless, to be forced
to pretend she believes their lies;
to be unable to go rushing to her people,
to go out and shout to the Hebrews,
to tell all, tell them how the murder was carried out.

ΚΑΙΣΑΡΙΩΝ

Ἐν μέρει γιὰ νὰ ἐξακριβώσω μιὰ ἐποχή,
ἐν μέρει καὶ τὴν ὥρα νὰ περάσω,
τὴν νύχτα χθὲς πῆρα μιὰ συλλογὴ
ἐπιγραφῶν τῶν Πτολεμαίων νὰ διαβάσω.
Οἱ ἄφθονοι ἔπαινοι κ' ἡ κολακεῖες
εἰς ὅλους μοιάζουν. Ὅλοι εἶναι λαμπροί,
ἔνδοξοι, κραταιοί, ἀγαθοεργοί·
κάθ' ἐπιχείρησίς των σοφοτάτη.
Ἂν πεῖς γιὰ τὲς γυναῖκες τῆς γενιᾶς, κι αὐτές,
ὅλες ἡ Βερενίκες κ' ἡ Κλεοπάτρες θαυμαστές.

Ὅταν κατόρθωσα τὴν ἐποχὴ νὰ ἐξακριβώσω
θ' ἄφινα τὸ βιβλίο ἂν μιὰ μνεία μικρή,
κι ἀσήμαντη, τοῦ βασιλέως Καισαρίωνος
δὲν εἵλκυε τὴν προσοχή μου ἀμέσως …

Ἄ, νά, ἦρθες σὺ μὲ τὴν ἀόριστη
γοητεία σου. Στὴν ἱστορία λίγες
γραμμὲς μονάχα βρίσκονται γιὰ σένα,
κ' ἔτσι πιὸ ἐλεύθερα σ' ἔπλασα μὲς στὸν νοῦ μου.
Σ' ἔπλασα ὡραῖο κ' αἰσθηματικό.
Ἡ τέχνη μου στὸ πρόσωπό σου δίνει
μιὰν ὀνειρώδη συμπαθητικὴ ἐμορφιά.
Καὶ τόσο πλήρως σὲ φαντάσθηκα,
ποὺ χθὲς τὴν νύχτα ἀργά, σὰν ἔσβυνεν
ἡ λάμπα μου—ἄφισα ἐπίτηδες νὰ σβύνει—
ἐθάρρεψα ποὺ μπῆκες μὲς στὴν κάμαρά μου,
μὲ φάνηκε ποὺ ἐμπρός μου στάθηκες· ὡς θὰ ἤσουν
μὲς στὴν κατακτημένην Ἀλεξάνδρεια,
χλωμὸς καὶ κουρασμένος, ἰδεώδης ἐν τῇ λύπῃ σου,
ἐλπίζοντας ἀκόμη νὰ σὲ σπλαχνισθοῦν
οἱ φαῦλοι—ποὺ ψιθύριζαν τὸ «Πολυκαισαρίη».

KAISARION

In part to research a certain era,
in part to pass the time for a while,
I picked up last night a collection
of Ptolemaic inscriptions to read.
The many praises and the flatteries are much
the same for all of them. All are bright,
glorious, mighty, with good deeds to their name;
with every undertaking, full of wisdom.
If you speak of the women of their line, all those
are worthy, all Berenikes and Kleopatras.

When I thought I'd examined the period I wanted,
I would have left the book, were it not for a small,
unimportant detail: the noting of King Kaisarion
who attracted my attention at once …

And there you were, you came with
your indefinable appeal. Only a few lines
are found in history about you,
and so I might form you more freely in my mind.
I made you beautiful and full of sentiment.
My art gives to your face
a dreamlike, engaging beauty.
And so fully did I imagine you
that yesterday, late into the night, as my lamp
died out—I let myself die out—
I wondered that you came into my room,
you seemed to stand before me, as you might have
in conquered Alexandria,
pale and weary, ideal in your grief,
hoping that they would still take pity on you,
those lowlifes who whispered: "Too many Caesars."

Η ΔΙΟΡΙΑ ΤΟΥ ΝΕΡΩΝΟΣ

Δὲν ἀνησύχησεν ὁ Νέρων ὅταν ἄκουσε
τοῦ Δελφικοῦ Μαντείου τὸν χρησμό.
«Τὰ ἑβδομῆντα τρία χρόνια νὰ φοβᾶται.»
Εἶχε καιρὸν ἀκόμη νὰ χαρεῖ.
Τριάντα χρονῶ εἶναι. Πολὺ ἀρκετὴ
εἶν' ἡ διορία ποὺ ὁ θεὸς τὸν δίδει
γιὰ νὰ φροντίσει γιὰ τοὺς μέλλοντας κινδύνους.

Τώρα στὴν Ρώμη θὰ ἐπιστρέψει κουρασμένος λίγο,
ἀλλὰ ἐξαίσια κουρασμένος ἀπὸ τὸ ταξεῖδι αὐτό,
ποὺ ἦταν ὅλο μέρες ἀπολαύσεως—
στὰ θέατρα, στοὺς κήπους, στὰ γυμνάσια ...
Τῶν πόλεων τῆς Ἀχαΐας ἑσπέρες ...
Ἆ τῶν γυμνῶν σωμάτων ἡ ἡδονὴ πρὸ πάντων ...

Αὐτὰ ὁ Νέρων. Καὶ στὴν Ἰσπανία ὁ Γάλβας
κρυφὰ τὸ στράτευμά του συναθροίζει καὶ τὸ ἀσκεῖ,
ὁ γέροντας ὁ ἑβδομῆντα τριῶ χρονῶ.

NERO'S TERM

It didn't disturb Nero, not a bit, when he heard
the prediction of the oracle at Delphi:
"Beware the age of seventy-three."
He still has time to enjoy himself.
He's only thirty. More than enough
is the time the god has given him
to take care of future dangers.

Now, he'll return to Rome a little tired,
but exquisitely tired, due to the journey,
for the days there were pure enjoyment—
in theatres, in gardens, in sports …
evenings spent in the cities of Achaia …
and above all, the sexual desire of naked bodies …

That, for Nero's part. While Galba in Spain
pulls together his armies and drills them in secret—
that old man in his seventy-third year.

ΕΙΣ ΤΟ ΕΠΙΝΕΙΟΝ

Νέος, εἴκοσι ὀκτὼ ἐτῶν, μὲ πλοῖον τήνιον
ἔφθασε εἰς τοῦτο τὸ συριακὸν ἐπίνειον
ὁ Ἔμης, μὲ τὴν πρόθεσι νὰ μάθει μυροπώλης.
Ὅμως ἀρρώστησε εἰς τὸν πλοῦν. Καὶ μόλις
ἀπεβιβάσθη, πέθανε. Ἡ ταφή του, πτωχοτάτη,
ἔγιν᾽ ἐδῶ. Ὀλίγες ὥρες πρὶν πεθάνει, κάτι
ψιθύρισε γιὰ «οἰκίαν», γιὰ «πολὺ γέροντας γονεῖς».
Μὰ ποιοὶ ἦσαν τοῦτοι δὲν ἐγνώριζε κανείς,
μήτε ποιὰ ἡ πατρίς του μὲς στὸ μέγα πανελλήνιον.
Καλλίτερα. Γιατὶ ἔτσι ἐνῶ
κεῖται νεκρὸς σ᾽ αὐτὸ τὸ ἐπίνειον,
θὰ τὸν ἐλπίζουν πάντα οἱ γονεῖς του ζωντανό.

IN THE HARBOR TOWN

Young, all of twenty-eight years, on a Tenian ship,
he came here to this Syrian harbor town—
Emes by name, he intends to learn the incense trade.
But he fell ill during the journey. And just as
he was put ashore, he died. His burial, the poorest,
took place here. A few hours before he died he spoke
faintly, something about "home," and "very old parents."
But who they might be, nobody here knew,
or what country he called home in the great panhellenic world.
Better this way. For although
he lies dead in this harbor town,
his parents will always hope he is alive.

ΕΝΑΣ ΘΕΟΣ ΤΩΝ

Ὅταν κανένας των περνοῦσεν ἀπ' τῆς Σελευκείας
τὴν ἀγορά, περὶ τὴν ὥρα ποὺ βραδυάζει,
σὰν ὑψηλὸς καὶ τέλεια ὡραῖος ἔφηβος,
μὲ τὴν χαρὰ τῆς ἀφθαρσίας μὲς στὰ μάτια,
μὲ τ' ἀρωματισμένα μαῦρα του μαλλιά,
οἱ διαβάται τὸν ἐκύτταζαν
κι ὁ ἕνας τὸν ἄλλονα ρωτοῦσεν ἂν τὸν γνώριζε,
κι ἂν ἦταν Ἕλλην τῆς Συρίας, ἢ ξένος. Ἀλλὰ μερικοί,
ποὺ μὲ περισσοτέρα προσοχὴ παρατηροῦσαν,
ἐκαταλάμβαναν καὶ παραμέριζαν·
κ' ἐνῶ ἐχάνετο κάτω ἀπ' τὲς στοές,
μὲς στὲς σκιὲς καὶ μὲς στὰ φῶτα τῆς βραδυᾶς,
πηαίνοντας πρὸς τὴν συνοικία ποὺ τὴν νύχτα
μονάχα ζεῖ, μὲ ὄργια καὶ κραιπάλη,
καὶ κάθε εἴδους μέθη καὶ λαγνεία,
ἐρέμβαζαν ποιὸς τάχα ἦταν ἐξ Αὐτῶν,
καὶ γιὰ ποιὰν ὕποπτην ἀπόλαυσί του
στῆς Σελευκείας τοὺς δρόμους ἐκατέβηκεν
ἀπ' τὰ Προσκυνητά, Πάνσεπτα Δώματα.

ONE OF THEIR GODS

When one of them appeared, walking through Seleukeia's
marketplace, just at the hour of nightfall,
moving like a young ephebe, tall, of perfect beauty,
and with the joy of immortality in his eyes,
with his jet-black hair perfumed,
the passers-by kept gazing at him,
one asked the other if anyone knew him,
if he were a Greek from Syria or a stranger.
But some who scrutinized him with greater care
would understand and step aside;
and as he vanished beneath the arcades,
in the shadows and the night lights,
going toward that quarter which comes alive
only at night, with orgies and debauchery,
with all kinds of intoxication and lust,
they wondered which of Them could he be,
and for what secret pleasure of his
had he descended to walk Seleukeia's streets
from the Hallowed, Celestial Mansions.

ΛΑΝΗ ΤΑΦΟΣ

Ὁ Λάνης ποὺ ἀγάπησες ἐδῶ δὲν εἶναι, Μάρκε,
στὸν τάφο ποὺ ἔρχεσαι καὶ κλαῖς, καὶ μένεις ὧρες κι ὧρες.
Τὸν Λάνη ποὺ ἀγάπησες τὸν ἔχεις πιὸ κοντά σου
στὸ σπίτι σου ὅταν κλείεσαι καὶ βλέπεις τὴν εἰκόνα,
ποὺ αὐτὴ κάπως διατήρησεν ὅ,τ' εἶχε ποὺ ν' ἀξίζει,
ποὺ αὐτὴ κάπως διατήρησεν ὅ,τ' εἶχες ἀγαπήσει.

Θυμᾶσαι, Μάρκε, ποὺ ἔφερες ἀπὸ τοῦ ἀνθυπάτου
τὸ μέγαρον τὸν Κυρηναῖο περίφημο ζωγράφο,
καὶ μὲ τί καλλιτεχνικὴν ἐκεῖνος πανουργία
μόλις εἶδε τὸν φίλο σου κ' ἤθελε νὰ σᾶς πείσει
ποὺ ὡς Ὑάκινθον ἐξ ἅπαντος ἔπρεπε νὰ τὸν κάμει
(μ' αὐτὸν τὸν τρόπο πιὸ πολὺ θ' ἀκούονταν ἡ εἰκών του).

Μὰ ὁ Λάνης σου δὲν δάνειζε τὴν ἐμορφιά του ἔτσι·
καὶ σταθερὰ ἐναντιωθεὶς εἶπε νὰ παρουσιάσει
ὄχι διόλου τὸν Ὑάκινθον, ὄχι κανέναν ἄλλον,
ἀλλὰ τὸν Λάνη, υἱὸ τοῦ Ραμετίχου, Ἀλεξανδρέα.

TOMB OF LANES

The Lanes you loved, Markos, is no longer here
in this tomb where you come and weep, and spend hours on end.
The Lanes you loved you have nearer you now, at your home,
when you shut yourself inside and watch the painting,
a portrait that still keeps what was of value in him,
that still keeps what it was you loved in him.

Remember, Markos, when you brought the famed Kyrenian
painter from the Proconsul's palace, with what artistic tact
he tried to persuade the two of you, and especially when
he laid eyes on your friend, that he most definitely had to
convince you both to do Lanes as Hyacinth
(for in that way his portrait would be more famous.)

But your Lanes did not lend out his beauty so;
and, opposing him with conviction, told him to portray
neither Hyacinth, nor anyone else,
but only Lanes, son of Rametichos, an Alexandrian.

ΙΑΣΗ ΤΑΦΟΣ

Κεῖμαι ὁ Ἰασῆς ἐνταῦθα. Τῆς μεγάλης ταύτης πόλεως
ὁ ἔφηβος ὁ φημισμένος γιὰ ἐμορφιά.
Μ' ἐθαύμασαν βαθεῖς σοφοί· κ' ἐπίσης ὁ ἐπιπόλαιος,
ὁ ἁπλοῦς λαός. Καὶ χαίρομουν ἴσα καὶ γιὰ

τὰ δυό. Μὰ ἀπ' τὸ πολὺ νὰ μ' ἔχει ὁ κόσμος Νάρκισσο κ' Ἑρμῆ,
ἡ καταχρήσεις μ' ἔφθειραν, μ' ἐσκότωσαν. Διαβάτη,
ἂν εἶσαι Ἀλεξανδρεύς, δὲν θὰ ἐπικρίνεις. Ξέρεις τὴν ὁρμὴ
τοῦ βίου μας· τί θέρμην ἔχει· τί ἡδονὴ ὑπερτάτη.

TOMB OF IASES

I, Iases, lie here. Belonging to this great city,
the youth most renowned for his beauty.
Men of deep wisdom admired me; no less the simple,
run-of-the-mill ones. And I took equal pleasure

in both. But from people seeing me as a Narcissus
and a Hermes—excess wore my body out. They killed me.
Passerby, if you're an Alexandrian, you'll not reproach.
You know the drive of our lives: its fever, its sensual excess.

ΕΝ ΠΟΛΕΙ ΤΗΣ ΟΣΡΟΗΝΗΣ

Ἀπ' τῆς ταβέρνας τὸν καυγᾶ μᾶς φέραν πληγωμένο
τὸν φίλον Ρέμωνα χθὲς περὶ τὰ μεσάνυχτα.
Ἀπ' τὰ παράθυρα ποὺ ἀφίσαμεν ὁλάνοιχτα,
τ' ὡραῖο του σῶμα στὸ κρεββάτι φώτιζε ἡ σελήνη.
Εἴμεθα ἕνα κρᾶμα ἐδῶ· Σύροι, Γραικοί, Ἀρμένιοι, Μῆδοι.
Τέτοιος κι ὁ Ρέμων εἶναι. Ὅμως χθὲς σὰν φώτιζε
τὸ ἐρωτικό του πρόσωπο ἡ σελήνη,
ὁ νοῦς μας πῆγε στὸν πλατωνικὸ Χαρμίδη.

A TOWN IN OSROENE

From that tavern brawl, around midnight, they brought to us
wounded our dear friend Rhemon.
Through the windows we'd left wide open,
the moon glistened against his beautiful body on the bed.
We're a mixture of youths here: Syrians, Greeks,
Armenians, Medes. Rhemon, too, is one such. Last night,
yes, when the moon illumined his erotic face,
our mind sought out the time of Plato's Charmides.

ΙΓΝΑΤΙΟΥ ΤΑΦΟΣ

Ἐδῶ δὲν εἶμαι ὁ Κλέων ποὺ ἀκούσθηκα
στὴν Ἀλεξάνδρεια (ὅπου δύσκολα ξιπάζονται)
γιὰ τὰ λαμπρά μου σπίτια, γιὰ τοὺς κήπους,
γιὰ τ᾽ ἄλογα καὶ γιὰ τ᾽ ἀμάξια μου,
γιὰ τὰ διαμαντικὰ καὶ τὰ μετάξια ποὺ φοροῦσα.
Ἄπαγε· ἐδῶ δὲν εἶμαι ὁ Κλέων ἐκεῖνος·
τὰ εἴκοσι ὀκτώ του χρόνια νὰ σβυσθοῦν.
Εἶμ᾽ ὁ Ἰγνάτιος, ἀναγνώστης, ποὺ πολὺ ἀργὰ
συνῆλθα· ἀλλ᾽ ὅμως κ᾽ ἔτσι δέκα μῆνες ἔζησα εὐτυχεῖς
μὲς στὴν γαλήνη καὶ μὲς στὴν ἀσφάλεια τοῦ Χριστοῦ.

114

TOMB OF IGNATIOS

Here I'm not that Kleon everybody's heard of
in Alexandria (where it's hard to boast)
for my exquisite houses, my gardens,
for my horses and for my chariots,
or for the diamonds and pure silks I wore.
Be that far from me now; here I'm not Kleon.
Let them be wiped out, his twenty-eight years.
I am Ignatios, lay-recitor, who came to my senses
very late; but even so, I lived ten happy months
in tranquility, happily secure with Christ.

ΕΝ ΤΩ ΜΗΝΙ ΑΘΥΡ

Μὲ δυσκολία διαβάζω   στὴν πέτρα τὴν ἀρχαία.
«Κύ[ρι]ε Ἰησοῦ Χριστέ».   Ἕνα «Ψυ[χ]ὴν» διακρίνω.
«Ἐν τῷ μη[νὶ] Ἀθὺρ»   «Ὁ Λεύκιο[ς] ἐ[κοιμ]ήθη».
Στὴ μνεία τῆς ἡλικίας   «Ἐβί[ωσ]εν ἐτῶν»,
τὸ Κάππα Ζῆτα δείχνει   ποὺ νέος ἐκοιμήθη.
Μὲς στὰ φθαρμένα βλέπω   «Αὐτὸ[ν] ... Ἀλεξανδρέα».
Μετὰ ἔχει τρεῖς γραμμὲς   πολὺ ἀκρωτηριασμένες·
μὰ κάτι λέξεις βγάζω—   σὰν «δ[ά]κρυα ἡμῶν», «ὀδύνην»,
κατόπιν πάλι «δάκρυα»,   καὶ «[ἡμ]ῖν τοῖς [φ]ίλοις πένθος».
Μὲ φαίνεται ποὺ ὁ Λεύκιος   μεγάλως θ᾽ ἀγαπήθη.
Ἐν τῷ μηνὶ Ἀθὺρ   ὁ Λεύκιος ἐκοιμήθη.

IN THE MONTH OF ATHYR

I read with difficulty   on this ancient stone:
"Lo[r]d Jesus Christ."   A "so[u]l" is clear to me.
"In the mon[th] of Athyr"   "Leukio[s] was laid to [sle]ep."
Here is something about age   "He li[ve]d to the age of"—
the Kappa-Zeta indicates   how very young he went to sleep.
In the worn-out part, I see   "Hi[m] ... Alexandrian."
Then follow three lines   badly broken apart;
but I can make out words   like "our t[ea]rs," "grief;"
then "tears" again,   and [we] his [f]riends do mourn."
It seems to me Leukios   was greatly loved.
In the month of Athyr   Leukios was laid to sleep.

ΓΙΑ ΤΟΝ ΑΜΜΟΝΗ, ΠΟΥ ΠΕΘΑΝΕ 29 ΕΤΩΝ,
ΣΤΑ 610

Ραφαήλ, ὀλίγους στίχους σὲ ζητοῦν
γιὰ ἐπιτύμβιον τοῦ ποιητοῦ Ἀμμόνη νὰ συνθέσεις.
Κάτι πολὺ καλαίσθητον καὶ λεῖον. Σὺ θὰ μπορέσεις,
εἶσαι ὁ κατάλληλος, νὰ γράψεις ὡς ἁρμόζει
γιὰ τὸν ποιητὴν Ἀμμόνη, τὸν δικό μας.

Βέβαια θὰ πεῖς γιὰ τὰ ποιήματά του—
ἀλλὰ νὰ πεῖς καὶ γιὰ τὴν ἐμορφιά του,
γιὰ τὴν λεπτὴ ἐμορφιά του ποὺ ἀγαπήσαμε.

Πάντοτε ὡραῖα καὶ μουσικὰ τὰ ἑλληνικά σου εἶναι.
Ὅμως τὴν μαστοριά σου ὅληνα τὴ θέμε τώρα.
Σὲ ξένη γλῶσσα ἡ λύπη μας κ᾽ ἡ ἀγάπη μας περνοῦν.
Τὸ αἰγυπτιακό σου αἴσθημα χύσε στὴν ξένη γλῶσσα.

Ραφαήλ, οἱ στίχοι σου ἔτσι νὰ γραφοῦν
ποὺ νά ᾽χουν, ξέρεις, ἀπὸ τὴν ζωή μας μέσα των,
ποὺ κι ὁ ρυθμὸς κ᾽ ἡ κάθε φράσις νὰ δηλοῦν
ποὺ γι᾽ Ἀλεξανδρινὸ γράφει Ἀλεξανδρινός.

FOR AMMONES, WHO DIED AT 29,
IN A.D. 610

Raphael, a few verses they ask of you, an
epitaph for the poet Ammones; do compose them:
something of refined taste and polish. You can
do it, you are most suited to write what's just
for the poet Ammones, one of our own.

You will of course speak of his poems—
but you must speak too of his beauty,
of his delicate beauty that we so loved.

Your Greek is always graceful and musical.
Now it's your superb craftsmanship we need.
Our sorrow and our love let pass into the foreign tongue.
Pour all your Egyptian feeling into the Greek you use.

And, Raphael, let your verses be written just
so they may have, you know, something of our life
within them, where every rhythm and every phrase
may show an Alexandrian writing of an Alexandrian.

ΑΙΜΙΛΙΑΝΟΣ ΜΟΝΑΗ, ΑΛΕΞΑΝΔΡΕΥΣ,
628–655 Μ.Χ.

Μὲ λόγια, μὲ φυσιογνωμία, καὶ μὲ τρόπους
μιὰ ἐξαίρετη θὰ κάμω πανοπλία·
καὶ θ' ἀντικρύζω ἔτσι τοὺς κακοὺς ἀνθρώπους
χωρὶς νὰ ἔχω φόβον ἢ ἀδυναμία.

Θὰ θέλουν νὰ μὲ βλάψουν. Ἀλλὰ δὲν θὰ ξέρει
κανεὶς ἀπ' ὅσους θὰ μὲ πλησιάζουν
ποῦ κεῖνται ἡ πληγές μου, τὰ τρωτά μου μέρη,
κάτω ἀπὸ τὰ ψεύδη ποὺ θὰ μὲ σκεπάζουν.—

Ῥήματα τῆς καυχήσεως τοῦ Αἰμιλιανοῦ Μονάη.
Ἄραγε νά 'καμε ποτὲ τὴν πανοπλία αὐτή;
Ἐν πάσῃ περιπτώσει, δὲν τὴν φόρεσε πολύ.
Εἴκοσι ἑπτὰ χρονῶ, στὴν Σικελία πέθανε.

AIMILIANOS MONAE, ALEXANDRIAN,
A.D. 628–655

With the right expression, appearance, and deportment
I will build me a fine suit of armor.
And that's how I intend to face the malicious,
without fearing anything, not even my own weakness.

They'll surely want to harm me. But no one
of those who come near me will know
where my wounds are, my vulnerable parts,
beneath the layer of lies that will shelter me.—

Boastful words of Aimilianos Monae.
I'm wondering: did he ever make that suit of armor?
In any case, he never wore it much.
At age twenty-seven, in Sicily, he died.

ΟΤΑΝ ΔΙΕΓΕΙΡΟΝΤΑΙ

Προσπάθησε νὰ τὰ φυλάξεις, ποιητή,
ὅσο κι ἂν εἶναι λίγα αὐτὰ ποὺ σταματιοῦνται.
Τοῦ ἐρωτισμοῦ σου τὰ ὁράματα.
Βάλ᾽ τα, μισοκρυμένα, μὲς στὲς φράσεις σου.
Προσπάθησε νὰ τὰ κρατήσεις, ποιητή,
ὅταν διεγείρονται μὲς στὸ μυαλό σου,
τὴν νύχτα ἢ μὲς στὴν λάμψι τοῦ μεσημεριοῦ.

WHEN THEY ARE ROUSED

Safeguard them, do try, Poet,
however few they are that you can hold on to—
visions of your erotic life.
Phrase them, half-hidden, in your rhythms.
Hold on to them, do try, Poet—
when they are roused in your brain
at night or in the glare of noontime.

ΗΔΟΝΗ

Χαρὰ καὶ μύρο τῆς ζωῆς μου ἡ μνήμη τῶν ὡρῶν
ποὺ ηὗρα καὶ ποὺ κράτηξα τὴν ἡδονὴ ὡς τὴν ἤθελα.
Χαρὰ καὶ μύρο τῆς ζωῆς μου ἐμένα, ποὺ ἀποστράφηκα
τὴν κάθε ἀπόλαυσιν ἐρώτων τῆς ρουτίνας.

·

TO SENSUAL PLEASURE

Joy and myrrh, incense of my life, memory of the hours
I found and held fast to the pleasure I most wanted.
Joy and myrrh, incense of my life, alone mine, when I turned
away from the place where common love sojourns.

ΕΤΣΙ ΠΟΛΥ ΑΤΕΝΙΣΑ—

Τὴν ἐμορφιὰ ἔτσι πολὺ ἀτένισα,
ποὺ πλήρης εἶναι αὐτῆς ἡ ὅρασίς μου.

Γραμμὲς τοῦ σώματος. Κόκκινα χείλη. Μέλη ἡδονικά.
Μαλλιὰ σὰν ἀπὸ ἀγάλματα ἑλληνικὰ παρμένα·
πάντα ἔμορφα, κι ἀχτένιστα σὰν εἶναι,
καὶ πέφτουν, λίγο, ἐπάνω στ᾽ ἄσπρα μέτωπα.
Πρόσωπα τῆς ἀγάπης, ὅπως τά 'θελεν
ἡ ποίησίς μου ... μὲς στὲς νύχτες τῆς νεότητός μου,
μέσα στὲς νύχτες μου, κρυφά, συναντημένα ...

I'VE FACED HEAD-ON—

I've faced beauty head-on for so long
that my gaze overflows with it.

The body's shape. Red lips. Sexual limbs.
Greek statues' hair:
always lovely, always tousled,
falling lightly on pale foreheads.
Faces of love, those my poetry
most desired ... in the dark nights of my youth,
in my dark nights, met with in secret ...

ΕΝ ΤΗ ΟΔΩ

Τὸ συμπαθητικό του πρόσωπο, κομμάτι ὠχρό·
τὰ καστανά του μάτια, σὰν κομένα·[1]
εἴκοσι πέντ᾽ ἐτῶν, πλὴν μοιάζει μᾶλλον εἴκοσι·
μὲ κάτι καλλιτεχνικὸ στὸ ντύσιμό του
—τίποτε χρῶμα τῆς κραβάτας, σχῆμα τοῦ κολλάρου—
ἀσκόπως περπατεῖ μὲς στὴν ὁδό,
ἀκόμη σὰν ὑπνωτισμένος ἀπ᾽ τὴν ἄνομη ἡδονή,
ἀπὸ τὴν πολὺ ἄνομη ἡδονὴ ποὺ ἀπέκτησε.

---

[1] See Editor's Note, p. xvii, n. 1.

IN THE STREET

His handsome face, somewhat pale;
his chestnut eyes, exhausted;
twenty-five years old, yet looking about twenty;
with something of the artist in his attire
—the hue of his tie, the shape of his collar—
he drifts aimlessly in the street now,
as if still dazed by the pleasure of forbidden sex,
by the exhausting, illicit pleasure he received.

Η ΠΡΟΘΗΚΗ ΤΟΥ ΚΑΠΝΟΠΩΛΕΙΟΥ

Κοντὰ σὲ μιὰ κατάφωτη προθήκη
καπνοπωλείου ἐστέκονταν, ἀνάμεσα σ' ἄλλους πολλούς.
Τυχαίως τὰ βλέμματά των συναντήθηκαν,
καὶ τὴν παράνομην ἐπιθυμία τῆς σαρκός των
ἐξέφρασαν δειλά, διστακτικά.
Ἔπειτα, ὀλίγα βήματα στὸ πεζοδρόμιο ἀνήσυχα—
ὡς ποὺ ἐμειδίασαν, κ' ἔνευσαν ἐλαφρῶς.

Καὶ τότε πιὰ τὸ ἀμάξι τὸ κλεισμένο ...
τὸ αἰσθητικὸ πλησίασμα τῶν σωμάτων·
τὰ ἐνωμένα χέρια, τὰ ἐνωμένα χείλη.

THE TOBACCONIST'S WINDOW

They both stood among a crowd of others,
near the brightly lit window of the tobacconist's shop.
Their eyes met as by chance,
and the illicit desire of each other's body—
they expressed it shyly, hesitantly.
Then, a few paces on the sidewalk, uneasy,
until they smiled and nodded slightly.

Then followed the closed carriage …
the sensual closeness of bodies,
the touch of hands, the touch of lips.

ΠΕΡΑΣΜΑ

Ἐκεῖνα ποὺ δειλὰ φαντάσθη μαθητής, εἶν' ἀνοιχτά,
φανερωμένα ἐμπρός του. Καὶ γυρνᾶ, καὶ ξενυχτᾶ,
καὶ παρασύρεται. Κι ὡς εἶναι (γιὰ τὴν τέχνη μας) σωστό,
τὸ αἷμα του, καινούριο καὶ ζεστό,
ἡ ἡδονὴ τὸ χαίρεται. Τὸ σῶμα του νικᾶ
ἔκνομη ἐρωτικὴ μέθη· καὶ τὰ νεανικὰ
μέλη ἐνδίδουνε σ' αὐτήν.

                 Κ' ἔτσι ἕνα παιδὶ ἁπλὸ
γένεται ἄξιο νὰ τὸ δοῦμε, κι ἀπ' τὸν Ὑψηλὸ
τῆς Ποιήσεως Κόσμο μιὰ στιγμὴ περνᾶ κι αὐτό—
τὸ αἰσθητικὸ παιδὶ μὲ τὸ αἷμα του καινούριο καὶ ζεστό.

PASSAGE

His timid daydreams as a schoolboy are now open
reality before him. Now he roams the night till the small hours,
often led astray. And as it is (for our art) so true,
his blood so warm and new,
enjoyed so by sexual passion itself. His body prizes
the unnatural, erotic, and drunken; and his youthful
limbs surrender to it.

                    And so a simple boy
becomes worthy of our attention, and from the High
World of Poetry, for an instant, he too passes through—
the sensitive boy with his warm blood and new.

ΕΝ ΕΣΠΕΡᾼ

Πάντως δὲν θὰ διαρκούσανε πολύ. Ἡ πεῖρα
τῶν χρόνων μὲ τὸ δείχνει. Ἀλλ' ὅμως κάπως βιαστικὰ
ἦλθε καὶ τὰ σταμάτησεν ἡ Μοῖρα.
Ἤτανε σύντομος ὁ ὡραῖος βίος.
Ἀλλὰ τί δυνατὰ ποὺ ἦσαν τὰ μύρα,
σὲ τί ἐξαίσια κλίνην ἐπλαγιάσαμε,
σὲ τί ἡδονὴ τὰ σώματά μας δώσαμε.

Μιὰ ἀπήχησις τῶν ἡμερῶν τῆς ἡδονῆς,
μιὰ ἀπήχησις τῶν ἡμερῶν κοντά μου ἦλθε,
κάτι ἀπ' τῆς νεότητός μας τῶν δυονῶ τὴν πύρα·
στὰ χέρια μου ἕνα γράμμα ξαναπῆρα,
καὶ διάβαζα πάλι καὶ πάλι ὡς ποὺ ἔλειψε τὸ φῶς.

Καὶ βγῆκα στὸ μπαλκόνι μελαγχολικά—
βγῆκα ν' ἀλλάξω σκέψεις βλέποντας τουλάχιστον
ὀλίγη ἀγαπημένη πολιτεία,
ὀλίγη κίνησι τοῦ δρόμου καὶ τῶν μαγαζιῶν.

IN THE EVENING

Together, we wouldn't have lasted anyway.
Years of experience tell me that. Even so,
Fate came along and put a stop to us a bit abruptly.
It passed us too soon, that beautiful life.
And yet, how strong the fragrances,
how exquisite the bed we lay upon,
what searing pleasure we gave our bodies to.

An echo of the days of sexual pleasure,
an echo of those days came to brush near me,
something of our youth, the fire we two shared;
I lay my hands once more on the letter,
and I read it again and again until the waning of the light.

Then I stepped out on to the balcony, saddened—
I went outside to clear my mind, at least
to look upon some small part of my loving city,
some movement in the streets and the shops.

ΓΚΡΙΖΑ

Κυττάζοντας ἕνα ὀπάλλιο μισὸ γκρίζο
θυμήθηκα δυὸ ὡραῖα γκρίζα μάτια
ποὺ εἶδα· θά 'ναι εἴκοσι χρόνια πρίν ...

....

Γιὰ ἕναν μῆνα ἀγαπηθήκαμε.
Ἔπειτα ἔφυγε, θαρρῶ στὴν Σμύρνη,
γιὰ νὰ ἐργασθεῖ ἐκεῖ, καὶ πιὰ δὲν ἰδωθήκαμε.

Θ' ἀσχήμισαν—ἂν ζεῖ—τὰ γκρίζα μάτια·
θὰ χάλασε τ' ὡραῖο πρόσωπο.

Μνήμη μου, φύλαξέ τα σὺ ὡς ἦσαν.
Καί, μνήμη, ὅ,τι μπορεῖς ἀπὸ τὸν ἔρωτά μου αὐτόν,
ὅ,τι μπορεῖς φέρε με πίσω ἀπόψι.

GRAY

Looking through an opal, half-gray,
I remembered two beautiful gray eyes;
it must be twenty years ago I saw them …

. . . .

We were lovers for a month.
Then he took off, I think, for Smyrna,
searching for work, and we never met again.

They'll be less alluring—if he lives—those gray eyes;
the beautiful face will have broken down.

Memory, safeguard them in your knowledge.
And, memory, bring back what you can of my love,
whatever you can, bring back to me tonight.

ΚΑΤΩ ΑΠ' ΤΟ ΣΠΙΤΙ

Χθὲς περπατῶντας σὲ μιὰ συνοικία
ἀπόκεντρη, πέρασα κάτω ἀπὸ τὸ σπίτι
ποὺ ἔμπαινα σὰν ἤμουν νέος πολύ.
Ἐκεῖ τὸ σῶμα μου εἶχε λάβει ὁ Ἔρως
μὲ τὴν ἐξαίσια του ἰσχύν.

            Καὶ χθὲς
σὰν πέρασ' ἀπ' τὸν δρόμο τὸν παληό,
ἀμέσως ὡραΐσθηκαν ἀπ' τὴν γοητεία τοῦ ἔρωτος
τὰ μαγαζιά, τὰ πεζοδρόμια, ἡ πέτρες,
καὶ τοῖχοι, καὶ μπαλκόνια, καὶ παράθυρα·
τίποτε ἄσχημο δὲν ἔμεινεν ἐκεῖ.

Καὶ καθὼς στέκομουν, κ' ἐκύτταζα τὴν πόρτα,
καὶ στέκομουν, κ' ἐβράδυνα κάτω ἀπ' τὸ σπίτι,
ἡ ὑπόστασίς μου ὅλη ἀπέδιδε
τὴν φυλαχθεῖσα ἡδονικὴ συγκίνησι.

IN FRONT OF THE HOUSE

Yesterday, while walking around an out-of-the-way
neighborhood, I passed in front of the house
I used to frequent when I was very young.
There my body surrendered to Eros
under his exquisite force.

And yesterday,
as I passed along the old familiar street, at once,
it all turned beautiful before the loveliness of Eros:
the shops, the sidewalks, the stones,
and the walls too, and the balconies, and the windows;
nothing common remained in view.

And as I stood and looked at the door,
and lingered, standing in front of the house,
my whole being re-enacted
that pent-up, delirious pleasure.

ΤΟ ΔΙΠΛΑΝΟ ΤΡΑΠΕΖΙ

Θά 'ναι μόλις εἴκοσι δυὸ ἐτῶν.
Κι ὅμως ἐγὼ εἶμαι βέβαιος πού, σχεδὸν τὰ ἴσα
χρόνια προτήτερα, τὸ ἴδιο σῶμα αὐτὸ τὸ ἀπήλαυσα.

Δὲν εἶναι διόλου ἔξαψις ἐρωτισμοῦ.
Καὶ μοναχὰ πρὸ ὀλίγου μπῆκα στὸ καζίνο·
δὲν εἶχα οὔτε ὥρα γιὰ νὰ πιῶ πολύ.
Τὸ ἴδιο σῶμα ἐγὼ τὸ ἀπήλαυσα.

Κι ἂν δὲν θυμοῦμαι, ποῦ—ἕνα ξέχασμά μου δὲν σημαίνει.

Ἄ τώρα, νά, ποὺ κάθησε στὸ διπλανὸ τραπέζι
γνωρίζω κάθε κίνησι ποὺ κάμνει—κι ἀπ' τὰ ροῦχα κάτω
γυμνὰ τ' ἀγαπημένα μέλη ξαναβλέπω.

THE NEXT TABLE

He can't be more than twenty-two years of age.
Still, I feel certain that, almost the same number
of years earlier, I possessed him, the very same body.

No, it's not erotic fever speaking.
It's only a little while back I entered the casino;
I had no time yet to drink too much.
I did possess that very same body.

And if I don't remember where—a memory lapse is nothing.

Ah, there now, he is sitting down at the next table.
I know every motion his body makes—and under his clothes,
stark naked, I see again the limbs I loved.

ΘΥΜΗΣΟΥ, ΣΩΜΑ ...

Σῶμα, θυμήσου ὄχι μόνο τὸ πόσο ἀγαπήθηκες,
ὄχι μονάχα τὰ κρεββάτια ὅπου πλάγιασες,
ἀλλὰ κ' ἐκεῖνες τὲς ἐπιθυμίες ποὺ γιὰ σένα
γυάλιζαν μὲς στὰ μάτια φανερά,
κ' ἐτρέμανε μὲς στὴν φωνή—καὶ κάποιο
τυχαῖον ἐμπόδιο τὲς ματαίωσε.
Τώρα ποὺ εἶναι ὅλα πιὰ μέσα στὸ παρελθόν,
μοιάζει σχεδὸν καὶ στὲς ἐπιθυμίες
ἐκεῖνες σὰν νὰ δόθηκες—πῶς γυάλιζαν,
θυμήσου, μὲς στὰ μάτια ποὺ σὲ κύτταζαν·
πῶς ἔτρεμαν μὲς στὴν φωνή, γιὰ σέ, θυμήσου, σῶμα.

BODY, REMEMBER …

Body, remember not only how much you were loved,
not only the beds upon which you lay,
but those desires too that glowed openly
for you in their eyes,
and their voices that trembled for you—that only
some chance obstacle stopped them short.
Now that all this is safely in the past,
it almost feels as if you gave yourself
fully to those desires—as they glowed,
remember, the eyes that devoured you;
the voices, trembling for you, remember, body!

ΜΕΡΕΣ ΤΟΥ 1903

Δὲν τὰ ηὗρα πιὰ ξανά—τὰ τόσο γρήγορα χαμένα ...
τὰ ποιητικὰ τὰ μάτια, τὸ χλωμὸ
τὸ πρόσωπο ... στὸ νύχτωμα τοῦ δρόμου ...

Δὲν τὰ ηὗρα πιά—τ᾽ ἀποκτηθέντα κατὰ τύχην ὅλως,
ποὺ ἔτσι εὔκολα παραίτησα·
καὶ ποὺ κατόπι μὲ ἀγωνίαν ἤθελα.
Τὰ ποιητικὰ τὰ μάτια, τὸ χλωμὸ τὸ πρόσωπο,
τὰ χείλη ἐκεῖνα δὲν τὰ ηὗρα πιά.

DAYS OF 1903

I never found them again—those so soon lost …
the poetic eyes, that pale
face … along the darkening road …

No, I never found them—I had them by a chance encounter,
and so heartlessly let them go;
then, in time, I longed for them desperately.
The poetic eyes, the pale face,
those lips—I never ever found them again.

ΦΩΝΕΣ

Ἰδανικὲς φωνὲς κι ἀγαπημένες
ἐκείνων ποὺ πεθάναν, ἢ ἐκείνων ποὺ εἶναι
γιὰ μᾶς χαμένοι σὰν τοὺς πεθαμένους.

Κάποτε μὲς στὰ ὄνειρά μας ὁμιλοῦνε·
κάποτε μὲς στὴν σκέψι τὲς ἀκούει τὸ μυαλό.

Καὶ μὲ τὸν ἦχο των γιὰ μιὰ στιγμὴ ἐπιστρέφουν
ἦχοι ἀπὸ τὴν πρώτη ποίησι τῆς ζωῆς μας—
σὰ μουσική, τὴν νύχτα, μακρυνή, ποὺ σβύνει.

VOICES

Beloved voices, voices of perfection,
they're the ones who died, who are for us
as good as lost, lost like the dead.

They speak to us sometimes in our dreams,
the mind hears them sometimes in our thoughts.

It's with their sound that voices return for a moment,
echoes of our life's first poetry—
night music, distant and fading—snuffed out.

ΕΠΙΘΥΜΙΕΣ

Σὰν σώματα ὡραῖα νεκρῶν ποὺ δὲν ἐγέρασαν
καὶ τά 'κλεισαν, μὲ δάκρυα, σὲ μαυσωλεῖο λαμπρό,
μὲ ρόδα στὸ κεφάλι καὶ στὰ πόδια γιασεμιά—
ἔτσ' ἡ ἐπιθυμίες μοιάζουν ποὺ ἐπέρασαν
χωρὶς νὰ ἐκπληρωθοῦν· χωρὶς ν' ἀξιωθεῖ καμιὰ
τῆς ἡδονῆς μιὰ νύχτα, ἢ ἕνα πρωΐ της φεγγερό.

LONGINGS

Like beautiful bodies of the dead that never grew old,
shut away in brilliant mausoleums, tears shed for them,
their heads adorned with roses, jasmine at their feet—
that's what longings look like, gone long ago,
that were never satisfied; not once the hedonistic pleasure
of a night, or of a radiant morning's spent desires.

KERIA

Τοῦ μέλλοντος ἡ μέρες στέκοντ᾽ ἐμπροστά μας
σὰ μιὰ σειρὰ κεράκια ἀναμένα—
χρυσά, ζεστά, καὶ ζωηρὰ κεράκια.

Ἡ περασμένες μέρες πίσω μένουν,
μιὰ θλιβερὴ γραμμὴ κεριῶν σβυσμένων·
τὰ πιὸ κοντὰ βγάζουν καπνὸν ἀκόμη,
κρύα κεριά, λυωμένα, καὶ κυρτά.

Δὲν θέλω νὰ τὰ βλέπω· μὲ λυπεῖ ἡ μορφή των,
καὶ μὲ λυπεῖ τὸ πρῶτο φῶς των νὰ θυμοῦμαι.
Ἐμπρὸς κυττάζω τ᾽ ἀναμένα μου κεριά.

Δὲν θέλω νὰ γυρίσω νὰ μὴ διῶ καὶ φρίξω
τί γρήγορα ποὺ ἡ σκοτεινὴ γραμμὴ μακραίνει,
τί γρήγορα ποὺ τὰ σβυστὰ κεριὰ πληθαίνουν.

CANDLES

Days of future time standing before us
like a row of lighted candles—golden,
warm, and vibrant little candles.

Days of past time falling behind us,
a dismal line of snuffed-out candles;
the smoke of those nearest lingering,
cold candles, melted, and crooked.

I don't want to look upon them: their shape saddens me,
and it saddens me to remember their first light.
I look at my still lighted candles ahead.

I don't want to look back, don't want to see the horror
of that dark line, lengthening so quickly,
the snuffed-out candles multiplying so quickly.

ΕΝΑΣ ΓΕΡΟΣ

Στοῦ καφενείου τοῦ βοεροῦ τὸ μέσα μέρος
σκυμένος στὸ τραπέζι κάθετ᾽ ἕνας γέρος·
μὲ μιὰν ἐφημερίδα ἐμπρός του, χωρὶς συντροφιά.

Καὶ μὲς στῶν ἄθλιων γηρατειῶν τὴν καταφρόνια
σκέπτεται πόσο λίγο χάρηκε τὰ χρόνια
ποὺ εἶχε καὶ δύναμι, καὶ λόγο, κ᾽ ἐμορφιά.

Ξέρει ποὺ γέρασε πολύ· τὸ νοιώθει, τὸ κυττάζει.
Κ᾽ ἐν τούτοις ὁ καιρὸς ποὺ ἦταν νέος μοιάζει
σὰν χθές. Τί διάστημα μικρό, τί διάστημα μικρό.

Καὶ συλλογιέται ἡ Φρόνησις πῶς τὸν ἐγέλα·
καὶ πῶς τὴν ἐμπιστεύονταν πάντα—τί τρέλλα!—
τὴν ψεύτρα ποὺ ἔλεγε· «Αὔριο. Ἔχεις πολὺν καιρό.»

Θυμᾶται ὁρμὲς ποὺ βάσταγε· καὶ πόση
χαρὰ θυσίαζε. Τὴν ἄμυαλή του γνῶσι
κάθ᾽ εὐκαιρία χαμένη τώρα τὴν ἐμπαίζει.

... Μὰ ἀπ᾽ τὸ πολὺ νὰ σκέπτεται καὶ νὰ θυμᾶται
ὁ γέρος ἐζαλίσθηκε. Κι ἀποκοιμᾶται
στοῦ καφενείου ἀκουμπισμένος τὸ τραπέζι.

AN OLD MAN

In a corner, deep in the noisy café
sits an old man alone, bent over a table,
a newspaper open before him.

And in the indignity of miserable old age,
he reflects on how scant the joy he took from
the years he had strength, eloquence, and beauty.

He knows now he's old; he feels it, sees it.
Still, the years he was young seem like
yesterday. So brief a span of time, so brief.

And he thinks of Discretion, how she fooled him;
how he had always believed her—what madness!—
that cheat, saying, "You have all the time in the world."

He remembers the urges he suppressed, the joys
he sacrificed. Every lost opportunity
now mocks his mindless wisdom.

… But so much labor in thinking, in remembering,
makes the old man dizzy. And so he falls asleep,
head now resting on the café table.

ΔΕΗΣΙΣ

Ἡ θάλασσα στὰ βάθη της πῆρ' ἕναν ναύτη.—
Ἡ μάνα του, ἀνήξερη, πηαίνει κι ἀνάφτει

στὴν Παναγία μπροστὰ ἕνα ὑψηλὸ κερὶ
γιὰ νὰ ἐπιστρέψει γρήγορα καὶ νά 'ν' καλοὶ καιροί—

καὶ ὅλο πρὸς τὸν ἄνεμο στήνει τ' αὐτί.
Ἀλλὰ ἐνῶ προσεύχεται καὶ δέεται αὐτή,

ἡ εἰκὼν ἀκούει, σοβαρὴ καὶ λυπημένη,
ξεύροντας πὼς δὲν θά 'λθει πιὰ ὁ υἱὸς ποὺ περιμένει.

SUPPLIANCE

The sea took a sailor deep in her bosom.
His mother, unknowing, goes and lights

a tall candle to Our Lady's icon—for his
return in good time, for the weather to break—

while her ear is always cocked to the wind.
But even as she prays and supplicates,

the icon listens, saddened and solemn,
knowing the son she awaits will never return.

Η ΨΥΧΕΣ ΤΩΝ ΓΕΡΟΝΤΩΝ

Μὲς στὰ παληὰ τὰ σώματά των τὰ φθαρμένα
κάθονται τῶν γερόντων ἡ ψυχές.
Τί θλιβερὲς ποὺ εἶναι ἡ πτωχὲς
καὶ πῶς βαρυοῦνται τὴν ζωὴ τὴν ἄθλια ποὺ τραβοῦνε.
Πῶς τρέμουν μὴν τὴν χάσουνε καὶ πῶς τὴν ἀγαποῦνε
ἡ σαστισμένες κι ἀντιφατικὲς
ψυχές, ποὺ κάθονται—κωμικοτραγικές—
μὲς στὰ παληά των τὰ πετσιὰ τ' ἀφανισμένα.

THE SOULS OF OLD MEN

Inside their aging skin, in timeworn bodies,
sit the souls of old men.
How sad their poor souls
and how heavy the boring life they lead.
How they tremble lest they lose it, how they truly
love life, these baffled and contradictory
souls that sit—tragicomically—inside
their aging, transparent skins.

ΤΟ ΠΡΩΤΟ ΣΚΑΛΙ

Εἰς τὸν Θεόκριτο παραπονιοῦνταν
μιὰ μέρα ὁ νέος ποιητὴς Εὐμένης·
«Τώρα δυὸ χρόνια πέρασαν ποὺ γράφω
κ' ἕνα εἰδύλλιο ἔκαμα μονάχα.
Τὸ μόνον ἄρτιόν μου ἔργον εἶναι.
Ἀλλοίμονον, εἶν' ὑψηλὴ τὸ βλέπω,
πολὺ ὑψηλὴ τῆς Ποιήσεως ἡ σκάλα·
κι ἀπ' τὸ σκαλὶ τὸ πρῶτο ἐδῶ ποὺ εἶμαι,
ποτὲ δὲν θ' ἀνεβῶ ὁ δυστυχισμένος.»
Εἶπ' ὁ Θεόκριτος· «Αὐτὰ τὰ λόγια
ἀνάρμοστα καὶ βλασφημίες εἶναι.
Κι ἂν εἶσαι στὸ σκαλὶ τὸ πρῶτο, πρέπει
νά 'σαι ὑπερήφανος κ' εὐτυχισμένος.
Ἐδῶ ποὺ ἔφθασες, λίγο δὲν εἶναι·
τόσο ποὺ ἔκαμες, μεγάλη δόξα.
Κι αὐτὸ ἀκόμη τὸ σκαλὶ τὸ πρῶτο
πολὺ ἀπὸ τὸν κοινὸ τὸν κόσμο ἀπέχει.
Εἰς τὸ σκαλὶ γιὰ νὰ πατήσεις τοῦτο
πρέπει μὲ τὸ δικαίωμά σου νά 'σαι
πολίτης εἰς τῶν ἰδεῶν τὴν πόλι.
Καὶ δύσκολο στὴν πόλι ἐκείνην εἶναι
καὶ σπάνιο νὰ σὲ πολιτογραφήσουν.
Στὴν ἀγορά της βρίσκεις Νομοθέτας
ποὺ δὲν γελᾶ κανένας τυχοδιώκτης.
Ἐδῶ ποὺ ἔφθασες, λίγο δὲν εἶναι·
τόσο ποὺ ἔκαμες, μεγάλη δόξα.»

THE FIRST STEP

One day the young poet Eumenes
came complaining to Theokritos:
"It's now two years since I began to write
and I have composed only one idyll.
It remains my sole completed work.
Alas, I now see how high it is,
how very high this step-ladder of Poetry;
and from this first rung where I stand
I'll never climb any higher, unfortunate that I am."
And Theokritos answered: "These are not
fitting words; what you say is blasphemy.
And even if you find yourself on the first rung,
you must be proud and count yourself fortunate.
This height you've reached is no mean thing;
your achievement brings no small glory.
And even that one first step
stands far apart from ordinary men.
And just to stand still on this first step
you must have earned the right to
belong to the city of ideas.
What's hard in that city, what's really rare,
is for them to judge and naturalize you a citizen.
In their midst you'll find those who legislate,
and they cannot be fooled by charlatans.
This height you've reached is no mean thing;
your achievement brings no small glory."

ΔΙΑΚΟΠΗ

Τὸ ἔργον τῶν θεῶν διακόπτομεν ἐμεῖς,
τὰ βιαστικὰ κι ἄπειρα ὄντα τῆς στιγμῆς.
Στῆς Ἐλευσῖνος καὶ στῆς Φθίας τὰ παλάτια
ἡ Δήμητρα κ' ἡ Θέτις ἀρχινοῦν ἔργα καλὰ
μὲς σὲ μεγάλες φλόγες καὶ βαθὺν καπνόν. Ἀλλὰ
πάντοτε ὁρμᾶ ἡ Μετάνειρα ἀπὸ τὰ δωμάτια
τοῦ βασιλέως, ξέπλεγη καὶ τρομαγμένη,
καὶ πάντοτε ὁ Πηλεὺς φοβᾶται κ' ἐπεμβαίνει.

INTERRUPTION

We are the ones who interrupt the gods' work,
we hasty, half-baked creatures of the moment.
In the royal halls of Eleusis and Phthia
Demeter and Thetis initiate benevolent deeds
over high flames and dense smoke. But
always Metaneira, lurking in the King's quarters,
dashes out, hair loose and terror-stricken,
and always, Peleus, fearful, intervenes.

ΘΕΡΜΟΠΥΛΕΣ

Τιμὴ σ' ἐκείνους ὅπου στὴν ζωή των
ὥρισαν καὶ φυλάγουν Θερμοπύλες.
Ποτὲ ἀπὸ τὸ χρέος μὴ κινοῦντες·
δίκαιοι κ' ἴσιοι σ' ὅλες των τὲς πράξεις,
ἀλλὰ μὲ λύπη κιόλας κ' εὐσπλαχνία·
γενναῖοι ὁσάκις εἶναι πλούσιοι, κι ὅταν
εἶναι πτωχοί, πάλ' εἰς μικρὸν γενναῖοι,
πάλι συντρέχοντες ὅσο μποροῦνε·
πάντοτε τὴν ἀλήθεια ὁμιλοῦντες,
πλὴν χωρὶς μῖσος γιὰ τοὺς ψευδομένους.

Καὶ περισσότερη τιμὴ τοὺς πρέπει
ὅταν προβλέπουν (καὶ πολλοὶ προβλέπουν)
πὼς ὁ Ἐφιάλτης θὰ φανεῖ στὸ τέλος,
κ' οἱ Μῆδοι ἐπὶ τέλους θὰ διαβοῦνε.

THERMOPYLAI

Honor to those who in life
point the way to guard Thermopylai.
Never wavering from their duty;
just and even-keeled in their deeds,
yet with pity too and compassion;
generous when rich, and when
they are poor, generous still in small measure,
again helping when they can;
always speaking the truth,
yet without hatred for those who lie.

And even more honor is due to those
who do foresee (as many do foresee)
that Ephialtes will appear in the end,
and the Medes will finally break through.

CHE FECE... IL GRAN RIFIUTO

Σὲ μερικοὺς ἀνθρώπους ἔρχεται μιὰ μέρα
ποὺ πρέπει τὸ μεγάλο Ναὶ ἢ τὸ μεγάλο τὸ Ὄχι
νὰ ποῦνε. Φανερώνεται ἀμέσως ὅποιος τό 'χει
ἔτοιμο μέσα του τὸ Ναί, καὶ λέγοντάς το πέρα

πηγαίνει στὴν τιμὴ καὶ στὴν πεποίθησί του.
Ὁ ἀρνηθεὶς δὲν μετανοιώνει. Ἂν ρωτιοῦνταν πάλι,
ὄχι θὰ ξαναέλεγε. Κι ὅμως τὸν καταβάλλει
ἐκεῖνο τ' ὄχι—τὸ σωστό—εἰς ὅλην τὴν ζωή του.

CHE FECE ... IL GRAN RIFIUTO

To some people there comes the day
when they must speak out the great Yes
or the great No. He's at once revealed who
has it in him, ready to say the Yes,

and saying it, he marches on, honorable and self-assured.
He who refuses does not repent. Were he asked again,
he'd still say No. Yet it weighs him down that No—
the just No—his whole life through.

ΤΑ ΠΑΡΑΘΥΡΑ

Σ᾽ αὐτὲς τὲς σκοτεινὲς κάμαρες, ποὺ περνῶ
μέρες βαρυές, ἐπάνω κάτω τριγυρνῶ
γιὰ νά ᾽βρω τὰ παράθυρα.—Ὅταν ἀνοίξει
ἕνα παράθυρο θά ᾽ναι παρηγορία.—
Μὰ τὰ παράθυρα δὲν βρίσκονται, ἢ δὲν μπορῶ
νὰ τά ᾽βρω. Καὶ καλλίτερα ἴσως νὰ μὴν τὰ βρῶ.
Ἴσως τὸ φῶς θά ᾽ναι μιὰ νέα τυραννία.
Ποιὸς ξέρει τί καινούρια πράγματα θὰ δείξει.

WINDOWS

In these, these darkened rooms, I pass
burdensome days, pacing back and forth,
looking to find the windows. —When opened,
even one window will be a comfort.—
But the windows are not there, or I don't seem
to find them. Perhaps it's best I never find them.
Perhaps the light will prove one more tyranny.
And who knows what new things it will reveal?

ΠΕΡΙΜΕΝΟΝΤΑΣ ΤΟΥΣ ΒΑΡΒΑΡΟΥΣ

—Τί περιμένουμε στὴν ἀγορὰ συναθροισμένοι;

Εἶναι οἱ βάρβαροι νὰ φθάσουν σήμερα.

—Γιατί μέσα στὴν Σύγκλητο μιὰ τέτοια ἀπραξία;
Τί κάθοντ' οἱ Συγκλητικοὶ καὶ δὲν νομοθετοῦνε;

Γιατὶ οἱ βάρβαροι θὰ φθάσουν σήμερα.
Τί νόμους πιὰ θὰ κάμουν οἱ Συγκλητικοί;
Οἱ βάρβαροι σὰν ἔλθουν θὰ νομοθετήσουν.

—Γιατί ὁ αὐτοκράτωρ μας τόσο πρωῒ σηκώθη,
καὶ κάθεται στῆς πόλεως τὴν πιὸ μεγάλη πύλη
στὸν θρόνο ἐπάνω, ἐπίσημος, φορῶντας τὴν κορώνα;

Γιατὶ οἱ βάρβαροι θὰ φθάσουν σήμερα.
Κι ὁ αὐτοκράτωρ περιμένει νὰ δεχθεῖ
τὸν ἀρχηγό τους. Μάλιστα ἑτοίμασε
γιὰ νὰ τὸν δώσει μιὰ περγαμηνή. Ἐκεῖ
τὸν ἔγραψε τίτλους πολλοὺς κι ὀνόματα.

—Γιατί οἱ δυό μας ὕπατοι κ' οἱ πραίτορες ἐβγῆκαν
σήμερα μὲ τὲς κόκκινες, τὲς κεντημένες τόγες·
γιατί βραχιόλια φόρεσαν μὲ τόσους ἀμεθύστους,
καὶ δαχτυλίδια μὲ λαμπρά, γυαλιστερὰ σμαράγδια·
γιατί νὰ πιάσουν σήμερα πολύτιμα μπαστούνια
μ' ἀσήμια καὶ μαλάματα ἔκτακτα σκαλιγμένα;

Γιατὶ οἱ βάρβαροι θὰ φθάσουν σήμερα·
καὶ τέτοια πράγματα θαμπώνουν τοὺς βαρβάρους.

—Γιατί κ' οἱ ἄξιοι ρήτορες δὲν ἔρχονται σὰν πάντα
νὰ βγάλουνε τοὺς λόγους τους, νὰ ποῦνε τὰ δικά τους;

AWAITING THE BARBARIANS

—What are we waiting for, assembled in the marketplace?

      It's the barbarians who are coming today.

—Why this inactivity taking over the Senate?
What makes the Senators idle, not drafting our laws?

      Because the barbarians are to be here today.
      What laws can the Senators draw up now?
      When the barbarians come, they'll draft our laws.

—Why is our emperor out of bed this early,
sitting at the gate, the city's greatest gate,
formally enthroned, donning his crown?

      Because the barbarians will arrive today.
      And the emperor waits to receive
      their leader. He has naturally prepared
      a gift, a parchment to give him. He has
      emblazoned it with many a title and epithet.

—Why have our two consuls, together with their praetors,
emerged in red, their rich embroidered togas;
why do they wear their bracelets studded with amethysts,
their splendid rings with shining emeralds;
why take up today their precious walking sticks,
perfectly sculpted, inlaid with silver and with gold?

      Because the barbarians arrive today;
      and such things do dazzle the barbarians.

—Why have the worthy orators failed to show as usual,
to speak their lengthy speeches, to make their usual points?

Γιατὶ οἱ βάρβαροι θὰ φθάσουν σήμερα·
κι αὐτοὶ βαρυοῦντ᾽ εὐφράδειες καὶ δημηγορίες.

—Γιατί ν᾽ ἀρχίσει μονομιᾶς αὐτὴ ἡ ἀνησυχία
κ᾽ ἡ σύγχυσις. (Τὰ πρόσωπα τί σοβαρὰ ποὺ ἐγίναν).
Γιατί ἀδειάζουν γρήγορα οἱ δρόμοι κ᾽ ἡ πλατέες,
κι ὅλοι γυρνοῦν στὰ σπίτια τους πολὺ συλλογισμένοι;

Γιατὶ ἐνύχτωσε κ᾽ οἱ βάρβαροι δὲν ἦλθαν.
Καὶ μερικοὶ ἔφθασαν ἀπ᾽ τὰ σύνορα,
καὶ εἴπανε πὼς βάρβαροι πιὰ δὲν ὑπάρχουν.

Καὶ τώρα τί θὰ γένουμε χωρὶς βαρβάρους.
Οἱ ἄνθρωποι αὐτοὶ ἦσαν μιὰ κάποια λύσις.

Because the barbarians will arrive today;
and eloquence bores them, as do demagogues.

—Why this uneasiness come at once upon us,
why this disarray (people's faces so drawn and earnest).
Why do the streets empty out so quickly, and the squares,
with everyone lost in thought, returning to his home?

Because it's dark out and the barbarians never came.
And some men arriving from our borders
report: they don't exist, no more barbarians out there.

And now what will become of us without barbarians?
Those people were at least a kind of solution.

ΑΠΙΣΤΙΑ

Πολλὰ ἄρα Ὁμήρου ἐπαινοῦντες, ἀλλὰ τοῦτο οὐκ
ἐπαινεσόμεθα ... οὐδὲ Αἰσχύλου, ὅταν φῇ ἡ Θέτις
τὸν Ἀπόλλω ἐν τοῖς αὐτῆς γάμοις ᾄδοντα

ἐνδατεῖσθαι τὰς ἐὰς εὐπαιδίας,
νόσων τ᾽ ἀπείρους καὶ μακραίωνας βίους,
ξύμπαντά τ᾽ εἰπὼν θεοφιλεῖς ἐμὰς τύχας
παιῶν᾽ ἐπηυφήμησεν, εὐθυμῶν ἐμέ.
Κἀγὼ τὸ Φοίβου θεῖον ἀψευδὲς στόμα
ἤλπιζον εἶναι, μαντικῇ βρύον τέχνῃ·
ὁ δ᾽, αὐτὸς ὑμνῶν, ...
... αὐτός ἐστιν ὁ κτανὼν
τὸν παῖδα τὸν ἐμόν.

Πλάτων, Πολιτείας Β´

Σὰν πάντρευαν τὴν Θέτιδα μὲ τὸν Πηλέα
σηκώθηκε ὁ Ἀπόλλων στὸ λαμπρὸ τραπέζι
τοῦ γάμου, καὶ μακάρισε τοὺς νεονύμφους
γιὰ τὸν βλαστὸ ποὺ θά ᾽βγαινε ἀπ᾽ τὴν ἕνωσί των.
Εἶπε· Ποτὲ αὐτὸν ἀρρώστια δὲν θ᾽ ἀγγίξει
καὶ θά ᾽χει μακρυνὴ ζωή.—Αὐτὰ σὰν εἶπε,
ἡ Θέτις χάρηκε πολύ, γιατὶ τὰ λόγια
τοῦ Ἀπόλλωνος ποὺ γνώριζε ἀπὸ προφητεῖες
τὴν φάνηκαν ἐγγύησις γιὰ τὸ παιδί της.
Κι ὅταν μεγάλωνεν ὁ Ἀχιλλεύς, καὶ ἦταν
τῆς Θεσσαλίας ἔπαινος ἡ ἐμορφιά του,
ἡ Θέτις τοῦ θεοῦ τὰ λόγια ἐνθυμοῦνταν.
Ἀλλὰ μιὰ μέρα ἦλθαν γέροι μὲ εἰδήσεις,
κ᾽ εἶπαν τὸν σκοτωμὸ τοῦ Ἀχιλλέως στὴν Τροία.
Κ᾽ ἡ Θέτις ξέσχιζε τὰ πορφυρά της ροῦχα,
κ᾽ ἔβγαζεν ἀπὸ πάνω της καὶ ξεπετοῦσε
στὸ χῶμα τὰ βραχιόλια καὶ τὰ δαχτυλίδια.
Καὶ μὲς στὸν ὀδυρμό της τὰ παλιὰ θυμήθη·

DISLOYALTY

Although we may commend many things in Homer, this one we shall not commend ... nor shall we commend that perception in Aeschylus, when Thetis says that Apollo sang at her wedding and:

> dwelt on her [my] future blessed offspring,
> which would experience no illness and have a long life,
> and, after completing these words, he perfomed a paean-song over
> my good fortune in being loved by the gods, thus delighting my
> heart.
> And I hoped that Phoibos's divine mouth would not be mendacious,
> imbued as it is with the art of prophecy.
> But he, who himself sang that hymn, ...
> ... he himself is the one who killed my son.

Plato, *Republic II*

When they gave Thetis to Peleus in marriage,
Apollo stood up at the splendid wedding feast
and chanted blessings for the newlyweds
and for the boy that would come from their union.
He said: "Never will he be touched by illness
and his life will be a long one."— And, as he said this,
Thetis was overjoyed; for the words of Apollo,
who knew all about prophesies,
seemed to her a secure life for her boy.
And as Achilles was growing up
and his beauty became Thessaly's pride,
Thetis never forgot the god's words.
But one day some elders came with tidings,
they announced the slaying of Achilles at Troy.
And Thetis tore to pieces her purple robes,
took off her rings and her bracelets,
hurled them all to the ground,
and amid her grief came the memory of things past;

καὶ ρώτησε τί ἔκαμνε ὁ σοφὸς Ἀπόλλων,
ποῦ γύριζεν ὁ ποιητὴς ποὺ στὰ τραπέζια
ἔξοχα ὁμιλεῖ, ποῦ γύριζε ὁ προφήτης
ὅταν τὸν υἱό της σκότωναν στὰ πρῶτα νειάτα.
Κ' οἱ γέροι τὴν ἀπήντησαν πὼς ὁ Ἀπόλλων
αὐτὸς ὁ ἴδιος ἐκατέβηκε στὴν Τροία,
καὶ μὲ τοὺς Τρῶας σκότωσε τὸν Ἀχιλλέα.

and she asked what was he doing, where was the wise Apollo,
where was the poet roaming, who chanted at feasts,
where was this prophet wandering when her son
was slain in the bloom of his youth?
Then the elders gave her the answer: it was Apollo
himself who descended into Troy
and together with the Trojans killed Achilles.

ΤΑ ΑΛΟΓΑ ΤΟΥ ΑΧΙΛΛΕΩΣ

Τὸν Πάτροκλο σὰν εἶδαν σκοτωμένο,
ποὺ ἦταν τόσο ἀνδρεῖος, καὶ δυνατός, καὶ νέος,
ἄρχισαν τ' ἄλογα νὰ κλαῖνε τοῦ Ἀχιλλέως·
ἡ φύσις των ἡ ἀθάνατη ἀγανακτοῦσε
γιὰ τοῦ θανάτου αὐτὸ τὸ ἔργον ποὺ θωροῦσε.
Τίναζαν τὰ κεφάλια των καὶ τὲς μακρυὲς χαῖτες κουνοῦσαν,
τὴν γῆ χτυποῦσαν μὲ τὰ πόδια, καὶ θρηνοῦσαν
τὸν Πάτροκλο ποὺ ἐνοιώθανε ἄψυχο—ἀφανισμένο—
μιὰ σάρκα τώρα ποταπή—τὸ πνεῦμα του χαμένο—
ἀνυπεράσπιστο—χωρὶς πνοή—
εἰς τὸ μεγάλο Τίποτε ἐπιστραμένο ἀπ' τὴν ζωή.

Τὰ δάκρυα εἶδε ὁ Ζεὺς τῶν ἀθανάτων
ἀλόγων καὶ λυπήθη. «Στοῦ Πηλέως τὸν γάμο»
εἶπε «δὲν ἔπρεπ' ἔτσι ἄσκεπτα νὰ κάμω·
καλλίτερα νὰ μὴν σᾶς δίναμε, ἀλογά μου
δυστυχισμένα! Τί γυρεύατ' ἐκεῖ χάμου
στὴν ἄθλια ἀνθρωπότητα ποὺ εἶναι τὸ παίγνιον τῆς μοίρας.
Σεῖς ποὺ οὐδὲ ὁ θάνατος φυλάγει, οὐδὲ τὸ γῆρας
πρόσκαιρες συμφορὲς σᾶς τυραννοῦν. Στὰ βάσανά των
σᾶς ἔμπλεξαν οἱ ἄνθρωποι.»—Ὅμως τὰ δάκρυά των
γιὰ τοῦ θανάτου τὴν παντοτινὴ
τὴν συμφορὰν ἐχύνανε τὰ δυὸ τὰ ζῶα τὰ εὐγενή.

THE HORSES OF ACHILLES

As Patroklos lies dead before their eyes
—he was so young and strong and brave—
the horses, Achilles' stallions, begin to cry;
their immortal nature in outrage
over this handiwork Death laid before them.
They shake their heads and toss their hefty manes,
beating the ground with their hooves, mourning
Patroklos as they feel his soul depart—body empty—
a useless carcass—his spirit lost now—
vulnerable—without breath—
life gives it back to the void, the great Nothing.

Zeus's gaze fell on the immortal horses'
tears; he was struck with grief. "At Peleus's wedding,"
he said, "I acted in unthinking haste;
it were better had we not given you, my stallions,
to this misfortune! You had no calling
amidst unhappy humanity, the plaything of fate.
Death does not lie in wait for you, nor old age,
only passing disaster torments you. Here, in their miseries,
where these humans have entangled you."—Still, their tears
they shed for death's desolate
end, these two noble animals weeping.

ΤΕΙΧΗ

Χωρὶς περίσκεψιν, χωρὶς λύπην, χωρὶς αἰδὼ
μεγάλα κ᾽ ὑψηλὰ τριγύρω μου ἔκτισαν τείχη.

Καὶ κάθομαι καὶ ἀπελπίζομαι τώρα ἐδῶ.
Ἄλλο δὲν σκέπτομαι: τὸν νοῦν μου τρώγει αὐτὴ ἡ τύχη·

διότι πράγματα πολλὰ ἔξω νὰ κάμω εἶχον.
Ἀ ὅταν ἔκτιζαν τὰ τείχη πῶς νὰ μὴν προσέξω.

Ἀλλὰ δὲν ἄκουσα ποτὲ κρότον κτιστῶν ἢ ἦχον.
Ἀνεπαισθήτως μ᾽ ἔκλεισαν ἀπὸ τὸν κόσμον ἔξω.

WALLS

Without care, without pity, without shame,
they built these great, towering walls all round me.

And now I sit here, hopeless, in despair.
Empty of thought: this fate eats away at my mind;

for I had so many things still to do out there.
How did I not grasp their meaning, as they built these walls?

Yet never a sound, no pounding from builders did I hear.
Imperceptibly, they shut me away from the world out there.

Η ΚΗΔΕΙΑ ΤΟΥ ΣΑΡΠΗΔΟΝΟΣ

Βαρυὰν ὀδύνην ἔχει ὁ Ζεύς. Τὸν Σαρπηδόνα
ἐσκότωσεν ὁ Πάτροκλος· καὶ τώρα ὁρμοῦν
ὁ Μενοιτιάδης κ' οἱ Ἀχαιοὶ τὸ σῶμα
ν' ἁρπάξουνε καὶ νὰ τὸ ἐξευτελίσουν.

Ἀλλὰ ὁ Ζεὺς διόλου δὲν στέργει αὐτά.
Τὸ ἀγαπημένο του παιδί—ποὺ τὸ ἄφισε
καὶ χάθηκεν· ὁ Νόμος ἦταν ἔτσι—
τουλάχιστον θὰ τὸ τιμήσει πεθαμένο.
Καὶ στέλνει, ἰδού, τὸν Φοῖβο κάτω στὴν πεδιάδα
ἑρμηνευμένο πῶς τὸ σῶμα νὰ νοιασθεῖ.

Τοῦ ἥρωος τὸν νεκρὸ μ' εὐλάβεια καὶ μὲ λύπη
σηκώνει ὁ Φοῖβος καὶ τὸν πάει στὸν ποταμό.
Τὸν πλένει ἀπὸ τὲς σκόνες κι ἀπ' τ' αἵματα·
κλείει τὴν πληγή του, μὴ ἀφίνοντας
κανένα ἴχνος νὰ φανεῖ· τῆς ἀμβροσίας
τ' ἀρώματα χύνει ἐπάνω του· καὶ μὲ λαμπρὰ
Ὀλύμπια φορέματα τὸν ντύνει.
Τὸ δέρμα του ἀσπρίζει· καὶ μὲ μαργαριταρένιο
χτένι κτενίζει τὰ κατάμαυρα μαλλιά.
Τὰ ὡραῖα μέλη σχηματίζει καὶ πλαγιάζει.

Τώρα σὰν νέος μοιάζει βασιλεὺς ἁρματηλάτης—
στὰ εἴκοσι πέντε χρόνια του, στὰ εἴκοσι ἕξι—
ἀναπαυόμενος μετὰ ποὺ ἐκέρδισε,
μ' ἅρμα ὁλόχρυσο καὶ ταχυτάτους ἵππους,
σὲ ξακουστὸν ἀγῶνα τὸ βραβεῖον.

Ἔτσι σὰν ποὺ τελείωσεν ὁ Φοῖβος
τὴν ἐντολή του, κάλεσε τοὺς δυὸ ἀδελφοὺς
τὸν Ὕπνο καὶ τὸν Θάνατο, προστάζοντάς τους
νὰ πᾶν τὸ σῶμα στὴν Λυκία, τὸν πλούσιο τόπο.

THE FUNERAL OF SARPEDON

Zeus is in deep mourning. Patroklos
has slain Sarpedon; and he, the son of Menoitios,
and his Achaeans lunge across the field
to grab the body and dishonor it.

But Zeus will have none of that.
He did let his loving child die—
the Law compelled it—now he can
at least honor him in death. And, behold,
he sends Phoibos Apollo to the battlefield,
carefully instructing him how to care for the body.

The hero's corpse in reverence and in sorrow
Phoibos takes up in his arms and carries to the river.
He washes the dust and blood away;
closes the horrible wounds, leaving no visible
trace, pours many perfumes of ambrosia
on the body; and dresses him
in brilliant Olympian garments.
He makes his skin lifelike and with a pearl comb
he tends his raven-black hair.
He arranges the beautiful limbs into a natural sleep.

Now he resembles a young king, a royal charioteer,
in his twenty-fifth or twenty-sixth year,
resting after his victorious turn,
his chariot all gold and swiftest horses,
the prize he won at the famous race.

Phoibos, having completed his task,
summons forth the two brothers,
Sleep and Death, and commands them
to take the body to Lykia, that luscious land,

Καὶ κατὰ ἐκεῖ τὸν πλούσιο τόπο, τὴν Λυκία,
τοῦτοι ὁδοιπόρησαν οἱ δυὸ ἀδελφοὶ
Ὕπνος καὶ Θάνατος, κι ὅταν πιὰ ἔφθασαν
στὴν πόρτα τοῦ βασιλικοῦ σπιτιοῦ
παρέδωσαν τὸ δοξασμένο σῶμα,
καὶ γύρισαν στὲς ἄλλες τους φροντίδες καὶ δουλειές.

Κι ὡς τό 'λαβαν αὐτοῦ, στὸ σπίτι, ἀρχίνησε
μὲ συνοδεῖες, καὶ τιμές, καὶ θρήνους,
καὶ μ' ἄφθονες σπονδὲς ἀπὸ ἱεροὺς κρατῆρας,
καὶ μ' ὅλα τὰ πρεπὰ ἡ θλιβερὴ ταφή·
κ' ἔπειτα ἔμπειροι, τῆς πολιτείας ἐργάται,
καὶ φημισμένοι δουλευταὶ τῆς πέτρας,
ἥλθανε κ' ἔκαμαν τὸ μνῆμα καὶ τὴν στήλη.

and, taking that road to the rich land of Lykia,
the two brothers, Sleep and Death, traveled
on foot, and when at last they reached
the gate of the royal house,
they turned over the glorified body,
then went on their way to other cares, other labors.

Once the body is received into the house
it all begins: the processional dirges, the honors, laments and
threnodies, and endless libations from sacred craters;
then followed, in proper rituals, the solemn burial;
after a time, skilled workers from the town,
celebrated master-craftsmen in stone,
came and built the tomb and the *stēlē*.

Ο ΗΛΙΟΣ ΤΟΥ ΑΠΟΓΕΥΜΑΤΟΣ

Τὴν κάμαρην αὐτή, πόσο καλὰ τὴν ξέρω.
Τώρα νοικιάζονται κι αὐτὴ κ' ἡ πλαγινὴ
γιὰ ἐμπορικὰ γραφεῖα. Ὅλο τὸ σπίτι ἔγινε
γραφεῖα μεσιτῶν, κ' ἐμπόρων, κ' Ἑταιρεῖες.

Ἀ ἡ κάμαρη αὐτή, τί γνώριμη ποὺ εἶναι.

Κοντὰ στὴν πόρτα ἐδῶ ἦταν ὁ καναπές,
κ' ἐμπρός του ἕνα τουρκικὸ χαλί·
σιμὰ τὸ ράφι μὲ δυὸ βάζα κίτρινα.
Δεξιά· ὄχι, ἀντικρύ, ἕνα ντολάπι μὲ καθρέπτη.
Στὴ μέση τὸ τραπέζι ὅπου ἔγραφε·
κ' ἡ τρεῖς μεγάλες ψάθινες καρέγλες.
Πλάϊ στὸ παράθυρο ἦταν τὸ κρεββάτι
ποὺ ἀγαπηθήκαμε τόσες φορές.

Θὰ βρίσκονται ἀκόμη τὰ καϋμένα πουθενά.

Πλάϊ στὸ παράθυρο ἦταν τὸ κρεββάτι·
ὁ ἥλιος τοῦ ἀπογεύματος τὸ 'φθανε ὡς τὰ μισά.

... Ἀπόγευμα ἡ ὥρα τέσσερες, εἴχαμε χωρισθεῖ
γιὰ μιὰ ἑβδομάδα μόνο ... Ἀλλοίμονον,
ἡ ἑβδομὰς ἐκείνη ἔγινε παντοτινή.

THE AFTERNOON SUN

This room here, how well I know it.
Now it's up for rent, this and the one next door,
commercial rentals. The whole building is now
offices of agents, of merchants, and firms.

This room, yes, how familiar to me.

Near the door, here, was the sofa,
a Turkish rug in front of it;
close by, the shelf with two yellow vases.
On the right, no, opposite, a wardrobe with a mirror.
In the middle, the table where he would sit to write;
and the three large wicker chairs.
Next to the window was the bed
where we made love so many times.

Those dear old things must still be around somewhere.

Next to the window was the bed;
the afternoon sun covered about half.

… Afternoon, four o'clock, we separated
for one week only … o fate,
that one week became forever.

NA MEINEI

Ἡ ὥρα μιὰ τὴν νύχτα θά 'τανε,
ἢ μιάμισυ.

Σὲ μιὰ γωνιὰ τοῦ καπηλειοῦ·
πίσω ἀπ' τὸ ξύλινο τὸ χώρισμα.
Ἐκτὸς ἡμῶν τῶν δυὸ τὸ μαγαζὶ ὅλως διόλου ἄδειο.
Μιὰ λάμπα πετρελαίου μόλις τὸ φώτιζε.
Κοιμούντανε, στὴν πόρτα, ὁ ἀγρυπνισμένος ὑπηρέτης.

Δὲν θὰ μᾶς ἔβλεπε κανείς. Μὰ κιόλας
εἴχαμεν ἐξαφθεῖ τόσο πολύ,
ποὺ γίναμε ἀκατάλληλοι γιὰ προφυλάξεις.

Τὰ ἐνδύματα μισοανοίχθηκαν—πολλὰ δὲν ἦσαν
γιατὶ ἐπύρωνε θεῖος Ἰούλιος μῆνας.

Σάρκας ἀπόλαυσις ἀνάμεσα
στὰ μισοανοιγμένα ἐνδύματα·
γρήγορο σάρκας γύμνωμα—ποὺ τὸ ἴνδαλμά του
εἴκοσι ἔξι χρόνους διάβηκε· καὶ τώρα ἦλθε
νὰ μείνει μὲς στὴν ποίησιν αὐτή.

COMES TO CLAIM ITS PLACE

That time: one o'clock at night
or half past one.

      A corner of the wine-shop;
just behind the wood partition.
The shop altogether empty, except for us two,
the place barely lit by an oil lamp.
Half dozing at the door, the waiter watching …

Not a soul would see us. But then,
we were so far aroused
that we'd already gone beyond caution.

Our clothes half open—we wore so little
in this torrid, this heavenly month of July.

Sweet pleasure of flesh among
those half-opened clothes;
quick baring of flesh—a vision
that has traversed twenty-six years; and now
comes to claim a place in poetry.

ΤΩΝ ΕΒΡΑΙΩΝ (50 M.X.)

Ζωγράφος καὶ ποιητής, δρομεὺς καὶ δισκοβόλος,
σὰν Ἐνδυμίων ἔμορφος, ὁ Ἰάνθης Ἀντωνίου.
Ἀπὸ οἰκογένειαν φίλην τῆς Συναγωγῆς.

«Ἡ τιμιότερές μου μέρες εἶν' ἐκεῖνες
ποὺ τὴν αἰσθητικὴ ἀναζήτησιν ἀφίνω,
ποὺ ἐγκαταλείπω τὸν ὡραῖο καὶ σκληρὸν ἑλληνισμό,
μὲ τὴν κυρίαρχη προσήλωσι
σὲ τέλεια καμωμένα καὶ φθαρτὰ ἄσπρα μέλη.
Καὶ γένομαι αὐτὸς ποὺ θὰ ἤθελα
πάντα νὰ μένω· τῶν Ἐβραίων, τῶν ἱερῶν Ἐβραίων, ὁ υἱός.»

Ἔνθερμη λίαν ἡ δήλωσίς του. «Πάντα
νὰ μένω τῶν Ἐβραίων, τῶν ἱερῶν Ἐβραίων—»

Ὅμως δὲν ἔμενε τοιοῦτος διόλου.
Ὁ Ἡδονισμὸς κ' ἡ Τέχνη τῆς Ἀλεξανδρείας
ἀφοσιωμένο τους παιδὶ τὸν εἶχαν.

OF THE JEWS (A.D. 50)

Painter and poet, runner and discus-thrower,
beautiful as Endymion, this son of Antonios,
Ianthes, his family close to the Synagogue.

"My most honored days are those
when I leave behind aesthetic pursuits,
when I abandon beautiful, hard Hellenism,
with its overreaching fervor
for the perfection of white, corruptible limbs.
And I become who I've always wanted to remain:
the son of the Jews, the holy Jews."

Most fervent indeed his declaration: "Let me
forever be of the Jews, of the holy Jews …"

Even so, he never held to it for long.
Hedonism and the Art of Alexandria
held him fast, their dedicated son.

ΙΜΕΝΟΣ

« ... Ν' ἀγαπηθεῖ ἀκόμη περισσότερον
ἡ ἡδονὴ ποὺ νοσηρῶς καὶ μὲ φθορὰ ἀποκτᾶται·
σπάνια τὸ σῶμα βρίσκοντας ποὺ αἰσθάνεται ὅπως θέλει αὐτή—
ποὺ νοσηρῶς καὶ μὲ φθορά, παρέχει
μιὰν ἔντασιν ἐρωτική, ποὺ δὲν γνωρίζει ἡ ὑγεία ... »

Ἀπόσπασμα ἀπὸ μιὰν ἐπιστολὴ
τοῦ νέου Ἰμένου (ἐκ πατρικίων) διαβοήτου
ἐν Συρακούσαις ἐπὶ ἀσωτίᾳ,
στοὺς ἄσωτους καιροὺς τοῦ τρίτου Μιχαήλ.

IMENOS

"... let it be cherished more even,
this sensual pleasure, achieved in unhealthy and corrupt ways.
Its care for the body, finding passion where it wants it,
in an unhealthy and corrupt way, opens up to a desired,
erotic intensity, one that healthy love cannot know ..."

Extract from a letter
written by the youth Imenos (of a patrician family),
notorious in Syracuse for debauchery
in the debauched times of Michael the Third.

ΤΟΥ ΠΛΟΙΟΥ

Τὸν μοιάζει βέβαια ἡ μικρὴ αὐτή,
μὲ τὸ μολύβι ἀπεικόνισίς του.

Γρήγορα καμωμένη, στὸ κατάστρωμα τοῦ πλοίου·
ἕνα μαγευτικὸ ἀπόγευμα.
Τὸ Ἰόνιον Πέλαγος ὁλόγυρά μας.

Τὸν μοιάζει. Ὅμως τὸν θυμοῦμαι σὰν πιὸ ἔμορφο.
Μέχρι παθήσεως ἦταν αἰσθητικός,
κι αὐτὸ ἐφώτιζε τὴν ἔκφρασί του.
Πιὸ ἔμορφος μὲ φανερώνεται
τώρα ποὺ ἡ ψυχή μου τὸν ἀνακαλεῖ, ἀπ' τὸν Καιρό.

Ἀπ' τὸν Καιρό. Εἴν' ὅλ' αὐτὰ τὰ πράγματα πολὺ παληά—
τὸ σκίτσο, καὶ τὸ πλοῖο, καὶ τὸ ἀπόγευμα.

ON BOARD SHIP

It looks just like him, of course, this little
portrait done in pencil.

Sketched in haste, on ship's deck.
A magical afternoon.
The Ionian Sea embracing us.

It does look like him. Only I remember him more lovely.
He was sensual to the point of madness,
and this lit up his whole face, his expression.
He appears more beautiful to me
now that my soul brings him back, out of Time past.

Out of Time past. All these things are very old indeed—
the sketch, and the ship, and the afternoon.

ΔΗΜΗΤΡΙΟΥ ΣΩΤΗΡΟΣ (162–150 Π.Χ.)

Κάθε του προσδοκία βγῆκε λανθασμένη!

Φαντάζονταν ἔργα νὰ κάμει ξακουστά,
νὰ παύσει τὴν ταπείνωσι ποὺ ἀπ' τὸν καιρὸ τῆς μάχης
τῆς Μαγνησίας τὴν πατρίδα του πιέζει.
Νὰ γίνει πάλι κράτος δυνατὸ ἡ Συρία,
μὲ τοὺς στρατούς της, μὲ τοὺς στόλους της,
μὲ τὰ μεγάλα κάστρα, μὲ τὰ πλούτη.

Ὑπέφερε, πικραίνονταν στὴν Ρώμη
σὰν ἔνοιωθε στὲς ὁμιλίες τῶν φίλων του,
τῆς νεολαίας τῶν μεγάλων οἴκων,
μὲς σ' ὅλην τὴν λεπτότητα καὶ τὴν εὐγένεια
ποὺ ἔδειχναν σ' αὐτόν, τοῦ βασιλέως
Σελεύκου Φιλοπάτορος τὸν υἱό—
σὰν ἔνοιωθε ποὺ ὅμως πάντα ὑπῆρχε μιὰ κρυφή
ὀλιγωρία γιὰ τὲς δυναστεῖες τὲς ἑλληνίζουσες·
ποὺ ξέπεσαν, ποὺ γιὰ τὰ σοβαρὰ ἔργα δὲν εἶναι,
γιὰ τῶν λαῶν τὴν ἀρχηγία πολὺ ἀκατάλληλες.
Τραβιοῦνταν μόνος του, κι ἀγανακτοῦσε, κι ὅμνυε
ποὺ ὅπως τὰ θαρροῦν διόλου δὲν θά 'ναι·
ἰδού ποὺ ἔχει θέλησιν αὐτός·
θ' ἀγωνισθεῖ, θὰ κάμει, θ' ἀνυψώσει.

Ἀρκεῖ νὰ βρεῖ ἕναν τρόπο στὴν Ἀνατολὴ νὰ φθάσει,
νὰ κατορθώσει νὰ ξεφύγει ἀπὸ τὴν Ἰταλία—
κι ὅλην αὐτὴν τὴν δύναμι ποὺ ἔχει
μὲς στὴν ψυχή του, ὅλην τὴν ὁρμὴν
αὐτὴ θὰ μεταδώσει στὸν λαό.

Ἀ στὴν Συρία μονάχα νὰ βρεθεῖ!
Ἔτσι μικρὸς ἀπ' τὴν πατρίδα ἔφυγε
ποὺ ἀμυδρῶς θυμοῦνταν τὴν μορφή της.

OF DEMETRIOS SOTER (162–150 B.C.)

His every expectation turned out a mistake!

He had imagined he might do great things,
bringing to an end the humiliation his country endured
since the battle of Magnesia, a heavy burden;
to make Syria once more a country of strength,
with its armies, with its fleet,
its great fortresses, its riches.

He had suffered in Rome, feeling embittered
when he sensed in overhearing his friends talk,
those youths of distinguished families,
in all their delicate manners and the respect
they showed toward him, son
of the King Seleukos Philopator—
when he sensed that even so there was always an unstated
apprehension about those Hellenized dynasties:
they were in full decline, not fit for any serious works,
and as for leading their people, entirely inept.
So he would pull away, alone, and turn indignant and swear
that things would not be at all as they believed.
See! Isn't he himself full of resolve!
He would struggle, accomplish, he'll bring all back again.

If he could only find a way himself to reach the East,
to manage a way of escaping Italy—
then all this strength he carries
in his soul, all this drive,
he would pass on to his people.

If only he could find himself in Syria!
So young when he left his country,
so vaguely remembering what it looked like.

Μὰ μὲς στὴν σκέψι του τὴν μελετοῦσε πάντα
σὰν κάτι ἱερὸ ποὺ προσκυνῶντας τὸ πλησιάζεις,
σὰν ὀπτασία τόπου ὡραίου, σὰν ὅραμα
ἑλληνικῶν πόλεων καὶ λιμένων.—

Καὶ τώρα;
        Τώρα ἀπελπισία καὶ καϋμός.
Εἴχανε δίκιο τὰ παιδιὰ στὴν Ρώμη.
Δὲν εἶναι δυνατὸν νὰ βασταχθοῦν ἡ δυναστεῖες
ποὺ ἔβγαλε ἡ Κατάκτησις τῶν Μακεδόνων.

Ἀδιάφορον· ἐπάσχισεν αὐτός,
ὅσο μποροῦσεν ἀγωνίσθηκε.
Καὶ μὲς στὴν μαύρη ἀπογοήτευσί του,
ἕνα μονάχα λογαριάζει πιὰ
μὲ ὑπερηφάνειαν· πού, κ᾽ ἐν τῇ ἀποτυχίᾳ του,
τὴν ἴδιαν ἀκατάβλητην ἀνδρεία στὸν κόσμο δείχνει.

Τ᾽ ἄλλα—ἦσαν ὄνειρα καὶ ματαιοπονίες.
Αὐτὴ ἡ Συρία—σχεδὸν δὲν μοιάζει σὰν πατρίς του,
αὐτὴ εἶν᾽ ἡ χώρα τοῦ Ἡρακλείδη καὶ τοῦ Βάλα.

But in his thoughts he had always imagined it
as something sacred, something you approach praying,
as a beautiful land, a chimera, a vision
of Greek cities and Greek ports.

And now?
        Now despair and longing.
They were right, those youths in Rome.
It's not possible to keep up those dynasties
that sprung from the Makedonian Conquest.

It's no matter: he himself took great pains,
fought as hard as he could.
And in his bleak disappointment,
there's only one thing he figures
fills him with pride; that, even in his failure,
he shows the world the same resolute daring.

The rest—they were futility itself and bold dreams.
This Syria now—she barely resembles his native land.
This is the country of Herakleides, the country of Balas.

ΕΙΓΕ ΕΤΕΛΕΥΤΑ

«Ποῦ ἀπεσύρθηκε, ποῦ ἐχάθηκε ὁ Σοφός;
Ἔπειτ' ἀπὸ τὰ θαύματά του τὰ πολλά,
τὴν φήμη τῆς διδασκαλίας του
ποὺ διεδόθηκεν εἰς τόσα ἔθνη,
ἐκρύφθηκ' αἴφνης καὶ δὲν ἔμαθε κανεὶς
μὲ θετικότητα τί ἔγινε
(οὐδὲ κανεὶς ποτὲ εἶδε τάφον του).
Ἔβγαλαν μερικοὶ πὼς πέθανε στὴν Ἔφεσο.
Δὲν τό 'γραψεν ὁ Δάμις ὅμως· τίποτε
γιὰ θάνατο τοῦ Ἀπολλωνίου δὲν ἔγραψεν ὁ Δάμις.
Ἄλλοι εἴπανε πὼς ἔγινε ἄφαντος στὴν Λίνδο.
Ἢ μήπως εἶν' ἐκείν' ἡ ἱστορία
ἀληθινή, ποὺ ἀνελήφθηκε στὴν Κρήτη,
στὸ ἀρχαῖο τῆς Δικτύννης ἱερόν.—
Ἀλλ' ὅμως ἔχουμε τὴν θαυμασία,
τὴν ὑπερφυσικὴν ἐμφάνισί του
εἰς ἕναν νέον σπουδαστὴ στὰ Τύανα.—
Ἴσως δὲν ἦλθεν ὁ καιρὸς γιὰ νὰ ἐπιστρέψει,
γιὰ νὰ φανερωθεῖ στὸν κόσμο πάλι·
ἢ μεταμορφωμένος, ἴσως, μεταξύ μας
γυρίζει ἀγνώριστος.—Μὰ θὰ ξαναφανερωθεῖ
ὡς ἤτανε, διδάσκοντας τὰ ὀρθά· καὶ τότε βέβαια
θὰ ἐπαναφέρει τὴν λατρεία τῶν θεῶν μας,
καὶ τὲς καλαίσθητες ἑλληνικές μας τελετές.»

Ἔτσι ἐρέμβαζε στὴν πενιχρή του κατοικία—
μετὰ μιὰ ἀνάγνωσι τοῦ Φιλοστράτου
«Τὰ ἐς τὸν Τυανέα Ἀπολλώνιον»—
ἕνας ἀπὸ τοὺς λίγους ἐθνικούς,
τοὺς πολὺ λίγους ποὺ εἶχαν μείνει. Ἄλλωστε—ἀσήμαντος
ἄνθρωπος καὶ δειλός—στὸ φανερὸν
ἔκανε τὸν Χριστιανὸ κι αὐτὸς κ' ἐκκλησιάζονταν.

IF ACTUALLY DEAD

"Where did the Sage go to, where did he disappear?
Following his many miracles,
and the fame of his teaching,
which spread to so many countries,
he went abruptly into hiding, and no one knew
with certainty what happened to him
(nor did anyone ever see his grave).
Some spread it around that he died at Ephesos.
But Damis did not record this in his memoir; nothing
about the death of Apollonios did Damis write down.
Some others said that he vanished at Lindos.
Or maybe it's the other story that's
true, about his assumption in Crete,
at the ancient sanctuary of Diktynna.—
But then again we have that incredible,
that supernatural apparition of his
popping up to a young student at Tyana.—
Maybe the time has not come for him to return
and make his appearance in the world again.
Or maybe, transfigured, he wanders among us
unrecognized.—But he will reappear in the manner
he was, teaching the ways of truth; then, of course,
he will return to the worship of our gods,
and our graceful Hellenic rituals."

So he mused in his shabby dwelling—
after he sat down to read Philostratos's
On Apollonios of Tyana—
he, one of the few, the very few pagans,
remaining now. Yet even he—an insignificant
and cowardly man—in public he was
a Christian and went regularly to church.

Ἦταν ἡ ἐποχὴ καθ' ἣν βασίλευεν,
ἐν ἄκρᾳ εὐλαβείᾳ, ὁ γέρων Ἰουστῖνος,
κ' ἡ Ἀλεξάνδρεια, πόλις θεοσεβής,
ἀθλίους εἰδωλολάτρας ἀποστρέφονταν.

It was the period when Justin the Elder reigned
and Alexandria, a God-fearing city,
abhorred disgraceful idolaters.

ΝΕΟΙ ΤΗΣ ΣΙΔΩΝΟΣ (400 Μ.Χ.)

Ὁ ἠθοποιὸς ποὺ ἔφεραν γιὰ νὰ τοὺς διασκεδάσει
ἀπήγγειλε καὶ μερικὰ ἐπιγράμματα ἐκλεκτά.

Ἡ αἴθουσα ἄνοιγε στὸν κῆπο ἐπάνω·
κ' εἶχε μιὰν ἐλαφρὰ εὐωδία ἀνθέων
ποὺ ἑνώνονταν μὲ τὰ μυρωδικὰ
τῶν πέντε ἀρωματισμένων Σιδωνίων νέων.

Διαβάσθηκαν Μελέαγρος, καὶ Κριναγόρας, καὶ Ριανός.
Μὰ σὰν ἀπήγγειλεν ὁ ἠθοποιός,
«Αἰσχύλον Εὐφορίωνος Ἀθηναῖον τόδε κεύθει—»
(τονίζοντας ἴσως ὑπὲρ τὸ δέον
τὸ «ἀλκὴν δ' εὐδόκιμον», τὸ «Μαραθώνιον ἄλσος»),
πετάχθηκεν εὐθὺς ἕνα παιδὶ ζωηρό,
φανατικὸ γιὰ γράμματα, καὶ φώναξε·

«Ἀ δὲν μ' ἀρέσει τὸ τετράστιχον αὐτό.
Ἐκφράσεις τοιούτου εἴδους μοιάζουν κάπως σὰν λιποψυχίες.
Δῶσε—κηρύττω—στὸ ἔργον σου ὅλην τὴν δύναμί σου,
ὅλην τὴν μέριμνα, καὶ πάλι τὸ ἔργον σου θυμήσου
μὲς στὴν δοκιμασίαν, ἢ ὅταν ἡ ὥρα σου πιὰ γέρνει.
Ἔτσι ἀπὸ σένα περιμένω κι ἀπαιτῶ.
Κι ὄχι ἀπ' τὸν νοῦ σου ὁλότελα νὰ βγάλεις
τῆς Τραγωδίας τὸν Λόγο τὸν λαμπρό—
τί Ἀγαμέμνονα, τί Προμηθέα θαυμαστό,
τί Ὀρέστου, τί Κασσάνδρας παρουσίες,
τί Ἑπτὰ ἐπὶ Θήβας—καὶ γιὰ μνήμη σου νὰ βάλεις
μ ό ν ο ποὺ μὲς στῶν στρατιωτῶν τὲς τάξεις, τὸν σωρὸ
πολέμησες καὶ σὺ τὸν Δᾶτι καὶ τὸν Ἀρταφέρνη.»

YOUNG MEN OF SIDON (A.D. 400)

The actor they brought in to entertain them
also recited a few choice epigrams.

The room opened wide onto the garden,
and had its own light scent of blossoms
mingled with the fragrance
of the five perfumed young Sidonians.

The readings: from Meleager, Krinagoras, Rhianos.
But when the actor declaimed
"Aeschylus, the Athenian son of Euphorion, lies here"
(accenting maybe more than he needed to
the "renowned bravery" and the "Marathonian grove"),
suddenly a feisty youth jumped up, clearly
a lover of literature and began shouting:

"No, I really don't like that quatrain.
Phrasing of that sort seems like our soul fails us.
Give—I say—all your strength to your work,
all your mind and soul and think it through again,
in difficult times too, and again when you near your end.
That is my expectation, what I demand of you.
Not that you put out of your mind entirely
the brilliant art, the great Word of Tragedy—
your *Agamemnon*, the miraculous *Prometheus*,
how you present Orestes or Kassandra,
your *Seven Against Thebes*—and so to write for your
memorial *only* that, as an ordinary soldier among the hordes,
you too fought against Datis and Artaphernes."

ΓΙΑ ΝΑ 'ΡΘΟΥΝ—

Ἕνα κερὶ ἀρκεῖ.　　Τὸ φῶς του τὸ ἀμυδρὸ
ἁρμόζει πιὸ καλά,　　θά 'ναι πιὸ συμπαθὲς
σὰν ἔρθουν τῆς Ἀγάπης,　　σὰν ἔρθουν ἡ Σκιές.

Ἕνα κερὶ ἀρκεῖ.　　Ἡ κάμαρη ἀπόψι
νὰ μὴ ἔχει φῶς πολύ.　　Μέσα στὴν ρέμβην ὅλως
καὶ τὴν ὑποβολή,　　καὶ μὲ τὸ λίγο φῶς—
μέσα στὴν ρέμβην ἔτσι　　θὰ ὁραματισθῶ
γιὰ νά 'ρθουν τῆς Ἀγάπης,　　γιὰ νά 'ρθουν ἡ Σκιές.

SO THEY MIGHT COME—

One candle is enough.   The light flickering dim
is more fitting,   will be more kind
when the Ghosts come,   the Ghosts of Love.

One candle is enough.   Tonight the room
mustn't have too much light. Given over to reverie
and all suggestive rapture,   with light flickering dim
in reverie, just so,   I will shape visions
for the Ghosts to come,   the Ghosts of Love.

Ο ΔΑΡΕΙΟΣ

Ὁ ποιητὴς Φερνάζης τὸ σπουδαῖον μέρος
τοῦ ἐπικοῦ ποιήματός του κάμνει.
Τὸ πῶς τὴν βασιλεία τῶν Περσῶν
παρέλαβε ὁ Δαρεῖος Ὑστάσπου. (Ἀπὸ αὐτὸν
κατάγεται ὁ ἔνδοξός μας βασιλεύς,
ὁ Μιθριδάτης, Διόνυσος κ' Εὐπάτωρ). Ἀλλ' ἐδῶ
χρειάζεται φιλοσοφία· πρέπει ν' ἀναλύσει
τὰ αἰσθήματα ποὺ θὰ εἶχεν ὁ Δαρεῖος:
ἴσως ὑπεροψίαν καὶ μέθην· ὄχι ὅμως—μᾶλλον
σὰν κατανόησι τῆς ματαιότητος τῶν μεγαλείων.
Βαθέως σκέπτεται τὸ πρᾶγμα ὁ ποιητής.

Ἀλλὰ τὸν διακόπτει ὁ ὑπηρέτης του ποὺ μπαίνει
τρέχοντας, καὶ τὴν βαρυσήμαντην εἴδησι ἀγγέλλει.
Ἄρχισε ὁ πόλεμος μὲ τοὺς Ρωμαίους.
Τὸ πλεῖστον τοῦ στρατοῦ μας πέρασε τὰ σύνορα.

Ὁ ποιητὴς μένει ἐνεός. Τί συμφορά!
Ποῦ τώρα ὁ ἔνδοξός μας βασιλεύς,
ὁ Μιθριδάτης, Διόνυσος κ' Εὐπάτωρ,
μ' ἑλληνικὰ ποιήματα ν' ἀσχοληθεῖ.
Μέσα σὲ πόλεμο—φαντάσου, ἑλληνικὰ ποιήματα.

Ἀδημονεῖ ὁ Φερνάζης. Ἀτυχία!
Ἐκεῖ ποὺ τὸ εἶχε θετικὸ μὲ τὸν Δαρεῖο
ν' ἀναδειχθεῖ, καὶ τοὺς ἐπικριτάς του,
τοὺς φθονερούς, τελειωτικὰ ν' ἀποστομώσει.
Τί ἀναβολή, τί ἀναβολὴ στὰ σχέδιά του.

Καὶ νά 'ταν μόνο ἀναβολή, πάλι καλά.
Ἀλλὰ νὰ δοῦμε ἂν ἔχουμε κι ἀσφάλεια
στὴν Ἀμισό. Δὲν εἶναι πολιτεία ἐκτάκτως ὀχυρή.
Εἶναι φρικτότατοι ἐχθροὶ οἱ Ρωμαῖοι.

DAREIOS

The poet Phernazes is at a critical point
in his important epic work:
how the kingdom of the Persians
passed to Dareios, son of Hystaspes. (It's from him
that our glorious king Mithridates,
Dionysos and Eupator, descends.) Here, though, he would
need philosophical reflection; Phernazes must
analyze the emotional state of Dareios at the time:
perhaps arrogance and intoxication; but surely not—maybe
more an awareness of the vanities of greatness.
Now the poet thinks deeply on the matter.

But his servant interrupts him, enters
running, and announces the gravest news:
the war with the Romans has begun;
the better part of our army has crossed the border.

The poet remains speechless. What a disaster!
How can our glorious king,
Mithridates, Dionysos and Eupator,
trouble himself with Greek poems now?
In the middle of a war—imagine, Greek poems!

Phernazes is irritated. What bad luck!
Just as he felt sure he'd win all praise for himself
with his own *Dareios*, and silence
his envious critics once and for all.—
What a setback, what a setback to his tactics.

And were it only a setback, it wouldn't be so bad.
But let's see if we can even consider ourselves safe
in Amisos. It's not exactly a well-fortified city.
And the Romans are the most horrible enemies.

Μπορούμε νὰ τὰ βγάλουμε μ' αὐτούς,
οἱ Καππαδόκες; Γένεται ποτέ;
Εἶναι νὰ μετρηθοῦμε τώρα μὲ τὲς λεγεῶνες;
Θεοὶ μεγάλοι, τῆς Ἀσίας προστάται, βοηθῆστε μας.—

Ὅμως μὲς σ' ὅλη του τὴν ταραχὴ καὶ τὸ κακό,
ἐπίμονα κ' ἡ ποιητικὴ ἰδέα πάει κ' ἔρχεται—
τὸ πιθανότερο εἶναι, βέβαια, ὑπεροψίαν καὶ μέθην·
ὑπεροψίαν καὶ μέθην θὰ εἶχεν ὁ Δαρεῖος.

Are we any kind of match for them,
we Kappadocians? Can it ever be possible?
Are we now to place ourselves before the legions?
Great gods, patrons of Asia, help us.—

But through all his agony, all the chaos,
the poetic idea persists, it comes and goes—
most likely it's arrogance and intoxication;
Dareios was feeling arrogance and intoxication.

ΑΝΝΑ ΚΟΜΝΗΝΗ

Στὸν πρόλογο τῆς Ἀλεξιάδος της θρηνεῖ,
γιὰ τὴν χηρεία της ἡ Ἄννα Κομνηνή.

Εἰς ἴλιγγον εἶν' ἡ ψυχή της. «Καὶ
ρείθροις δακρύων» μᾶς λέγει «περιτέγγω
τοὺς ὀφθαλμούς ... Φεῦ τῶν κυμάτων» τῆς ζωῆς της,
«φεῦ τῶν ἐπαναστάσεων». Τὴν καίει ἡ ὀδύνη
«μέχρις ὀστέων καὶ μυελῶν καὶ μερισμοῦ ψυχῆς».

Ὅμως ἡ ἀλήθεια μοιάζει ποὺ μιὰ λύπη μόνην
καιρίαν ἐγνώρισεν ἡ φίλαρχη γυναῖκα·
ἕναν καϋμὸ βαθὺ μονάχα εἶχε
(κι ἂς μὴν τ' ὁμολογεῖ) ἡ ἀγέρωχη αὐτὴ Γραικιά,
ποὺ δὲν κατάφερε, μ' ὅλην τὴν δεξιότητά της,
τὴν Βασιλείαν ν' ἀποκτήσει· μὰ τὴν πῆρε
σχεδὸν μέσ' ἀπ' τὰ χέρια της ὁ προπετὴς Ἰωάννης.

ANNA KOMNENE

In the prologue to her *Alexiad,*
Anna Komnene laments her widowhood.

Her soul is in confusion. "And my eyes
run with tears," she tells us, "rivers of tears
from the eyes … Ah, for the waves of fate" of her life,
"alas for the revolutions." Grief consumes her,
"to the bones and marrow, the rending of her soul."

But the truth seems to be—this power-hungry woman
knew only one grief;
she had one burning obsession, this proud Greek
(never mind, she never admits it),
that she never, with all her dexterity,
managed to take the throne,
virtually grabbed out of her hands by impudent Ioannes.

ΒΥΖΑΝΤΙΝΟΣ ΑΡΧΩΝ, ΕΞΟΡΙΣΤΟΣ, ΣΤΙΧΟΥΡΓΩΝ

Οἱ ἐλαφροὶ ἄς μὲ λέγουν ἐλαφρόν.
Στὰ σοβαρὰ πράγματα ἤμουν πάντοτε
ἐπιμελέστατος. Καὶ θὰ ἐπιμείνω,
ὅτι κανεὶς καλλίτερά μου δὲν γνωρίζει
Πατέρας ἢ Γραφάς, ἢ τοὺς Κανόνας τῶν Συνόδων.
Εἰς κάθε ἀμφιβολίαν του ὁ Βοτανειάτης,
εἰς κάθε δυσκολίαν στὰ ἐκκλησιαστικά,
ἐμένα συμβουλεύονταν, ἐμένα πρῶτον.
Ἀλλὰ ἐξόριστος ἐδῶ (νὰ ὄψεται ἡ κακεντρεχὴς
Εἰρήνη Δούκαινα), καὶ δεινῶς ἀνιῶν,
οὐδόλως ἄτοπον εἶναι νὰ διασκεδάζω
ἑξάστιχα κι ὀκτάστιχα ποιῶν—
νὰ διασκεδάζω μὲ μυθολογήματα
Ἑρμοῦ, καὶ Ἀπόλλωνος, καὶ Διονύσου,
ἢ ἡρώων τῆς Θεσσαλίας καὶ τῆς Πελοποννήσου·
καὶ νὰ συνθέτω ἰάμβους ὀρθοτάτους,
ὅπως—θὰ μ' ἐπιτρέψετε νὰ πῶ—οἱ λόγιοι
τῆς Κωνσταντινουπόλεως δὲν ξέρουν νὰ συνθέσουν.
Αὐτὴ ἡ ὀρθότης, πιθανόν, εἶν' ἡ αἰτία τῆς μομφῆς.

A BYZANTINE NOBLEMAN, IN EXILE, COMPOSING VERSES

Let the lightweight call me lightweight.
In serious matters, I have always been
most scrupulous. And I'll insist
that no one knows better than myself
the Church Fathers, or the Scriptures, or the Canons of the Councils.
Whenever Botaneiates had any doubt,
whenever an ecclesiastical difficulty came up,
it was me he consulted, me first.
But, exiled here (for that I have to thank the spiteful
Eirene Doukaina), and painfully bored,
it is not entirely unseemly to have some fun
writing six- and eight-line poems—
to have fun making up, mythologizing, bits of poems
about Hermes, Apollo, and Dionysos,
or heroes of Thessaly and the Peloponnese;
and to compose the most exact iambics
just as—you'll allow me to say—the intellectuals
of Constantinople never could compose.
It must be this perfection that draws their censure.

Η ΑΡΧΗ ΤΩΝ

Ἡ ἐκπλήρωσις τῆς ἔκνομής των ἡδονῆς
ἔγινεν. Ἀπ' τὸ στρῶμα σηκωθῆκαν,
καὶ βιαστικὰ ντύνονται χωρὶς νὰ μιλοῦν.
Βγαίνουνε χωριστά, κρυφὰ ἀπ' τὸ σπίτι· καὶ καθὼς
βαδίζουνε κάπως ἀνήσυχα στὸν δρόμο, μοιάζει
σὰν νὰ ὑποψιάζονται ποὺ κάτι ἐπάνω των προδίδει
σὲ τί εἴδους κλίνην ἔπεσαν πρὸ ὀλίγου.

Πλὴν τοῦ τεχνίτου πῶς ἐκέρδισε ἡ ζωή.
Αὔριο, μεθαύριο, ἢ μὲ τὰ χρόνια θὰ γραφοῦν
οἱ στίχ' οἱ δυνατοὶ ποὺ ἐδῶ ἦταν ἡ ἀρχή των.

THEIR BEGINNING

They have just had illicit sex.
They get up from the mattress
and dress quickly, without speaking.
Separate, they come out of the house, furtively;
and as they move along the street a bit unsettled,
they feel as if their demeanor betrays
the kind of bed they have just shared.

How precious this, for the life of the artist:
tomorrow, the day after, or in years to come, potent
verses will be written that had their beginning here.

ΕΥΝΟΙΑ ΤΟΥ ΑΛΕΞΑΝΔΡΟΥ ΒΑΛΑ

Ἄ δὲν συγχίζομαι ποὺ ἔσπασε μιὰ ρόδα
τοῦ ἁμαξιοῦ, καὶ ποὺ ἔχασα μιὰ ἀστεία νίκη.
Μὲ τὰ καλὰ κρασιά, καὶ μὲς στὰ ὡραῖα ρόδα
τὴν νύχτα θὰ περάσω. Ἡ Ἀντιόχεια μὲ ἀνήκει.
Εἶμαι ὁ νέος ὁ πιὸ δοξαστός.
Τοῦ Βάλα εἶμ' ἐγὼ ἡ ἀδυναμία, ὁ λατρευτός.
Αὔριο, νὰ δεῖς, θὰ ποῦν πὼς ὁ ἀγὼν δὲν ἔγινε σωστός.
(Μὰ ἂν ἤμουν ἀκαλαίσθητος, κι ἂν μυστικὰ τὸ εἶχα προστάξει—
θά 'βγαζαν πρῶτο, οἱ κόλακες, καὶ τὸ κουτσό μου ἁμάξι).

·

THE FAVOR OF ALEXANDER BALAS

No, I'm not upset that my chariot wheel broke
and I lost that laughable race.
I'll pass the evening with fine wines, and rest
all night on lovely roses. Antioch belongs to me.
I'm the most glorious youth in town.
I'm Balas's weakness, he adores me.
Tomorrow, you'll see, they'll say the race was not fair.
(And if, inelegant enough, I ordered it in secret, the flatterers
would surely give first place to my crippled chariot.)

ΜΕΛΑΓΧΟΛΙΑ ΤΟΥ ΙΑΣΟΝΟΣ ΚΛΕΑΝΔΡΟΥ·
ΠΟΙΗΤΟΥ ΕΝ ΚΟΜΜΑΓΗΝῌ, 595 Μ.Χ.

Τὸ γήρασμα τοῦ σώματος καὶ τῆς μορφῆς μου
εἶναι πληγὴ ἀπὸ φρικτὸ μαχαῖρι.
Δὲν ἔχω ἐγκαρτέρησι καμιά.
Εἰς σὲ προστρέχω, Τέχνη τῆς Ποιήσεως,
ποὺ κάπως ξέρεις ἀπὸ φάρμακα·
νάρκης τοῦ ἄλγους δοκιμές, ἐν Φαντασίᾳ καὶ Λόγῳ.

Εἶναι πληγὴ ἀπὸ φρικτὸ μαχαῖρι.—
Τὰ φάρμακά σου φέρε, Τέχνη τῆς Ποιήσεως,
ποὺ κάμνουνε—γιὰ λίγο—νὰ μὴ νοιώθεται ἡ πληγή.

MELANCHOLY OF IASON KLEANDROS,
POET IN KOMMAGENE, A.D. 595

The aging of my body and face
is a wound from a ghastly knife.
I will not be resigned to it, no.
I turn to you, Art of Poetry,
you have a thing or two among your drugs; you know
to numb the pain: Imagination and the Word.

It's a wound from a ghastly knife.
Bring your drugs, Art of Poetry, make it so
—for a time—take away feeling from the wound.

Ο ΔΗΜΑΡΑΤΟΣ

Τὸ θέμα, ὁ Χαρακτὴρ τοῦ Δημαράτου,
ποὺ τὸν ἐπρότεινε ὁ Πορφύριος, ἐν συνομιλίᾳ,
ἔτσι τὸ ἐξέφρασεν ὁ νέος σοφιστὴς
(σκοπεύοντας, μετά, ῥητορικῶς νὰ τὸ ἀναπτύξει).

«Πρῶτα τοῦ βασιλέως Δαρείου, κ᾽ ἔπειτα
τοῦ βασιλέως Ξέρξη ὁ αὐλικός·
καὶ τώρα μὲ τὸν Ξέρξη καὶ τὸ στράτευμά του,
νά ἐπὶ τέλους θὰ δικαιωθεῖ ὁ Δημάρατος.

» Μεγάλη ἀδικία τὸν ἔγινε.
Ἦ τ α ν τοῦ Ἀρίστωνος ὁ υἱός. Ἀναίσχυντα
ἐδωροδόκησαν οἱ ἐχθροί του τὸ μαντεῖον.
Καὶ δὲν τοὺς ἔφθασε ποὺ τὸν ἐστέρησαν τὴν βασιλεία,
ἀλλ᾽ ὅταν πιὰ ὑπέκυψε, καὶ τὸ ἀπεφάσισε
νὰ ζήσει μ᾽ ἐγκαρτέρησιν ὡς ἰδιώτης,
ἔπρεπ᾽ ἐμπρὸς καὶ στὸν λαὸ νὰ τὸν προσβάλουν,
ἔπρεπε δημοσίᾳ νὰ τὸν ταπεινώσουν στὴν γιορτή.

» Ὅθεν τὸν Ξέρξη μὲ πολὺν ζῆλον ὑπηρετεῖ.
Μὲ τὸν μεγάλο Περσικὸ στρατό,
κι αὐτὸς στὴν Σπάρτη θὰ ξαναγυρίσει·
καὶ βασιλεὺς σὰν πρίν, πῶς θὰ τὸν διώξει
ἀμέσως, πῶς θὰ τὸν ἐξευτελίσει
ἐκεῖνον τὸν ραδιοῦργον Λεωτυχίδη.

» Κ᾽ ἡ μέρες του περνοῦν γεμάτες μέριμνα·
νὰ δίδει συμβουλὲς στοὺς Πέρσας, νὰ τοὺς ἐξηγεῖ
τὸ πῶς νὰ κάμουν γιὰ νὰ κατακτήσουν τὴν Ἑλλάδα.

» Πολλὲς φροντίδες, πολλὴ σκέψις καὶ γιὰ τοῦτο
εἶν᾽ ἔτσι ἀνιαρὲς τοῦ Δημαράτου ἡ μέρες·
πολλὲς φροντίδες, πολλὴ σκέψις καὶ γιὰ τοῦτο

DEMARATOS

The subject, "The Character of Demaratos,"
Porphyry suggested it in conversation.
This is how the young sophist phrased it
(intending to develop it rhetorically later):

"See him as the courtier of Kings,
first of Dareios, after that of Xerxes,
and now with Xerxes and his mighty army—
watch how at last Demaratos will be vindicated.

A grave injustice was done to him.
There's no question *he was* Ariston's son.
But his enemies bribed the oracle shamelessly.
"Nor were they content to deprive him of his kingdom,
but when at last he capitulated and decided
to live, persevering, as a private citizen,
they had to insult him even before the people,
they had to humiliate him in public at the festival.

Now he repays them by serving Xerxes with great zeal.
Together with the great Persian armies,
he will surely return to Sparta too;
and king as before he will be, and then watch how
swiftly he will oust, how he will vilify and shame
that conspirator Leotychides.

But now his days pass burdened with anxiety;
guiding the Persians, explaining patiently
what they should do to conquer Greece.

Much to be alert for, much to think out, that's why
Demaratos is world-weary, his days so tedious;
much to be alert for, much to think out, that's why

καμιὰ στιγμὴ χαρᾶς δὲν ἔχει ὁ Δημάρατος·
γιατὶ χαρὰ δὲν εἶν' αὐτὸ ποὺ αἰσθάνεται
(δὲν εἶναι· δὲν τὸ παραδέχεται·
πῶς νὰ τὸ πεῖ χαρά; ἐκορυφώθ' ἡ δυστυχία του)
ὅταν τὰ πράγματα τὸν δείχνουν φανερὰ
ποὺ οἱ Ἕλληνες θὰ βγοῦνε νικηταί.»

there's not a moment's joy in Demaratos's life;
he cannot call it joy, this thing he experiences
(it really is not; he cannot admit as much;
how can he name this joy? his misery is at a peak),
when things point clearly in one direction:
that the Greeks will surely be the victors."

ΕΚΟΜΙΣΑ ΕΙΣ ΤΗΝ ΤΕΧΝΗΝ

Κάθομαι καὶ ρεμβάζω.   Ἐπιθυμίες κ' αἰσθήσεις
ἐκόμισα εἰς τὴν Τέχνην—   κάτι μισοειδωμένα,
πρόσωπα ἤ γραμμές·   ἐρώτων ἀτελῶν
κάτι ἀβέβαιες μνῆμες.   Ἄς ἀφεθῶ σ' αὐτήν.
Ξέρει νὰ σχηματίσει   Μορφὴν τῆς Καλλονῆς·
σχεδὸν ἀνεπαισθήτως   τὸν βίον συμπληροῦσα,
συνδυάζουσα ἐντυπώσεις,   συνδυάζουσα τὲς μέρες.

I BROUGHT TO ART

I sit here and contemplate: I brought to art
desires and feelings—   things half-seen,
faces or shapes;   indistinct memories
of unfulfilled loves.   Let me rely on her.
Art knows how to fashion   a Figure of Beauty;
almost imperceptibly   rounding out life,
mingling together impressions,   mingling the days.

ΑΠΟ ΤΗΝ ΣΧΟΛΗΝ ΤΟΥ ΠΕΡΙΩΝΥΜΟΥ ΦΙΛΟΣΟΦΟΥ

Ἔμεινε μαθητὴς τοῦ Ἀμμωνίου Σακκᾶ δυὸ χρόνια·
ἀλλὰ βαρέθηκε καὶ τὴν φιλοσοφία καὶ τὸν Σακκᾶ.

Κατόπι μπῆκε στὰ πολιτικά.
Μὰ τὰ παραίτησεν. Ἦταν ὁ Ἔπαρχος μωρός·
κ' οἱ πέριξ του ξόανα ἐπίσημα καὶ σοβαροφανῆ·
τρισβάρβαρα τὰ ἑλληνικά των, οἱ ἄθλιοι.

Τὴν περιέργειάν του εἵλκυσε
κομμάτ' ἡ Ἐκκλησία· νὰ βαπτισθεῖ
καὶ νὰ περάσει Χριστιανός. Μὰ γρήγορα
τὴν γνώμη του ἄλλαξε. Θὰ κάκιωνε ἀσφαλῶς
μὲ τοὺς γονεῖς του, ἐπιδεικτικὰ ἐθνικούς·
καὶ θὰ τοῦ ἔπαυαν—πρᾶγμα φρικτόν—
εὐθὺς τὰ λίαν γενναῖα δοσίματα.

Ἔπρεπεν ὅμως καὶ νὰ κάμει κάτι. Ἔγινε ὁ θαμὼν
τῶν διεφθαρμένων οἴκων τῆς Ἀλεξανδρείας,
κάθε κρυφοῦ καταγωγίου κραιπάλης.

Ἡ τύχη τοῦ ἐφάν' εἰς τοῦτο εὐμενής·
τὸν ἔδωσε μορφὴν εἰς ἄκρον εὐειδῆ.
Καὶ χαίρονταν τὴν θείαν δωρεάν.

Τουλάχιστον γιὰ δέκα χρόνια ἀκόμη
ἡ καλλονή του θὰ διαρκοῦσεν. Ἔπειτα—
ἴσως ἐκ νέου στὸν Σακκᾶ νὰ πήγαινε.
Κι ἂν ἐν τῷ μεταξὺ ἀπέθνησκεν ὁ γέρος,
πήγαινε σ' ἄλλου φιλοσόφου ἢ σοφιστοῦ·
πάντοτε βρίσκεται κατάλληλος κανείς.

Ἢ τέλος, δυνατὸν καὶ στὰ πολιτικὰ
νὰ ἐπέστρεφεν—ἀξιεπαίνως ἐνθυμούμενος

FROM THE SCHOOL OF THE RENOWNED PHILOSOPHER

He was a student of Ammonios Sakkas for two years;
but philosophy bored him, and so did Sakkas.

Then he went into politics.
But he gave that up too. The Prefect was an idiot;
and those around him, haughty officious blockheads;
their Greek, most barbaric, the miserable lot of them.

To satisfy his curiosity he became somewhat attracted
to the Church; he might go ahead and be baptized
and pass as a Christian. But he soon
changed his mind: he'd be sure to turn his parents
against him, showy pagans that they were;
and—horrible idea—they would cut off
at once their most generous allowance.

And yet he had to do something. He became a habitual
client of the shady houses of Alexandria,
of every secret, depraved den of debauchery.

But in this, his luck would prove propitious;
it had endowed him with the most attractive looks.
And he was thrilled with his divine gift.

His beauty would keep for at least
ten more years. After that?—
maybe he'd go back and start anew with Sakkas.
And if, meantime, the old man should die,
he'd go to another philosopher or sophist;
there's always one suitable around.

Or, in the end, he might even
return to politics—commendably remembering anew

227

τὲς οἰκογενειακές του παραδόσεις,
τὸ χρέος πρὸς τὴν πατρίδα, κι ἄλλα ἠχηρὰ παρόμοια.

his family's way of life,
duty to country, and more such resounding trivialities.

ΤΕΧΝΟΥΡΓΟΣ ΚΡΑΤΗΡΩΝ

Εἰς τὸν κρατῆρα αὐτὸν   ἀπὸ ἀγνὸν ἀσῆμι—
ποὺ γιὰ τοῦ Ἡρακλείδη   ἔγινε τὴν οἰκία,
ἔνθα καλαισθησία   πολλὴ ἐπικρατεῖ—
ἰδοὺ ἄνθη κομψά, καὶ ῥύακες, καὶ θύμοι,
κ' ἔθεσα ἐν τῷ μέσῳ   ἕναν ὡραῖον νέον,
γυμνόν, ἐρωτικόν·   μὲς στὸ νερὸ τὴν κνήμη
τὴν μιά του ἔχει ἀκόμη.—   Ἱκέτευσα, ὦ μνήμη,
νὰ σ' εὕρω βοηθὸν   ἀρίστην, γιὰ νὰ κάμω
τοῦ νέου ποὺ ἀγαποῦσα   τὸ πρόσωπον ὡς ἦταν.
Μεγάλη ἡ δυσκολία   ἀπέβη ἐπειδὴ
ὡς δέκα πέντε χρόνια   πέρασαν ἀπ' τὴν μέρα
ποὺ ἔπεσε, στρατιώτης,   στῆς Μαγνησίας τὴν ἧτταν.

CRAFTSMAN OF WINE BOWLS

On the face of this wine bowl   of the purest silver—
made specially for   the House of Herakleides,
a place where exquisite   good taste prevails—
you can see stylish flowers,   running brooks, and thyme.
Amid all that, I placed   a beautiful young man,
naked, erotic;   one leg is still
immersed in the water.   I begged you, Memory,
to stand by me with your skill that I might shape the face
of this youth that I loved,   the face as it was.
The task proves most   difficult because
some fifteen years   have passed since the day
he fell, a soldier,   in the defeat of Magnesia.

ΥΠΕΡ ΤΗΣ ΑΧΑΪΚΗΣ ΣΥΜΠΟΛΙΤΕΙΑΣ
ΠΟΛΕΜΗΣΑΝΤΕΣ

Ἀνδρεῖοι σεῖς ποὺ πολεμήσατε καὶ πέσατ᾽ εὐκλεῶς·
τοὺς πανταχοῦ νικήσαντας μὴ φοβηθέντες.
Ἄμωμοι σεῖς, ἂν ἔπταισαν ὁ Δίαιος κι ὁ Κριτόλαος.
Ὅταν θὰ θέλουν οἱ Ἕλληνες νὰ καυχηθοῦν,
«Τέτοιους βγάζει τὸ ἔθνος μας» θὰ λένε
γιὰ σᾶς. Ἔτσι θαυμάσιος θὰ ᾽ναι ὁ ἔπαινός σας.—

Ἐγράφη ἐν Ἀλεξανδρείᾳ ὑπὸ Ἀχαιοῦ·
ἕβδομον ἔτος Πτολεμαίου, Λαθύρου.

THOSE WHO FOUGHT FOR THE ACHAEAN LEAGUE

Brave men you are, you who fought and fell so famously;
those who were victors everywhere never made you fear.
Unblemished you are, even if Diaios and Kritolaos were at fault.
When the Greeks will want to boast,
"these are the kinds of men our nation breeds," they'll speak
of you. That's how great their paean will be.—

Written in Alexandria by an Achaean
during the seventh year of the reign of Ptolemy Lathyros.

ΠΡΟΣ ΤΟΝ ΑΝΤΙΟΧΟΝ ΕΠΙΦΑΝΗ

Ὁ νέος Ἀντιοχεὺς   εἶπε στὸν βασιλέα,
«Μὲς στὴν καρδιά μου πάλλει   μιὰ προσφιλὴς ἐλπίς·
οἱ Μακεδόνες πάλι,   Ἀντίοχε Ἐπιφανῆ,
οἱ Μακεδόνες εἶναι   μὲς στὴν μεγάλη πάλη.
Ἂς ἦ τ α ν νὰ νικήσουν—   καὶ σ᾿ ὅποιον θέλει δίδω
τὸν λέοντα καὶ τοὺς ἵππους,   τὸν Πᾶνα ἀπὸ κοράλλι,
καὶ τὸ κομψὸ παλάτι,   καὶ τοὺς ἐν Τύρῳ κήπους,
κι ὅσ᾿ ἄλλα μ᾿ ἔχεις δώσει,   Ἀντίοχε Ἐπιφανῆ.»

Ἴσως νὰ συγκινήθη   κομμάτι ὁ βασιλεύς.
Μὰ πάραυτα θυμήθη   πατέρα κι ἀδελφόν,
καὶ μήτε ἀπεκρίθη.   Μποροῦσε ὠτακουστὴς
νὰ ἐπαναλάβει κάτι.—   Ἄλλωστε, ὡς φυσικόν,
ταχέως ἐπῆλθε εἰς Πύδναν   ἡ ἀπαισία λῆξις.

TO ANTIOCHOS EPIPHANES

The young Antiochian   said to the king:
"My heart pulsates   with a dearly loved hope.
The Makedonians are again,   Antiochos Epiphanes,
the Makedonians are now   embroiled in the great conflict.
If only they could win—   I would give away to any who wants them
the lion and the horses,   the Pan made of coral,
the elegant palace,   and the gardens of Tyre,
and all else you've given me,   O Antiochos Epiphanes."

Maybe the king was   moved, in a small way.
But for all that he remembered   his father and brother,
he never answered.   There might be an eavesdropper,
might repeat what he heard.—   In any case, as expected,
the disastrous end   came swiftly at Pydna.

Σ' ΕΝΑ ΒΙΒΛΙΟ ΠΑΛΗΟ—

Σ' ἕνα βιβλίο παληό—περίπου ἑκατὸ ἐτῶν—
ἀνάμεσα στὰ φύλλα του λησμονημένη,
ηὗρα μιὰν ὑδατογραφία ἄνευ ὑπογραφῆς.
Θά 'ταν τὸ ἔργον καλλιτέχνου λίαν δυνατοῦ.
Ἔφερ' ὡς τίτλον, «Παρουσίασις τοῦ Ἔρωτος».

Πλὴν μᾶλλον ἥρμοζε, «—τοῦ ἔρωτος τῶν ἄκρως αἰσθητῶν».

Γιατὶ ἦταν φανερὸ σὰν ἔβλεπες τὸ ἔργον
(εὔκολα νοιώθονταν ἡ ἰδέα τοῦ καλλιτέχνου)
ποὺ γιὰ ὅσους ἀγαποῦνε κάπως ὑγιεινά,
μὲς στ' ὁπωσδήποτε ἐπιτετραμμένον μένοντες,
δὲν ἦταν προωρισμένος ὁ ἔφηβος
τῆς ζωγραφιᾶς—μὲ καστανά, βαθύχροα μάτια·
μὲ τοῦ προσώπου του τὴν ἐκλεκτὴ ἐμορφιά,
τὴν ἐμορφιὰ τῶν ἀνωμάλων ἕλξεων·
μὲ τὰ ἰδεώδη χείλη του ποὺ φέρνουνε
τὴν ἡδονὴ εἰς ἀγαπημένο σῶμα·
μὲ τὰ ἰδεώδη μέλη του πλασμένα γιὰ κρεββάτια
ποὺ ἀναίσχυντα τ' ἀποκαλεῖ ἡ τρεχάμενη ἠθική.

IN AN OLD BOOK—

In an old book—about a hundred years old—
forgotten inside its pages,
I found a watercolor without a signature.
It must have been the work of a very fine artist.
It had the title, "The Appearance of Eros."

A more fitting title might have been, "… of Eros for excessive
                    sensualists."

For it was clear as you looked at the work
(it was easy to discern the artist's mind)
that for those who love in a more or less healthy way,
who stay within what's proper and permissible,
this watercolor ephebe was never intended
—a youth with deep chestnut eyes;
a face graced with exquisite beauty,
the beauty of unnatural desires;
ideal lips that bring
sensual pleasure to a loving body;
ideal limbs sculpted for beds
that current morality calls shameless.

ΕΝ ΑΠΟΓΝΩΣΕΙ

Τὸν ἔχασ' ἐντελῶς.　Καὶ τώρα πιὰ ζητεῖ
στὰ χείλη καθενὸς　καινούριου ἐραστῆ
τὰ χείλη τὰ δικά του·　στὴν ἔνωσι μὲ κάθε
καινούριον ἐραστὴ　ζητεῖ νὰ πλανηθεῖ
πὼς εἶναι ὁ ἴδιος νέος,　πὼς δίδεται σ' ἐκεῖνον.

Τὸν ἔχασ' ἐντελῶς,　σὰν νὰ μὴ ὑπῆρχε κάν.
Γιατὶ ἤθελε—εἶπ' ἐκεῖνος—　ἤθελε νὰ σωθεῖ
ἀπ' τὴν στιγματισμένη,　τὴν νοσηρὰ ἡδονή·
ἀπ' τὴν στιγματισμένη,　τοῦ αἴσχους ἡδονή.
Ἦταν καιρὸς ἀκόμη—　ὡς εἶπε— νὰ σωθεῖ.

Τὸν ἔχασ' ἐντελῶς,　σὰν νὰ μὴ ὑπῆρχε κάν.
Ἀπὸ τὴν φαντασίαν,　ἀπὸ τὲς παραισθήσεις
στὰ χείλη ἄλλων νέων　τὰ χείλη του ζητεῖ·
γυρεύει νὰ αἰσθανθεῖ　ξανὰ τὸν ἔρωτά του.

IN DESPAIR

He lost him now for good.   And now he looks to find
on each new   lover's lips
those lips of his;   locked in embrace
with each new lover   he longs to fantasize
that he's still the same youth,   that it's to him he gives himself.

He lost him now for good,   as if he never was at all.
For he wanted—said he—   to save himself
from this tainted,   this sick pleasure;
from this tainted,   this shameful, tainted pleasure
There was still time—   as he said—to save himself.

He lost him now for good,   as if he never was at all.
In his fantasies,   through hallucination,
on the lips of other youths   he looks to find his lips;
he longs to feel   once more his love.

Ο ΙΟΥΛΙΑΝΟΣ, ΟΡΩΝ ΟΛΙΓΩΡΙΑΝ

«Ὁρῶν οὖν πολλὴν μὲν ὀλιγωρίαν οὖσαν
ἡμῖν πρὸς τοὺς θεούς»—λέγει μὲ ὕφος σοβαρόν.
Ὀλιγωρίαν. Μὰ τί περίμενε λοιπόν;
Ὅσο ἤθελεν ἂς ἔκαμνεν ὀργάνωσι θρησκευτική,
ὅσο ἤθελεν ἂς ἔγραφε στὸν ἀρχιερέα Γαλατίας,
ἢ εἰς ἄλλους τοιούτους, παροτρύνων κι ὁδηγῶν.
Οἱ φίλοι του δὲν ἦσαν Χριστιανοί·
αὐτὸ ἦταν θετικόν. Μὰ δὲν μποροῦσαν κιόλας
νὰ παίζουν σὰν κι αὐτόνα (τὸν Χριστιανομαθημένο)
μὲ σύστημα καινούριας ἐκκλησίας,
ἀστεῖον καὶ στὴν σύλληψι καὶ στὴν ἐφαρμογή.
Ἕλληνες ἦσαν ἐπὶ τέλους. Μηδὲν ἄγαν, Αὔγουστε.

JULIAN SEEING NEGLECT

"Seeing, then, that there is much neglect
of the gods among us"—he says in a solemn way.
Neglect. Just what did he expect?
So let him do it, organize religion as he likes, let him
write to the High Priest of Galatia as much as he likes,
or to others like himself, inciting and advising them.
His friends were not Christians;
that much was certain. But even so they couldn't
fool about as he could (reared a Christian)
with a new religious system,
ludicrous both in thought and in practice.
They were Greeks, after all. Nothing in excess, Augustus.

ΕΠΙΤΥΜΒΙΟΝ ΑΝΤΙΟΧΟΥ, ΒΑΣΙΛΕΩΣ ΚΟΜΜΑΓΗΝΗΣ

Μετὰ ποὺ ἐπέστρεψε, περίλυπη, ἀπ᾽ τὴν κηδεία του,
ἡ ἀδελφὴ τοῦ ἐγκρατῶς καὶ πράως ζήσαντος,
τοῦ λίαν ἐγγραμμάτου Ἀντιόχου, βασιλέως
Κομμαγηνῆς, ἤθελ᾽ ἕνα ἐπιτύμβιον γι᾽ αὐτόν.
Κι ὁ Ἐφέσιος σοφιστὴς Καλλίστρατος—ὁ κατοικῶν
συχνὰ ἐν τῷ κρατιδίῳ τῆς Κομμαγηνῆς,
κι ἀπὸ τὸν οἶκον τὸν βασιλικὸν
ἀσμένως κ᾽ ἐπανειλημμένως φιλοξενηθείς—
τὸ ἔγραψε, τῇ ὑποδείξει Σύρων αὐλικῶν,
καὶ τὸ ἔστειλε εἰς τὴν γραῖαν δέσποιναν.

«Τοῦ Ἀντιόχου τοῦ εὐεργέτου βασιλέως
νὰ ὑμνηθεῖ ἐπαξίως, ὦ Κομμαγηνοί, τὸ κλέος.
Ἦταν τῆς χώρας κυβερνήτης προνοητικός.
Ὑπῆρξε δίκαιος, σοφός, γενναῖος.
Ὑπῆρξεν ἔτι τὸ ἄριστον ἐκεῖνο, Ἑλληνικός—
ἰδιότητα δὲν ἔχ᾽ ἡ ἀνθρωπότης τιμιοτέραν·
εἰς τοὺς θεοὺς εὑρίσκονται τὰ πέραν.»

EPITAPH FOR ANTIOCHOS, KING OF KOMMAGENE

When she returned, full of sorrow, from the funeral,
the sister of Antiochos, King of Kommagene, whose life
was one of self-restraint, a life of scholarly pursuit,
for him she wanted a proper epitaph.
And the Ephesian sophist Kallistratos—who often
came to stay in the tiny state of Kommagene,
a frequent and welcome guest at the royal house—
wrote the epitaph, as the Syrian courtiers advised,
and sent it to the elderly lady.

"Give the beneficent king, Antiochos, the high
and just praise he deserves, O Kommagenians.
For he was the country's provident leader.
He was just, wise, courageous.
He had, too, that special excellence: he was Hellenic—
a bent of life humanity has never equaled;
what's beyond may be found only with the gods."

ΘΕΑΤΡΟΝ ΤΗΣ ΣΙΔΩΝΟΣ (400 Μ.Χ.)

Πολίτου ἐντίμου υἱός— πρὸ πάντων, εὐειδὴς
ἔφηβος τοῦ θεάτρου, ποικίλως ἀρεστός,
ἐνίοτε συνθέτω ἐν γλώσσῃ ἑλληνικῇ
λίαν εὐτόλμους στίχους, ποὺ τοὺς κυκλοφορῶ
πολὺ κρυφά, ἐννοεῖται— θεοί! νὰ μὴν τοὺς δοῦν
οἱ τὰ φαιὰ φοροῦντες, περὶ ἠθικῆς λαλοῦντες—
στίχους τῆς ἡδονῆς τῆς ἐκλεκτῆς, ποὺ πηαίνει
πρὸς ἄγονην ἀγάπη κι ἀποδοκιμασμένη.

THE THEATRE OF SIDON (A.D. 400)

Son of an esteemed citizen—   above all, striking to look at,
a youth of the theatre,   desirable in many ways,
I occasionally write   using the Greek language
most daring verses   that I circulate in secret,
(it goes without saying)—   gods! may they not see them,
those grey-clad brains   ranting about morality—
verses of erotic pleasure,   of a special pleasure, veering toward
an uncharted act of love,   a condemned, barren love.

Ο ΙΟΥΛΙΑΝΟΣ ΕΝ ΝΙΚΟΜΗΔΕΙᾼ

Ἄστοχα πράγματα καὶ κινδυνώδη.
Οἱ ἔπαινοι γιὰ τῶν Ἑλλήνων τὰ ἰδεώδη.

Ἡ θεουργίες κ᾽ ἡ ἐπισκέψεις στοὺς ναοὺς
τῶν ἐθνικῶν. Οἱ ἐνθουσιασμοὶ γιὰ τοὺς ἀρχαίους θεούς.

Μὲ τὸν Χρυσάνθιον ἡ συχνὲς συνομιλίες.
Τοῦ φιλοσόφου—τοῦ ἄλλωστε δεινοῦ—Μαξίμου ἡ θεωρίες.

Καὶ νά τὸ ἀποτέλεσμα. Ὁ Γάλλος δείχνει ἀνησυχία
μεγάλην. Ὁ Κωνστάντιος ἔχει κάποιαν ὑποψία.

Ἀ οἱ συμβουλεύσαντες δὲν ἦσαν διόλου συνετοί.
Παρέγινε—λέγει ὁ Μαρδόνιος—ἡ ἱστορία αὐτή,

καὶ πρέπει ἐξ ἅπαντος νὰ παύσει ὁ θόρυβός της.—
Ὁ Ἰουλιανὸς πηγαίνει πάλιν ἀναγνώστης

στὴν ἐκκλησία τῆς Νικομηδείας,
ὅπου μεγαλοφώνως καὶ μετ᾽ εὐλαβείας

πολλῆς τὲς ἱερὲς Γραφὲς διαβάζει,
καὶ τὴν χριστιανική του εὐσέβεια ὁ λαὸς θαυμάζει.

JULIAN IN NIKOMEDEIA

Foolish things and, worse, hazardous things:
the praising of Greek ideals.

Taking part in all manner of mysteries, visits
to Pagan temples. Enthusiasm for the ancient gods.

And those frequent consultations with Chrysanthios.
Talks on the theories of Maximos, the astute thinker.

And here's what comes of all that. Gallos shows
great concern. Constantios begins to have suspicions.

And Julian's advisers show no prudence at all.
Too far—Mardonios says—the matter's gone too far,

this whole commotion must be stopped at any cost.
So Julian in good time goes back as a lay-reader

at the church of Nikomedeia, where
with his loud voice and true reverence

he reads passages of Holy Scriptures,
while the people marvel at his Christian piety.

ΠΡΙΝ ΤΟΥΣ ΑΛΛΑΞΕΙ Ο ΧΡΟΝΟΣ

Λυπήθηκαν μεγάλως   στὸν ἀποχωρισμό των.
Δὲν τό 'θελαν αὐτοί·   ἦταν ἡ περιστάσεις.
Βιοτικὲς ἀνάγκες   ἐκάμνανε τὸν ἕνα
νὰ φύγει μακρυά—   Νέα Ὑόρκη ἢ Καναδᾶ.
Ἡ ἀγάπη των βεβαίως   δὲν ἦταν ἴδια ὡς πρίν·
εἶχεν ἐλαττωθεῖ   ἡ ἕλξις βαθμηδόν,
εἶχεν ἐλαττωθεῖ   ἡ ἕλξις της πολύ.
Ὅμως νὰ χωρισθοῦν,   δὲν τό 'θελαν αὐτοί.
Ἦταν ἡ περιστάσεις.—   Ἢ μήπως καλλιτέχνις
ἐφάνηκεν ἡ Τύχη   χωρίζοντάς τους τώρα
πρὶν σβύσει τὸ αἴσθημά των,   πρὶν τοὺς ἀλλάξει ὁ Χρόνος·
ὁ ἕνας γιὰ τὸν ἄλλον   θὰ εἶναι ὡς νὰ μένει πάντα
τῶν εἴκοσι τεσσάρων   ἐτῶν τ' ὡραῖο παιδί.

BEFORE TIME CHANGES THEM

Both were greatly saddened   at their parting.
They never meant it to happen;   it was those bad times.
The need to make a living   forced them: the one
would go far away—   New York or Canada.
Their love, of course, was not   the love it had been;
attraction for each other   lessened with time,
it lessened by far   the attraction between them.
Though parting   was not their choosing.
It was those bad times.—   Or might it have been
that Fate the artist   crafted their separation now,
before their love subsides,   before Time changes them;
—each will remain for the other,   forever for the other
the beautiful youth   of twenty-four years.

ΗΛΘΕ ΓΙΑ ΝΑ ΔΙΑΒΑΣΕΙ—

Ἦλθε γιὰ νὰ διαβάσει. Εἶν' ἀνοιχτὰ
δυό, τρία βιβλία· ἱστορικοὶ καὶ ποιηταί.
Μὰ μόλις διάβασε δέκα λεπτά,
καὶ τὰ παραίτησε. Στὸν καναπὲ
μισοκοιμᾶται. Ἀνήκει πλήρως στὰ βιβλία—
ἀλλ' εἶναι εἴκοσι τριῶ ἐτῶν, κ' εἶν' ἔμορφος πολύ·
καὶ σήμερα τὸ ἀπόγευμα πέρασ' ὁ ἔρως
στὴν ἰδεώδη σάρκα του, στὰ χείλη.
Στὴ σάρκα του ποὺ εἶναι ὅλο καλλονὴ
ἡ θέρμη πέρασεν ἡ ἐρωτική·
χωρὶς ἀστείαν αἰδῶ γιὰ τὴν μορφὴ τῆς ἀπολαύσεως …

HE CAME HERE TO READ—

He came here to read. They lie open,
his two or three books: historians and poets.
But he barely read for ten minutes,
before he put the books aside. He is now
half-asleep on the sofa. He belongs entirely to books—
but he's only twenty-three, and he's much too lovely;
and just this afternoon Eros brushed him,
rode over his ideal flesh, his lips.
Over his flesh that is sheer beauty,
the heat of Eros passed through,
with no absurd shame for this kind of pleasure ...

ΤΟ 31 Π.Χ. ΣΤΗΝ ΑΛΕΞΑΝΔΡΕΙΑ

Ἀπ' τὴν μικρή του, στὰ περίχωρα πλησίον, κώμη,
καὶ σκονισμένος ἀπὸ τὸ ταξεῖδι ἀκόμη

ἔφθασεν ὁ πραγματευτής. Καὶ «Λίβανον!» καὶ «Κόμμι!»
«Ἄριστον Ἔλαιον!» «Ἄρωμα γιὰ τὴν κόμη!»

στοὺς δρόμους διαλαλεῖ. Ἀλλ' ἡ μεγάλη ὀχλοβοή,
κ' ἡ μουσικές, κ' ἡ παρελάσεις ποῦ ἀφίνουν ν' ἀκουσθεῖ.

Τὸ πλῆθος τὸν σκουντᾶ, τὸν σέρνει, τὸν βροντᾶ.
Κι ὅταν πιὰ τέλεια σαστισμένος, Τί εἶναι ἡ τρέλλα αὐτή; ρωτᾶ,

ἕνας τοῦ ρίχνει κι αὐτουνοῦ τὴν γιγαντιαία ψευτιὰ
τοῦ παλατιοῦ—ποὺ στὴν Ἑλλάδα ὁ Ἀντώνιος νικᾶ.

IN ALEXANDRIA, 31 B.C.

From his small village near the outskirts,
still covered with dust from his journey,

the peddler arrives. He bellows: "Frankincense!" and "Gum!"
"Excellent olive oil!" "Scented oils for your hair!"

So he hawks his ware in the street. But with all the clamor,
the music, the parades, who can hear him?

The crowd bumps into him, drags him along, he takes his knocks.
And, when perfectly off balance, he asks, "What does this madness
          mean?"

someone drops the great lie the palace
has been passing off: Anthony is triumphant in Greece.

Ο ΙΩΑΝΝΗΣ ΚΑΝΤΑΚΟΥΖΗΝΟΣ ΥΠΕΡΙΣΧΥΕΙ

Τοὺς κάμπους βλέπει ποὺ ἀκόμη ὁρίζει
μὲ τὸ σιτάρι, μὲ τὰ ζῶα, μὲ τὰ καρποφόρα
δένδρα. Καὶ πιὸ μακρυὰ τὸ σπίτι του τὸ πατρικό,
γεμάτο ροῦχα κ' ἔπιπλα πολύτιμα, κι ἀσημικό.

Θὰ τοῦ τὰ πάρουν—Ἰησοῦ Χριστέ!—θὰ τοῦ τὰ πάρουν τώρα.

Ἄραγε νὰ τὸν λυπηθεῖ ὁ Καντακουζηνὸς
ἂν πάει στὰ πόδια του νὰ πέσει. Λὲν πὼς εἶν' ἐπιεικής,
λίαν ἐπιεικής. Ἀλλ' οἱ περὶ αὐτόν; ἀλλ' ὁ στρατός;—
Ἤ, στὴν κυρία Εἰρήνη νὰ προσπέσει, νὰ κλαυθεῖ;

Κουτός! στὸ κόμμα νὰ μπλεχθεῖ τῆς Ἄννας—
ποὺ νὰ μὴν ἔσωνε νὰ τὴν στεφανωθεῖ
ὁ κὺρ Ἀνδρόνικος ποτέ. Εἴδαμε προκοπὴ
ἀπὸ τὸ φέρσιμό της, εἴδαμε ἀνθρωπιά;
Μὰ ὣς κ' οἱ Φράγκοι δὲν τὴν ἐκτιμοῦνε πιά.
Γελοῖα τὰ σχέδιά της, μωρὰ ἡ ἑτοιμασία της ὅλη.
Ἐνῶ φοβέριζαν τὸν κόσμο ἀπὸ τὴν Πόλι,
τοὺς ρήμαξεν ὁ Καντακουζηνός, τοὺς ρήμαξε ὁ κὺρ Γιάννης.

Καὶ ποὺ τὸ εἶχε σκοπὸ νὰ πάει μὲ τοῦ κὺρ Γιάννη
τὸ μέρος! Καὶ θὰ τό 'καμνε. Καὶ θά 'ταν τώρα εὐτυχισμένος,
μεγάλος ἄρχοντας πάντα, καὶ στεριωμένος,
ἂν ὁ δεσπότης δὲν τὸν ἔπειθε τὴν τελευταία στιγμή,
μὲ τὴν ἱερατική του ἐπιβολή,
μὲ τὲς ἀπὸ ἄκρου εἰς ἄκρον ἐσφαλμένες του πληροφορίες,
καὶ μὲ τὲς ὑποσχέσεις του, καὶ τὲς βλακεῖες.

IOANNES KANTAKOUZENOS TRIUMPHS

He sees the fields that still belong to him,
with the wheat, the domestic animals, the fruit
trees. And there, a little ways off, his paternal home,
full of clothes, valuable furniture, silverware.

It'll all be taken—Jesus Christ—they'll take it away from him now.

Would Kantakouzenos take pity on him were he
to go and fall at his feet. They say he's kindhearted,
very kindhearted. But, of those around him? And the army?—
Or should he prostrate himself, pleading, to Lady Eirene?

Stupid! That he should get mixed up in Anna's party—
curse the moment Lord Andronikos went
and married her. Did we see any benefit from her,
has she shown us any humanity?
Even the Franks have no longer any respect for her.
Her plans were foolish, all her preparations idiotic.
As they were threatening everybody from Constantinople,
Kantakouzenos ruined them, Lord Ioannes ruined them.

And to think he'd intended to go with Lord Ioannes'
side! And he would have done it. And he'd be happy now,
great nobleman that he is, and time-honored,
had the bishop not won him over at the last moment,
with his daunting hieratic aura,
with his mistaken information from beginning to end,
his promises, and all his stupidities.

ΤΕΜΕΘΟΣ, ΑΝΤΙΟΧΕΥΣ· 400 Μ.Χ.

Στίχοι τοῦ νέου Τεμέθου   τοῦ ἐρωτοπαθοῦς.
Μὲ τίτλον «Ὁ Ἐμονίδης»—   τοῦ Ἀντιόχου Ἐπιφανοῦς
ὁ προσφιλὴς ἑταῖρος·   ἕνας περικαλλὴς
νέος ἐκ Σαμοσάτων.   Μὰ ἂν ἔγιναν οἱ στίχοι
θερμοί, συγκινημένοι   εἶναι ποὺ ὁ Ἐμονίδης
(ἀπὸ τὴν παλαιὰν   ἐκείνην ἐποχή·
τὸ ἑκατὸν τριάντα ἑπτὰ   τῆς βασιλείας Ἑλλήνων!—
ἴσως καὶ λίγο πρίν)   στὸ ποίημα ἐτέθη
ὡς ὄνομα ψιλόν·   εὐάρμοστον ἐν τούτοις.
Μιὰ ἀγάπη τοῦ Τεμέθου   τὸ ποίημα ἐκφράζει,
ὡραίαν κι ἀξίαν αὐτοῦ.   Ἐμεῖς οἱ μυημένοι
οἱ φίλοι του οἱ στενοί·   ἐμεῖς οἱ μυημένοι
γνωρίζουμε γιὰ ποιόνα   ἐγράφησαν οἱ στίχοι.
Οἱ ἀνίδεοι Ἀντιοχεῖς   διαβάζουν, Ἐμονίδην.

TEMETHOS, ANTIOCHIAN (A.D. 400)

Verses written by the youth   Temethos, the lovelorn.
With the title: "Emonides"—   the beloved
of Antiochos Epiphanes;   an exquisitely beautiful
youth from Samosata.   And if the written verses turned out
all fiery and emotional,   it is because Emonides
(from that old,   that ancient period,
the hundred and thirty-seventh   year of the Greek dynasty!—
or maybe just before) appears   in the poem
as a casual name;   but fitting all the same.
The poem puts forth a kind   of love that Temethos feels,
a beautiful love, every bit worthy of him.   We the initiated,
we his intimate friends,   we the initiated
know well for whom   these verses were written.
The unsuspecting Antiochians   just read: "Emonides."

ΑΠΟ ΥΑΛΙ ΧΡΩΜΑΤΙΣΤΟ

Πολὺ μὲ συγκινεῖ μιὰ λεπτομέρεια
στὴν στέψιν, ἐν Βλαχέρναις, τοῦ Ἰωάννη Καντακουζηνοῦ
καὶ τῆς Εἰρήνης Ἀνδρονίκου Ἀσάν.
Ὅπως δὲν εἶχαν παρὰ λίγους πολυτίμους λίθους
(τοῦ ταλαιπώρου κράτους μας ἦταν μεγάλ᾽ ἡ πτώχεια)
φόρεσαν τεχνητούς. Ἕνα σωρὸ κομμάτια ἀπὸ ὑαλί,
κόκκινα, πράσινα ἢ γαλάζια. Τίποτε
τὸ ταπεινὸν ἢ τὸ ἀναξιοπρεπὲς
δὲν ἔχουν κατ᾽ ἐμὲ τὰ κομματάκια αὐτὰ
ἀπὸ ὑαλὶ χρωματιστό. Μοιάζουνε τουναντίον
σὰν μιὰ διαμαρτυρία θλιβερὴ
κατὰ τῆς ἄδικης κακομοιριᾶς τῶν στεφομένων.
Εἶναι τὰ σύμβολα τοῦ τί ἥρμοζε νὰ ἔχουν,
τοῦ τί ἐξ ἅπαντος ἦταν ὀρθὸν νὰ ἔχουν
στὴν στέψι των ἕνας Κὺρ Ἰωάννης Καντακουζηνός,
μιὰ Κυρία Εἰρήνη Ἀνδρονίκου Ἀσάν.

OF COLORED GLASS

I am deeply moved by one detail
in the coronation of Ioannes Kantakouzenos and Eirene,
daughter of Andronikos Asan, at Vlachernai.
As they had nothing more than a few precious stones
(our miserable country had fallen into great poverty)
they put on artificial ones. A bunch of pieces made of glass,
red, green, or blue. Nothing
lowly or unbecoming,
in my opinion, nothing undignified
in these pieces of colored glass. They resemble,
on the contrary, a saddened protest against
the unjust poverty of the couple to be crowned.
They are symbols of what they ought to have,
of what it would be fitting, without fail, for them to have
at their coronation: a Lord such as Ioannes Kantakouzenos
and a Lady such as Eirene Andronikos Asan.

ΤΟ 25^{ΟΝ} ΕΤΟΣ ΤΟΥ ΒΙΟΥ ΤΟΥ

Πηγαίνει στὴν ταβέρνα τακτικὰ
ποὺ εἴχανε γνωρισθεῖ τὸν περασμένο μῆνα.
Ρώτησε· μὰ δὲν ἤξεραν τίποτε νὰ τὸν ποῦν.
Ἀπὸ τὰ λόγια των, κατάλαβε πὼς εἶχε γνωρισθεῖ
μ' ἕνα ὅλως ἄγνωστο ὑποκείμενον·
μιὰ ἀπ' τὲς πολλὲς ἄγνωστες κ' ὕποπτες
νεανικὲς μορφὲς ποὺ ἀπ' ἐκεῖ περνοῦσαν.
Πηγαίνει ὅμως στὴν ταβέρνα τακτικά, τὴν νύχτα,
καὶ κάθεται καὶ βλέπει πρὸς τὴν εἴσοδο·
μέχρι κοπώσεως βλέπει πρὸς τὴν εἴσοδο.
Ἴσως νὰ μπεῖ. Ἀπόψ' ἴσως νά 'ρθεῖ.

Κοντὰ τρεῖς ἑβδομάδες ἔτσι κάμνει.
Ἀρρώστησεν ὁ νοῦς του ἀπὸ λαγνεία.
Στὸ στόμα του μείνανε τὰ φιλιά.
Παθαίνεται ἀπ' τὸν διαρκῆ πόθον ἡ σάρκα του ὅλη.
Τοῦ σώματος ἐκείνου ἡ ἁφὴ εἶν' ἐπάνω του.
Θέλει τὴν ἕνωσι μαζύ του πάλι.

Νὰ μὴν προδίδεται, τὸ προσπαθεῖ ἐννοεῖται.
Μὰ κάποτε σχεδὸν ἀδιαφορεῖ.—
Ἐξ ἄλλου, σὲ τί ἐκτίθεται τὸ ξέρει,
τὸ πῆρε ἀπόφασι. Δὲν εἶν' ἀπίθανον ἡ ζωή του αὐτὴ
σὲ σκάνδαλον ὀλέθριο νὰ τὸν φέρει.

THE 25TH YEAR OF HIS LIFE

He goes regularly to the taverna, where
they'd met the month before.
He queried within; but they had nothing to tell him.
He understood from their careful words
that he'd met an entirely unknown drifter;
one of the many unknown and suspect
youthful forms that pass through there.
Still, he goes regularly to the taverna, at night,
and sits and looks toward the entrance;
he looks at the entrance till he's exhausted.
Maybe he'll walk in. Maybe tonight he'll come.

He does this, going on three weeks now.
His mind has grown sick from longing.
The kisses are still there on his mouth.
His whole flesh aches with incessant lust,
the touch of that body is still all over him.
He wants to be joined with it once again.

Of course he tries not to give himself away.
But there are times he couldn't care less.—
Besides, he knows what he's exposing himself to,
he's accepted it. It's not impossible the life he leads
will bring him up against final and ruinous scandal.

ΕΙΣ ΙΤΑΛΙΚΗΝ ΠΑΡΑΛΙΑΝ

Ὁ Κῆμος Μενεδώρου,   Ἰταλιώτης νέος,
τὸν βίον του περνᾶ   μέσα στὲς διασκεδάσεις·
ὡς συνειθίζουν τοῦτοι   οἱ ἀπ' τὴν Μεγάλη Ἑλλάδα
μὲς στὰ πολλὰ τὰ πλούτη   ἀναθρεμένοι νέοι.

Μὰ σήμερα εἶναι λίαν,   παρὰ τὸ φυσικό του,
σύννους καὶ κατηφής.   Κοντὰ στὴν παραλίαν,
μὲ ἄκραν μελαγχολίαν   βλέπει ποὺ ἐκφορτώνουν
τὰ πλοῖα μὲ τὴν λείαν   ἐκ τῆς Πελοποννήσου.

Λάφυρα ἑλληνικά· ἡ λεία τῆς Κορίνθου.

Ἀ σήμερα βεβαίως   δὲν εἶναι θεμιτόν,
δὲν εἶναι δυνατὸν   ὁ Ἰταλιώτης νέος
νά 'χει γιὰ διασκεδάσεις   καμιὰν ἐπιθυμίαν.

ON AN ITALIAN SHORE

Kemos, son of Menedoros,   a Greek-Italian youth,
goes through life   simply having a good time,
as these young men do   from Greater Greece
with their ample wealth   and rich upbringing.

But this day makes him,   much against his nature,
moody and depressed.   Near the shore,
he sees with great sadness   where they unload
ships with spoils   grabbed from the Peloponnese.

Greek spoils: the plunder of Corinth.

Ah, today, surely   it is not fitting,
not possible   this Greek-Italian youth
to want a good time   in any way at all.

ΣΤΟ ΠΛΗΚΤΙΚΟ ΧΩΡΙΟ

Στὸ πληκτικὸ χωριὸ ποὺ ἐργάζεται—
ὑπάλληλος σ' ἕνα κατάστημα
ἐμπορικό· νεότατος—καὶ ποὺ ἀναμένει
ἀκόμη δυὸ τρεῖς μῆνες νὰ περάσουν,
ἀκόμη δυὸ τρεῖς μῆνες γιὰ νὰ λιγοστέψουν ἡ δουλειές,
κ' ἔτσι νὰ μεταβεῖ στὴν πόλιν νὰ ριχθεῖ
στὴν κίνησι καὶ στὴν διασκέδασιν εὐθύς·
στὸ πληκτικὸ χωριὸ ὅπου ἀναμένει—
ἔπεσε στὸ κρεββάτι ἀπόψι ἐρωτοπαθής,
ὅλ' ἡ νεότης του στὸν σαρκικὸ πόθο ἀναμένη,
εἰς ἔντασιν ὡραίαν ὅλ' ἡ ὡραία νεότης του.
Καὶ μὲς στὸν ὕπνον ἡ ἡδονὴ προσῆλθε· μέσα
στὸν ὕπνο βλέπει κ' ἔχει τὴν μορφή, τὴν σάρκα ποὺ ἤθελε ...

IN THE LIFELESS VILLAGE

In the lifeless village where he works—
a sales clerk in retail,
a textile shop; so very young—there
he waits for the two or three months to end,
two or three months till business falls off,
till he moves to the city and plunges headlong
into the hustle and bustle of urban pleasures;
in the lifeless village where he bides his time—
tonight he falls into bed bursting with sex urges,
veritable lust, the bloom of his youth on fire:
the beauty of his youth succumbs to the beauty
of intensity. And while asleep he surrenders to
his vision of the figure, of the flesh he craved …

ΑΠΟΛΛΩΝΙΟΣ Ο ΤΥΑΝΕΥΣ ΕΝ ΡΟΔΩ

Γιὰ τὴν ἁρμόζουσα παίδευσι κι ἀγωγὴ
ὁ Ἀπολλώνιος ὁμιλοῦσε μ' ἕναν
νέον ποὺ ἔκτιζε πολυτελῆ
οἰκίαν ἐν Ρόδῳ. «Ἐγὼ δὲ ἐς ἱερὸν»
εἶπεν ὁ Τυανεὺς στὸ τέλος «παρελθὼν
πολλῷ ἂν ἥδιον ἐν αὐτῷ μικρῷ
ὄντι ἄγαλμα ἐλέφαντός τε καὶ χρυσοῦ
ἴδοιμι ἢ ἐν μεγάλῳ κεραμεοῦν τε καὶ φαῦλον.» —

Τὸ «κεραμεοῦν» καὶ «φαῦλον»· τὸ σιχαμερό:
ποὺ κιόλας μερικοὺς (χωρὶς προπόνησι ἀρκετή)
ἀγυρτικῶς ἐξαπατᾶ. Τὸ κεραμεοῦν καὶ φαῦλον.

266

APOLLONIOS OF TYANA IN RHODES

The talk was on proper education—
Apollonios was discussing this
with a youth who was building a luxury
home in Rhodes. "When I enter a temple," said
the Tyanian in the end, "even if the temple be small,
I would much prefer to view a statue
of gold and ivory there, rather than a common
statue of clay in a large temple."

"The one of clay" is surely "common"—and repulsive:
a thing that fools certain people (those inadequately trained)
—and that's "the one of clay" and "common."

Η ΑΡΡΩΣΤΙΑ ΤΟΥ ΚΛΕΙΤΟΥ

Ὁ Κλεῖτος, ἕνα συμπαθητικὸ
παιδί, περίπου εἴκοσι τριῶ ἐτῶν—
μὲ ἀρίστην ἀγωγή, μὲ σπάνια ἑλληνομάθεια—
εἶν' ἄρρωστος βαρειά. Τὸν ηὗρε ὁ πυρετὸς
ποὺ φέτος θέρισε στὴν Ἀλεξάνδρεια.

Τὸν ηὗρε ὁ πυρετὸς ἐξαντλημένο κιόλας ἠθικῶς
ἀπ' τὸν καϋμὸ ποὺ ὁ ἑταῖρος του, ἕνας νέος ἠθοποιός,
ἔπαυσε νὰ τὸν ἀγαπᾶ καὶ νὰ τὸν θέλει.

Εἶν' ἄρρωστος βαρειά, καὶ τρέμουν οἱ γονεῖς του.

Καὶ μιὰ γρηὰ ὑπηρέτρια ποὺ τὸν μεγάλωσε,
τρέμει κι αὐτὴ γιὰ τὴν ζωὴ τοῦ Κλείτου.
Μὲς στὴν δεινὴν ἀνησυχία της
στὸν νοῦ της ἔρχεται ἕνα εἴδωλο
ποὺ λάτρευε μικρή, πρὶν μπεῖ αὐτοῦ, ὑπηρέτρια,
σὲ σπίτι Χριστιανῶν ἐπιφανῶν, καὶ χριστιανέψει.
Παίρνει κρυφὰ κάτι πλακούντια, καὶ κρασί, καὶ μέλι.
Τὰ πάει στὸ εἴδωλο μπροστά. Ὅσα θυμᾶται μέλη
τῆς ἱκεσίας ψάλλει· ἄκρες, μέσες. Ἡ κουτὴ
δὲν νοιώθει ποὺ τὸν μαῦρον δαίμονα λίγο τὸν μέλει
ἂν γιάνει ἢ ἂν δὲν γιάνει ἕνας Χριστιανός.

KLEITOS'S ILLNESS

Kleitos, a likeable young man,
around twenty-three years old—
with an excellent education, rare knowledge of Greek—
has been taken seriously ill. He caught the fever
that mowed down many this year in Alexandria.

The fever found him already exhausted, in low morale,
from the hurt his friend, a young actor, caused him
now that he no longer loved or wanted him.

He's seriously ill, and his parents tremble with fear.

The old servant woman who brought him up
is also fearful for Kleitos's life.
Deep in her anxious distress, an idol
comes to mind, one she worshiped when she was
small, before she came a maid to this prominent
Christian home, and turned Christian herself.
She secretly gathers the votive cakes, wine, and honey;
takes and places them before the idol, chanting words
of supplication she still remembers: odds and ends.
Dumb woman, doesn't realize that the black demon
cares little if a Christian boy gets well or not.

ΕΝ ΔΗΜΩ ΤΗΣ ΜΙΚΡΑΣ ΑΣΙΑΣ

Ἡ εἰδήσεις γιὰ τὴν ἔκβασι τῆς ναυμαχίας, στὸ Ἄκτιον,
ἦσαν βεβαίως ἀπροσδόκητες.
Ἀλλὰ δὲν εἶναι ἀνάγκη νὰ συντάξουμε νέον ἔγγραφον.
Τ' ὄνομα μόνον ν' ἀλλαχθεῖ. Ἀντίς, ἐκεῖ
στὲς τελευταῖες γραμμές, «Λυτρώσας τοὺς Ρωμαίους
ἀπ' τὸν ὀλέθριον Ὀκτάβιον,
τὸν δίκην παρωδίας Καίσαρα,»
τώρα θὰ βάλουμε «Λυτρώσας τοὺς Ρωμαίους
ἀπ' τὸν ὀλέθριον Ἀντώνιον».
Ὅλο τὸ κείμενον ταιριάζει ὡραῖα.

«Στὸν νικητήν, τὸν ἐνδοξότατον, ·
τὸν ἐν παντὶ πολεμικῷ ἔργῳ ἀνυπέρβλητον,
τὸν θαυμαστὸν ἐπὶ μεγαλουργίᾳ πολιτικῇ,
ὑπὲρ τοῦ ὁποίου ἐνθέρμως εὔχονταν ὁ δῆμος,
τὴν ἐπικράτησι τοῦ Ἀντωνίου»
ἐδῶ, ὅπως εἴπαμεν, ἡ ἀλλαγή: «τοῦ Καίσαρος
ὡς δῶρον τοῦ Διὸς κάλλιστον θεωρῶν—
στὸν κραταιὸ προστάτη τῶν Ἑλλήνων,
τὸν ἔθη ἑλληνικὰ εὐμενῶς γεραίροντα,
τὸν προσφιλῆ ἐν πάσῃ χώρᾳ ἑλληνικῇ,
τὸν λίαν ἐνδεδειγμένον γιὰ ἔπαινο περιφανῆ,
καὶ γιὰ ἐξιστόρησι τῶν πράξεών του ἐκτενῆ
ἐν λόγῳ ἑλληνικῷ κ' ἐμμέτρῳ καὶ πεζῷ·
ἐν λόγῳ ἑλληνικῷ ποὺ εἶν' ὁ φορεὺς τῆς φήμης,»
καὶ τὰ λοιπά, καὶ τὰ λοιπά. Λαμπρὰ ταιριάζουν ὅλα.

IN A TOWNSHIP OF ASIA MINOR

The news of the naval battle at Actium
was of course unexpected.
But, no reason that we should draft a new decree.
Only the name needs be changed. In place of—there,
in the last lines—"Having freed the Romans
from that disastrous Octavian,
that parody of a Caesar,"
let it now read, "Having freed the Romans
from the disastrous Anthony."
Now the whole text fits quite well.

"For the victor, most glorious one,
unrivaled in warring actions,
impressive in his political conduct,
on whose behalf the whole city
prays for: victory to Anthony."
Here, just as we said, comes the shift: "For Caesar,
regarding his triumph the finest gift from Zeus—
the mighty protector of the Greeks,
who kindly honors the Greek ways of life;
beloved in every Hellenic land,
who well deserves exalted praise,
and whose exploits should be recited at length
in the Greek language, both in verse and prose,
in the *Greek language*, the vehicle of fame."
And so on, and so forth. Just right, it all fits brilliantly.

ΙΕΡΕΥΣ ΤΟΥ ΣΕΡΑΠΙΟΥ

Τὸν γέροντα καλὸν πατέρα μου,
τὸν ἀγαπῶντα με τὸ ἴδιο πάντα·
τὸν γέροντα καλὸν πατέρα μου θρηνῶ
ποὺ πέθανε προχθές, ὀλίγο πρὶν χαράξει.

Ἰησοῦ Χριστέ, τὰ παραγγέλματα
τῆς ἱεροτάτης ἐκκλησίας σου νὰ τηρῶ
εἰς κάθε πρᾶξιν μου, εἰς κάθε λόγον,
εἰς κάθε σκέψι εἶν' ἡ προσπάθεια μου
ἡ καθημερινή. Κι ὅσους σὲ ἀρνοῦνται
τοὺς ἀποστρέφομαι. —Ἀλλὰ τώρα θρηνῶ·
ὀδύρομαι, Χριστέ, γιὰ τὸν πατέρα μου
μ' ὅλο ποὺ ἤτανε—φρικτὸν εἰπεῖν—
στὸ ἐπικατάρατον Σεράπιον ἱερεύς.

PRIEST AT THE SERAPEION

My kindly old father,
whose love for me never waned,
my kindly old father, I mourn,
who died two days ago, just before dawn.

My Christ, Jesus, the set of laws
of your most sacred Church I keep
in my every action, my every word
in all my thoughts—it's my life's
daily struggle. And all those who deny you,
I abhor—but now I mourn;
I weep, my Christ, for my father,
though he was—horrible to say it—
a priest at the accursed Serapeion.

ΜΕΣΑ ΣΤΑ ΚΑΠΗΛΕΙΑ—

Μέσα στὰ καπηλειὰ   καὶ τὰ χαμαιτυπεῖα
τῆς Βηρυτοῦ κυλιέμαι.   Δὲν ἤθελα νὰ μένω
στὴν Ἀλεξάνδρεια ἐγώ.   Μ' ἄφισεν ὁ Ταμίδης·
κ' ἐπῆγε μὲ τοῦ Ἐπάρχου   τὸν υἱὸ γιὰ ν' ἀποκτήσει
μιὰ ἔπαυλι στὸν Νεῖλο,   ἕνα μέγαρον στὴν πόλιν.
Δὲν ἔκανε νὰ μένω   στὴν Ἀλεξάνδρεια ἐγώ.—
Μέσα στὰ καπηλειὰ   καὶ τὰ χαμαιτυπεῖα
τῆς Βηρυτοῦ κυλιέμαι.   Μὲς σ' εὐτελῆ κραιπάλη
διάγω ποταπῶς.   Τὸ μόνο ποὺ μὲ σώζει
σὰν ἐμορφιὰ διαρκής,   σὰν ἄρωμα ποὺ ἐπάνω
στὴν σάρκα μου ἔχει μείνει,   εἶναι ποὺ εἶχα δυὸ χρόνια
δικό μου τὸν Ταμίδη,   τὸν πιὸ ἐξαίσιο νέο,
δικό μου ὄχι γιὰ σπίτι   ἢ γιὰ ἔπαυλι στὸν Νεῖλο.

IN THE TAVERNAS—

I stagger along the tavernas   and the brothels,
the lowly bars of Beirut.   I didn't want to go on living
in Alexandria.   Tamides got up and left me;
and went off with the Prefect's   son to earn, to come by,
a villa on the Nile,   a mansion in the city.
It wasn't proper for me   to stay on in Alexandria.—
I stagger along the tavernas   and the brothels,
the lowly bars of Beirut.   In cheap debauchery, I lead
a squalid life.   Only one thing saves me,
like a lasting beauty,   like an aroma that
lingers on my flesh: it's those two years I had him,
had Tamides to myself,   the most beautiful youth,
all to myself, not for   a house or a villa on the Nile.

ΜΕΓΑΛΗ ΣΥΝΟΔΕΙΑ ΕΞ ΙΕΡΕΩΝ ΚΑΙ ΛΑΪΚΩΝ

Ἐξ ἱερέων καὶ λαϊκῶν μιὰ συνοδεία,
ἀντιπροσωπευμένα πάντα τὰ ἐπαγγέλματα,
διέρχεται ὁδούς, πλατέες, καὶ πύλες
τῆς περιωνύμου πόλεως Ἀντιοχείας.
Στῆς ἐπιβλητικῆς, μεγάλης συνοδείας τὴν ἀρχὴ
ὡραῖος, λευκοντυμένος ἔφηβος βαστᾶ
μὲ ἀνυψωμένα χέρια τὸν Σταυρόν,
τὴν δύναμιν καὶ τὴν ἐλπίδα μας, τὸν ἅγιον Σταυρόν.
Οἱ ἐθνικοί, οἱ πρὶν τοσοῦτον ὑπερφίαλοι,
συνεσταλμένοι τώρα καὶ δειλοὶ μὲ βίαν
ἀπομακρύνονται ἀπὸ τὴν συνοδείαν.
Μακρὰν ἡμῶν, μακρὰν ἡμῶν νὰ μένουν πάντα
(ὅσο τὴν πλάνη τους δὲν ἀπαρνοῦνται). Προχωρεῖ
ὁ ἅγιος Σταυρός. Εἰς κάθε συνοικίαν
ὅπου ἐν θεοσεβείᾳ ζοῦν οἱ Χριστιανοὶ
φέρει παρηγορίαν καὶ χαρά:
βγαίνουν, οἱ εὐλαβεῖς, στὲς πόρτες τῶν σπιτιῶν τους
καὶ πλήρεις ἀγαλλιάσεως τὸν προσκυνοῦν—
τὴν δύναμιν, τὴν σωτηρίαν τῆς οἰκουμένης, τὸν Σταυρόν.—

Εἶναι μιὰ ἐτήσια ἑορτὴ Χριστιανική.
Μὰ σήμερα τελεῖται, ἰδού, πιὸ ἐπιφανῶς.
Λυτρώθηκε τὸ κράτος ἐπὶ τέλους.
Ὁ μιαρότατος, ὁ ἀποτρόπαιος
Ἰουλιανὸς δὲν βασιλεύει πιά.

Ὑπὲρ τοῦ εὐσεβεστάτου Ἰοβιανοῦ εὐχηθῶμεν.

A GREAT PROCESSION OF PRIESTS AND LAYMEN

A procession of priests and laymen,
representing all professions, every walk of life,
moves through the streets, squares, and gates
of the celebrated city of Antioch.
At the head of the imposing, endless procession,
a beautiful, white-clad young ephebe, his arms
outstretched, holds high the Cross,
our strength and our hope, the holy Cross.
Pagans, so arrogant of late,
intimidated now and spineless, hurry
to walk away from the procession.
Far from us, let them stay far from us always
(so long as they refuse to renounce their error.)
And the holy Cross moves on. In every neighborhood,
where Christians live in godliness,
there it brings them comfort and joy:
the devout stand in the doorways of their homes
and, in utter elation, they kneel and worship
the power, the salvation of the world, the Cross.

It is an annual Christian festival.
But today, as you see, the celebration is more prominent.
The country is delivered at last.
The most profane, the outrageous
Julian reigns no longer.

Let us pray for the most pious Jovian.

ΣΟΦΙΣΤΗΣ ΑΠΕΡΧΟΜΕΝΟΣ ΕΚ ΣΥΡΙΑΣ

Δόκιμε σοφιστὴ   ποὺ ἀπέρχεσαι ἐκ Συρίας
καὶ περὶ Ἀντιοχείας   σκοπεύεις νὰ συγγράψεις,
ἐν τῷ ἔργῳ σου τὸν Μέβη   ἀξίζει ν' ἀναφέρεις.
Τὸν φημισμένο Μέβη   ποὺ ἀναντιρρήτως εἶναι
ὁ νέος ὁ πιὸ εὐειδής,   κι ὁ πιὸ ἀγαπηθεὶς
σ' ὅλην τὴν Ἀντιόχεια.   Κανέν' ἀπὸ τοὺς ἄλλους
τοῦ ἰδίου βίου νέους,   κανένα δὲν πληρώνουν
τόσο ἀκριβὰ ὡς αὐτόν.   Γιὰ νά 'χουνε τὸν Μέβη
μονάχα δυό, τρεῖς μέρες,   πολὺ συχνὰ τὸν δίνουν
ὡς ἑκατὸ στατῆρας.—   Εἶπα, Στὴν Ἀντιόχεια·
μὰ καὶ στὴν Ἀλεξάνδρεια,   μὰ καὶ στὴν Ρώμη ἀκόμη,
δὲν βρίσκετ' ἕνας νέος   ἐράσμιος σὰν τὸν Μέβη.

SOPHIST ABANDONING SYRIA

Notable Sophist,   now that you abandon Syria
and as your mind is set   to write a book on Antioch,
you will do well to mention   Mebes in your work,
the famed Mebes, you know,   without question
the finest looking young man,   the most loved
in all of Antioch.   No other youth, earning
his livelihood that way,   is paid as
handsomely as him.   To have Mebes
just two or three days,   they often give as much
as a hundred staters.   —Did I say in Antioch?
But in Alexandria, too,   and even in Rome,
no youth exists   as delectable and loving as Mebes.

Ο ΙΟΥΛΙΑΝΟΣ ΚΑΙ ΟΙ ΑΝΤΙΟΧΕΙΣ

Τὸ Χῖ, φασίν, οὐδὲν ἠδίκησε τὴν πόλιν οὐδὲ τὸ Κάππα
...Τυχόντες δ᾽ ἡμεῖς ἐξηγητῶν... ἐδιδάχθημεν ἀρχὰς
ὀνομάτων εἶναι τὰ γράμματα, δηλοῦν δ᾽ ἐθέλειν τὸ μὲν
Χριστόν, τὸ δὲ Κωνστάντιον.

Ἰουλιανοῦ, *Μισοπώγων*

Ἦτανε δυνατὸν ποτὲ ν᾽ ἀπαρνηθοῦν
τὴν ἔμορφή τους διαβίωσι· τὴν ποικιλία
τῶν καθημερινῶν τους διασκεδάσεων· τὸ λαμπρό τους
θέατρον ὅπου μιὰ ἕνωσις ἐγένονταν τῆς Τέχνης
μὲ τὲς ἐρωτικὲς τῆς σάρκας τάσεις!

Ἀνήθικοι μέχρι τινός—καὶ πιθανὸν μέχρι πολλοῦ—
ἦσαν. Ἀλλ᾽ εἶχαν τὴν ἱκανοποίησι ποὺ ὁ βίος τους
ἦταν ὁ π ε ρ ι λ ά λ η τ ο ς βίος τῆς Ἀντιοχείας,
ὁ ἐνήδονος, ὁ ἀπόλυτα καλαίσθητος.

Νὰ τ᾽ ἀρνηθοῦν αὐτά, γιὰ νὰ προσέξουν κιόλας τί;

Τὲς περὶ τῶν ψευδῶν θεῶν ἀερολογίες του,
τὲς ἀνιαρὲς περιαυτολογίες·
τὴν παιδαριώδη του θεατροφοβία·
τὴν ἄχαρι σεμνοτυφία του· τὰ γελοῖα του γένεια.

Ἀ βέβαια προτιμούσανε τὸ Χῖ,
ἀ βέβαια προτιμούσανε τὸ Κάππα· ἑκατὸ φορές.

JULIAN AND THE ANTIOCHIANS

> It is said the CHI never harmed the city, nor did the KAPPA.
> ... We found by chance some interpreters who taught us that
> these letters are the beginnings of names; the first of Christ
> and the second of Constantios.
>
> Julian, *Misopôgôn*

Was it ever possible to turn their back on
their beautiful way of life; the diversity
of their daily entertainment; their brilliant
theatre, where Art itself became one
with the erotic inclinations of their bodies!

Immoral to a point—and perhaps a little more than that—
they surely were. But they had the satisfaction that their life
was the *most talked about* life in all of Antioch,
the most hedonistic, and in absolute good taste.

Turn their back on all that, and do what instead?

Turn to his windbag words about false gods,
to his boring self-centred tirades;
his childish fear of the theatre;
his ugly prudery, his ridiculous beard.

Of course they preferred the CHI.
Of course they preferred the KAPPA—a hundred times over.

ΑΝΝΑ ΔΑΛΑΣΣΗΝΗ

Εἰς τὸ χρυσόβουλλον ποὺ ἔβγαλ' ὁ Ἀλέξιος Κομνηνὸς
γιὰ νὰ τιμήσει τὴν μητέρα του ἐπιφανῶς,
τὴν λίαν νοήμονα Κυρίαν Ἄννα Δαλασσηνή—
τὴν ἀξιόλογη στὰ ἔργα της, στὰ ἤθη—
ὑπάρχουν διάφορα ἐγκωμιαστικά:
ἐδῶ ἂς μεταφέρουμε ἀπὸ αὐτὰ
μιὰ φράσιν ἔμορφην, εὐγενικὴ
«Οὐ τὸ ἐμὸν ἢ τὸ σόν, τὸ ψυχρὸν τοῦτο ῥῆμα, ἐρρήθη».

ANNA DALASSENE

In the king's chrysobull decree by Alexios Komnenos,
issued especially to honor his mother,
that highly intelligent Lady Anna Dalassene—
remarkable both for her work and her principles—
there has been much praise for her.
Here, let us relate one phrase only,
one that is beautiful, sublime:
"She never let slip those cold words 'mine' or 'thine.'"

ΜΕΡΕΣ ΤΟΥ 1896

Ἐξευτελίσθη πλήρως.   Μιὰ ἐρωτικὴ ροπή του
λίαν ἀπαγορευμένη   καὶ περιφρονημένη
(ἔμφυτη μολοντοῦτο)   ὑπῆρξεν ἡ αἰτία:
ἦταν ἡ κοινωνία   σεμνότυφη πολύ.
Ἔχασε βαθμηδὸν   τὸ λιγοστό του χρῆμα·
κατόπι τὴν σειρά,   καὶ τὴν ὑπόληψί του.
Πλησίαζε τὰ τριάντα   χωρὶς ποτὲ ἕναν χρόνο
νὰ βγάλει σὲ δουλειά,   τουλάχιστον γνωστή.
Ἐνίοτε ἔξοδά του   τὰ κέρδιζεν ἀπὸ
μεσολαβήσεις ποὺ   θεωροῦνται ντροπιασμένες.
Κατήντησ' ἕνας τύπος   ποὺ ἂν σ' ἔβλεπαν μαζύ του
συχνά, ἦταν πιθανὸν   μεγάλως νὰ ἐκτεθεῖς.

Ἀλλ' ὄχι μόνον τοῦτα·   δὲν θά 'τανε σωστό.
Ἀξίζει παραπάνω   τῆς ἐμορφιᾶς του ἡ μνήμη.
Μιὰ ἄποψις ἄλλη ὑπάρχει   ποὺ ἂν ἰδωθεῖ ἀπὸ αὐτὴν
φαντάζει, συμπαθής·   φαντάζει, ἁπλὸ καὶ γνήσιο
τοῦ ἔρωτος παιδί,   ποὺ ἄνω ἀπ' τὴν τιμή,
καὶ τὴν ὑπόληψί του   ἔθεσε ἀνεξετάστως
τῆς καθαρῆς σαρκός του   τὴν καθαρὴ ἡδονή.

Ἀπ' τὴν ὑπόληψί του;   Μὰ ἡ κοινωνία ποὺ ἦταν
σεμνότυφη πολὺ   συσχέτιζε κουτά.

DAYS OF 1896

He fell so very low.　　His sexual passion,
altogether forbidden　　and disdained
(yet innate for all that),　　was the cause:
the people here　　were so very prudish.
In time he lost　　what little funds he had;
then his good standing,　　and his reputation.
He was nearing thirty　　without a solid year's
work anywhere,　　nothing he could call a job.
He often earned his keep　　as a go-between,
concluding deals　　thought sometimes shameful.
He fell so low　　that to be seen with him
too often, you'd risk　　greatly compromising yourself.

But that's not all of it;　　it would hardly be fair.
He deserves better,　　the memory of his beauty.
There is another picture,　　and when seen from that angle,
he appears more likeable;　　he seems a simple and honest
boy, given to Eros,　　who without hesitation placed
above honor,　　above reputation,
his pure flesh　　in the throes of sexual pleasure.

Above his reputation?　　Why, the people here
are prudes and hypocrites,　　they make lame assumptions.

ΔΥΟ ΝΕΟΙ, 23 ΕΩΣ 24 ΕΤΩΝ

Ἀπ' τὲς δεκάμισυ ἤτανε στὸ καφενεῖον,
καὶ τὸν περίμενε σὲ λίγο νὰ φανεῖ.
Πῆγαν μεσάνυχτα—καὶ τὸν περίμενεν ἀκόμη.
Πῆγεν ἡ ὥρα μιάμισυ· εἶχε ἀδειάσει
τὸ καφενεῖον ὁλοτελῶς σχεδόν.
Βαρέθηκεν ἐφημερίδες νὰ διαβάζει
μηχανικῶς. Ἀπ' τὰ ἔρημα, τὰ τρία σελίνια του
ἔμεινε μόνον ἕνα: τόση ὥρα ποὺ περίμενε
ξόδιασε τ' ἄλλα σὲ καφέδες καὶ κονιάκ.
Κάπνισεν ὅλα του τὰ σιγαρέτα.
Τὸν ἐξαντλοῦσε ἡ τόση ἀναμονή. Γιατὶ
κιόλας μονάχος ὅπως ἦταν γιὰ ὧρες, ἄρχισαν
νὰ τὸν καταλαμβάνουν σκέψεις ὀχληρὲς
τῆς παραστρατημένης του ζωῆς.

Μὰ σὰν εἶδε τὸν φίλο του νὰ μπαίνει—εὐθὺς
ἡ κούρασις, ἡ ἀνία, ἡ σκέψεις φύγανε.

Ὁ φίλος του ἔφερε μιὰ ἀνέλπιστη εἴδησι.
Εἶχε κερδίσει στὸ χαρτοπαικτεῖον ἑξήντα λίρες.

Τὰ ἔμορφά τους πρόσωπα, τὰ ἐξαίσιά τους νειάτα,
ἡ αἰσθητικὴ ἀγάπη ποὺ εἶχαν μεταξύ τους,
δροσίσθηκαν, ζωντάνεψαν, τονώθηκαν
ἀπ' τὲς ἑξήντα λίρες τοῦ χαρτοπαικτείου.

Κι ὅλο χαρὰ καὶ δύναμις, αἴσθημα κι ὡραιότης
πῆγαν—ὄχι στὰ σπίτια τῶν τιμίων οἰκογενειῶν τους
(ὅπου, ἄλλωστε, μήτε τοὺς θέλαν πιά):
σ' ἕνα γνωστό τους, καὶ λίαν εἰδικό,
σπίτι τῆς διαφθορᾶς πήγανε καὶ ζητῆσαν
δωμάτιον ὕπνου, κι ἀκριβὰ πιοτά, καὶ ξαναήπιαν.

TWO YOUNG MEN, 23 TO 24 YEARS OLD

It was ten-thirty when he came to the café,
and he waited for him to turn up any minute.
Midnight came—and he was still waiting for him.
One-thirty came round; the café
had almost emptied out.
He was bored, leafing through the newspapers
mechanically. Of the measly three shillings
he had only one left: all this time waiting
he'd spent the rest on coffees and cognac.
He'd smoked all of his cigarettes.
He was so weary with all this waiting. And,
all alone as he was for hours, certain
unsettling thoughts had taken hold of him,
thoughts of his life gone astray.

But when he saw his friend enter—exhaustion,
boredom, and all those lingering thoughts went away.

His friend brought unexpected news.
He'd won sixty pounds playing cards.

Their beautiful faces, their exquisite youth,
the desire they felt for each other,
came to life, refreshed, revitalized
with the sixty pounds from the card game.

With surging elation, passion and beauty,
they started out—not for their family homes
(where they were no longer wanted anyway):
but where they used to hang out, a most appropriate place,
a house of ill repute—that's where they went and asked
for a room, and expensive drinks, and drank some more.

287

Καὶ σὰν σωθῆκαν τ' ἀκριβὰ πιοτά,
καὶ σὰν πλησίαζε πιὰ ἡ ὥρα τέσσερες,
στὸν ἔρωτα δοθῆκαν εὐτυχεῖς.

And when the expensive drinks had run out,
and the hour was almost four,
happy, they gave themselves up to love.

ΠΑΛΑΙΟΘΕΝ ΕΛΛΗΝΙΣ

Καυχιέται ἡ Ἀντιόχεια   γιὰ τὰ λαμπρά της κτίρια,
καὶ τοὺς ὡραίους της δρόμους·   γιὰ τὴν περὶ αὐτὴν
θαυμάσιαν ἐξοχήν,   καὶ γιὰ τὸ μέγα πλῆθος
τῶν ἐν αὐτῇ κατοίκων.   Καυχιέται ποὺ εἶν' ἡ ἕδρα
ἐνδόξων βασιλέων·   καὶ γιὰ τοὺς καλλιτέχνας
καὶ τοὺς σοφοὺς ποὺ ἔχει,   καὶ γιὰ τοὺς βαθυπλούτους
καὶ γνωστικοὺς ἐμπόρους.   Μὰ πιὸ πολὺ ἀσυγκρίτως
ἀπ' ὅλα, ἡ Ἀντιόχεια   καυχιέται ποὺ εἶναι πόλις
παλαιόθεν ἑλληνίς·   τοῦ Ἄργους συγγενής:
ἀπ' τὴν Ἰώνη ποὺ   ἱδρύθη ὑπὸ Ἀργείων
ἀποίκων πρὸς τιμὴν   τῆς κόρης τοῦ Ἰνάχου.

GREEK SINCE ANCIENT TIMES

Antioch takes pride   in its magnificent buildings,
and its marvelous streets;   and the beauty of its
surrounding countryside,   the great crowds its
inhabitants make,   proud of being the seat
of glorious kings;   of the many artists it has
and of its intellectuals   and of the deeply wealthy,
yet practical, merchants.   But, above all else,
Antioch takes pride   in being a city,
Greek since ancient times;   a relative of Argos:
through Ione—   and it was founded by Argive
colonists to honor   Inachos's daughter.

ΜΕΡΕΣ ΤΟΥ 1901

Τοῦτο εἰς αὐτὸν ὑπῆρχε τὸ ξεχωριστό,
ποὺ μέσα σ' ὅλην του τὴν ἔκλυσι
καὶ τὴν πολλήν του πεῖραν ἔρωτος,
παρ' ὅλην τὴν συνειθισμένη του
στάσεως καὶ ἡλικίας ἐναρμόνισιν,
ἐτύχαιναν στιγμές—πλὴν βέβαια
σπανιότατες—ποὺ τὴν ἐντύπωσιν
ἔδιδε σάρκας σχεδὸν ἄθικτης.

Τῶν εἴκοσι ἐννιά του χρόνων ἡ ἐμορφιά,
ἡ τόσο ἀπὸ τὴν ἡδονὴ δοκιμασμένη,
ἦταν στιγμὲς ποὺ θύμιζε παράδοξα
ἔφηβο πού—κάπως ἀδέξια—στὴν ἀγάπη
πρώτη φορὰ τὸ ἁγνό του σῶμα παραδίδει.

DAYS OF 1901

This one thing in him set him truly apart:
in spite of his gutter debauchery,
his great expertise in love-making,
and his youthful attitude, aligned with
his sheer lust, equal to his years,
in spite of all this, there were moments—rare
to be sure—when he made one feel
that he gave over his body almost untouched.

His twenty-nine-year-old beauty,
time-tested by sexual pleasure:
there were moments when he strangely brought
to mind an ephebe who—somewhat awkward—
surrenders to love his pure body for the first time.

ΟΥΚ ΕΓΝΩΣ

Γιὰ τὲς θρησκευτικές μας δοξασίες—
ὁ κοῦφος Ἰουλιανὸς εἶπεν «Ἀνέγνων, ἔγνων,
κατέγνων». Τάχατες μᾶς ἐκμηδένισε
μὲ τὸ «κατέγνων» του, ὁ γελοιωδέστατος.

Τέτοιες ξυπνάδες ὅμως πέρασι δὲν ἔχουνε σ' ἐμᾶς
τοὺς Χριστιανούς. «Ἀνέγνως, ἀλλ' οὐκ ἔγνως· εἰ γὰρ ἔγνως,
οὐκ ἂν κατέγνως» ἀπαντήσαμεν ἀμέσως.

YOU DIDN'T UNDERSTAND

As for our religious beliefs—
the inane Julian had this to say: "I read, I understood,
I condemned." He thought he would destroy us
with his "condemned," that utterly laughable man.

We Christians do not fall so easily with such wisecracks.
We let him have it, our quick reply: "You read, but didn't
understand; had you understood, you wouldn't have condemned."

ΕΝΑΣ ΝΕΟΣ, ΤΗΣ ΤΕΧΝΗΣ ΤΟΥ ΛΟΓΟΥ—
ΣΤΟ 24^ON ΕΤΟΣ ΤΟΥ

Ὅπως μπορεῖς πιὰ δούλεψε, μυαλό.—
Τὸν φθείρει αὐτὸν μιὰ ἀπόλαυσις μισή.
Εἶναι σὲ μιὰ κατάστασι ἐκνευριστική.
Φιλεῖ τὸ πρόσωπο τὸ ἀγαπημένο κάθε μέρα,
τὰ χέρια του εἶναι πάνω στὰ πιὸ ἐξαίσια μέλη.
Ποτέ του δὲν ἀγάπησε μὲ τόσο μέγα
πάθος. Μὰ λείπει ἡ ὡραία πραγμάτωσις
τοῦ ἔρωτος· λείπει ἡ πραγμάτωσις
ποὺ πρέπει νά 'ναι κι ἀπ' τοὺς δυὸ μ' ἔντασιν ἐπιθυμητή.

(Δὲν εἶν' ὁμοίως δοσμένοι στὴν ἀνώμαλη ἡδονὴ κ' οἱ δυό.
Μονάχ' αὐτὸν κυρίεψε ἀπολύτως).

Καὶ φθείρεται, καὶ νεύριασε ἐντελῶς.
Ἐξ ἄλλου εἶναι κι ἄεργος· κι αὐτὸ πολὺ συντείνει.
Κάτι μικρὰ χρηματικὰ ποσὰ
μὲ δυσκολία δανείζεται (σχεδὸν
τὰ ζητιανεύει κάποτε) καὶ ψευτοσυντηρεῖται.
Φιλεῖ τὰ λατρεμένα χείλη· πάνω
στὸ ἐξαίσιο σῶμα—ποὺ ὅμως τώρα νοιώθει
πὼς στέργει μόνον—ἡδονίζεται.
Κ' ἔπειτα πίνει καὶ καπνίζει· πίνει καὶ καπνίζει·
καὶ σέρνεται στὰ καφενεῖα ὁλημερίς,
σέρνει μὲ ἀνία τῆς ἐμορφιᾶς του τὸ μαράζι.—
Ὅπως μπορεῖς πιὰ δούλεψε, μυαλό.

A YOUNG MAN OF LETTERS—
IN HIS 24TH YEAR

Work as you know how, brain, work at will on this:—
The youth wastes away with one-sided passion.
He's in a state, his nerves on edge.
He kisses the face he adores every day,
his hands are all over the exquisite limbs.
Never has he loved with such great
passion. But the beauty of love's fulfilment
is missing; fulfilment *is* missing,
something that both should want with passion.

(They aren't equally given to abnormal sexual pleasure.
It's only he who's been invaded so completely.)

And so he wastes away, and his nerves are frayed.
Then too, he's out of work, and this makes things worse.
Some small amounts of money with difficulty
he borrows (sometimes he almost
begs for it) and half gets by, a bare subsistence.
He kisses the adored lips; and atop
the exquisite body—which he now feels
is barely consenting—he takes his pleasure.
And afterwards he drinks and smokes; drinks and smokes;
and all day he trudges the beaten paths to the cafés.
Weary, he trudges his beauty's prickly thorns.—
Work as you know how, brain, work at will on this.

ΕΝ ΣΠΑΡΤΗ

Δὲν ἤξερεν ὁ βασιλεὺς Κλεομένης, δὲν τολμοῦσε—
δὲν ἤξερε ἕναν τέτοιον λόγο πῶς νὰ πεῖ
πρὸς τὴν μητέρα του: ὅτι ἀπαιτοῦσε ὁ Πτολεμαῖος
γιὰ ἐγγύησιν τῆς συμφωνίας των ν' ἀποσταλεῖ κι αὐτὴ
εἰς Αἴγυπτον καὶ νὰ φυλάττεται·
λίαν ταπεινωτικόν, ἀνοίκειον πρᾶγμα.
Κι ὅλο ἤρχονταν γιὰ νὰ μιλήσει· κι ὅλο δίσταζε.
Κι ὅλο ἄρχιζε νὰ λέγει· κι ὅλο σταματοῦσε.

Μὰ ἡ ὑπέροχη γυναῖκα τὸν κατάλαβε
(εἶχεν ἀκούσει κιόλα κάτι διαδόσεις σχετικές),
καὶ τὸν ἐνθάρρυνε νὰ ἐξηγηθεῖ.
Καὶ γέλασε· κ' εἶπε βεβαίως πηαίνει.
Καὶ μάλιστα χαίρονταν ποὺ μποροῦσε νά 'ναι
στὸ γῆρας της ὠφέλιμη στὴν Σπάρτη ἀκόμη.

Ὅσο γιὰ τὴν ταπείνωσι—μὰ ἀδιαφοροῦσε.
Τὸ φρόνημα τῆς Σπάρτης ἀσφαλῶς δὲν ἦταν ἱκανὸς
νὰ νοιώσει ἕνας Λαγίδης χθεσινός·
ὅθεν κ' ἡ ἀπαίτησίς του δὲν μποροῦσε
πραγματικῶς νὰ ταπεινώσει Δέσποιναν
Ἐπιφανῆ ὡς αὐτήν· Σπαρτιάτου βασιλέως μητέρα.

IN SPARTA

He didn't know, King Kleomenes, he didn't dare—
he didn't know just how to break it to his mother,
a thing like that: Ptolemy demanded,
as guarantee for their agreement, she too go to Egypt
and be held there hostage—
humiliating in the extreme and improper.
He kept coming by to speak to her; and he'd hesitate.
He'd begin to say something; and always he'd stop.

But this grand lady saw through him
(she had already heard the rumors),
and she encouraged him to come out and say it.
And she laughed; and said of course she'll go.
And she even showed how happy she was that she could be
in her ripe old age so useful still to Sparta.

As for being humiliated—she couldn't care less.
To be sure, the Spartan spirit is not easily graspable
by this Lagid king of yesterday;
so this demand of his could not in fact
really humiliate an Eminent Lady
like her: mother of a Spartan king.

ΕΙΚΩΝ ΕΙΚΟΣΙΤΡΙΕΤΟΥΣ ΝΕΟΥ ΚΑΜΩΜΕΝΗ
ΑΠΟ ΦΙΛΟΝ ΤΟΥ ΟΜΗΛΙΚΑ, ΕΡΑΣΙΤΕΧΝΗΝ

Τελείωσε τὴν εἰκόνα
λεπτομερῶς τὴν βλέπει.
ροῦχο ξεκουμπωμένο,
γελέκι καὶ κραβάτα.
πουκάμισο· ἀνοιγμένο,
ἀπὸ τὴν ἐμορφιὰ
Τὸ μέτωπο δεξιὰ
σκεπάζουν τὰ μαλλιά του,
(ὡς εἶναι ἡ χτενισιὰ
Ὑπάρχει ὁ τόνος πλήρως
ποὺ θέλησε νὰ βάλει
σὰν ἔκανε τὰ χείλη ...
ποὺ γιὰ ἐκπληρώσεις εἶναι

χθὲς μεσημέρι. Τώρα
 Τὸν ἔκαμε μὲ γκρίζο
γκρίζο βαθύ· χωρὶς
Μ' ἔνα τριανταφυλλὶ
 γιὰ νὰ φανεῖ καὶ κάτι
τοῦ στήθους, τοῦ λαιμοῦ.
ὁλόκληρο σχεδὸν
 τὰ ὡραῖα του μαλλιὰ
 ποὺ προτιμᾶ ἐφέτος).
ὁ ἡδονιστικὸς
σὰν ἔκανε τὰ μάτια,
 Τὸ στόμα του, τὰ χείλη
 ἐρωτισμοῦ ἐκλεκτοῦ.

A LIKENESS OF A TWENTY-THREE YEAR OLD YOUTH PAINTED
BY HIS FRIEND OF THE SAME AGE, AN AMATEUR

He finished the painting   yesterday noon. And now
he studies it in detail.   He put him in gray
clothes, unbuttoned,   a deep gray; without
vest or tie.   With a rose-colored
shirt, wide open,   so something of the beauty
of his chest   and neck might show through.
The hair falls over   his brow to the right,
covering much of it,   his lovely hair
(in the style   he favors this year).
And eros, all there,   that sensuality
he wanted to give him   when he did the eyes,
when he did the lips …   his mouth, those lips
made for love,   for special, discerning pleasures.

ΕΝ ΜΕΓΑΛΗ ΕΛΛΗΝΙΚΗ ΑΠΟΙΚΙΑ, 200 Π.Χ.

Ὅτι τὰ πράγματα δὲν βαίνουν κατ' εὐχὴν στὴν Ἀποικία
δὲν μέν' ἡ ἐλαχίστη ἀμφιβολία,
καὶ μ' ὅλο ποὺ ὁπωσοῦν τραβοῦμ' ἐμπρός,
ἴσως, καθὼς νομίζουν οὐκ ὀλίγοι, νὰ ἔφθασε ὁ καιρὸς
νὰ φέρουμε Πολιτικὸ Ἀναμορφωτή.

Ὅμως τὸ πρόσκομμα κ' ἡ δυσκολία
εἶναι ποὺ κάμνουνε μιὰ ἱστορία
μεγάλη κάθε πρᾶγμα οἱ Ἀναμορφωταὶ
αὐτοί. (Εὐτύχημα θὰ ἦταν ἂν ποτὲ
δὲν τοὺς χρειάζονταν κανείς.) Γιὰ κάθε τί,
γιὰ τὸ παραμικρὸ ρωτοῦνε κ' ἐξετάζουν,
κ' εὐθὺς στὸν νοῦ τους ριζικὲς μεταρρυθμίσεις βάζουν,
μὲ τὴν ἀπαίτησι νὰ ἐκτελεσθοῦν ἄνευ ἀναβολῆς.

Ἔχουνε καὶ μιὰ κλίσι στὲς θυσίες.
Παραιτηθεῖτε ἀπὸ τὴν κτῆσιν σας ἐκείνη·
ἡ κατοχή σας εἶν' ἐπισφαλής:
ἡ τέτοιες κτήσεις ἀκριβῶς βλάπτουν τὲς Ἀποικίες.
Παραιτηθεῖτε ἀπὸ τὴν πρόσοδον αὐτή,
κι ἀπὸ τὴν ἄλληνα τὴν συναφῆ,
κι ἀπὸ τὴν τρίτη τούτην: ὡς συνέπεια φυσική·
εἶναι μὲν οὐσιώδεις, ἀλλὰ τί νὰ γίνει;
σᾶς δημιουργοῦν μιὰ ἐπιβλαβῆ εὐθύνη.

Κι ὅσο στὸν ἔλεγχό τους προχωροῦνε,
βρίσκουν καὶ βρίσκουν περιττά, καὶ νὰ παυθοῦν ζητοῦνε·
πράγματα ποὺ ὅμως δύσκολα τὰ καταργεῖ κανείς.

Κι ὅταν, μὲ τὸ καλό, τελειώσουνε τὴν ἐργασία,
κι ὁρίσαντες καὶ περικόψαντες τὸ πᾶν λεπτομερῶς,
ἀπέλθουν, παίρνοντας καὶ τὴν δικαία μισθοδοσία,
νὰ δοῦμε τί ἀπομένει πιά, μετὰ

IN A LARGE GREEK COLONY, 200 B.C.

That things are not going well in the Colony
not the slightest doubt remains now,
and though, no matter what, we still go forward,
perhaps—as many believe—the time has come
to bring in a Political Reformer.

But here's what stands in the way, the difficulty:
each small thing they make into a big story, these
Political Reformers. (How fortunate if no one
ever needed them.) They question
the slightest thing, probe and examine,
and are quick to get into their heads radical reforms
with the demand they be executed without delay.

They also have a penchant for sacrifices:
Give up that possession of yours,
holding on to it is a bad risk:
it's these possessions that harm the Colonies.
Forgo this particular income,
the other as well, related to it,
and this third one too: it follows naturally;
yes, it is important, but what can one do?
They create an inevitable liability for you.

And as they forge ahead with their probing,
they find more and more spending to eliminate,
things that all the same are difficult to cut.

And when finally, in good time, they finish their work,
having examined every detail they'd cut to the bone,
they take their leave, along with just payment,
leaving us to see what remains after

τόση δεινότητα χειρουργική.—

Ἴσως δὲν ἔφθασεν ἀκόμη ὁ καιρός.
Νὰ μὴ βιαζόμεθα· εἶν' ἐπικίνδυνον πρᾶγμα ἡ βία.
Τὰ πρόωρα μέτρα φέρνουν μεταμέλεια.
Ἔχει ἄτοπα πολλά, βεβαίως καὶ δυστυχῶς, ἡ Ἀποικία.
Ὅμως ὑπάρχει τὶ τὸ ἀνθρώπινον χωρὶς ἀτέλεια;
Καὶ τέλος πάντων, νά, τραβοῦμ' ἐμπρός.

such miserable surgical finesse.—

Maybe the time has not yet come.
Let's not be hasty: there's danger in violent action.
Untimely measures bring regret.
Certainly, and unhappily, the Colony has many things crooked.
But is there anything human without imperfection?
And, when all is said and done, we do forge ahead.

ΗΓΕΜΩΝ ΕΚ ΔΥΤΙΚΗΣ ΛΙΒΥΗΣ

Ἄρεσε γενικῶς στὴν Ἀλεξάνδρεια,
τὲς δέκα μέρες ποὺ διέμεινεν αὐτοῦ,
ὁ ἡγεμὼν ἐκ Δυτικῆς Λιβύης
Ἀριστομένης, υἱὸς τοῦ Μενελάου.
Ὡς τ' ὄνομά του, κ' ἡ περιβολή, κοσμίως, ἑλληνική.
Δέχονταν εὐχαρίστως τὲς τιμές, ἀλλὰ
δὲν τὲς ἐπιζητοῦσεν· ἦταν μετριόφρων.
Ἀγόραζε βιβλία ἑλληνικά,
ἰδίως ἱστορικὰ καὶ φιλοσοφικά.
Πρὸ πάντων δὲ ἄνθρωπος λιγομίλητος.
Θά 'ταν βαθὺς στὲς σκέψεις, διεδίδετο,
κ' οἱ τέτοιοι τό 'χουν φυσικὸ νὰ μὴ μιλοῦν πολλά.

Μήτε βαθὺς στὲς σκέψεις ἦταν, μήτε τίποτε.
Ἕνας τυχαῖος, ἀστεῖος ἄνθρωπος.
Πῆρε ὄνομα ἑλληνικό, ντύθηκε σὰν τοὺς Ἕλληνας,
ἔμαθ' ἐπάνω, κάτω σὰν τοὺς Ἕλληνας νὰ φέρεται·
κ' ἔτρεμεν ἡ ψυχή του μὴ τυχὸν
χαλάσει τὴν καλούτσικην ἐντύπωσι
μιλῶντας μὲ βαρβαρισμοὺς δεινοὺς τὰ ἑλληνικά,
κ' οἱ Ἀλεξανδρινοὶ τὸν πάρουν στὸ ψιλό,
ὡς εἶναι τὸ συνήθειο τους, οἱ ἀπαίσιοι.

Γι' αὐτὸ καὶ περιορίζονταν σὲ λίγες λέξεις,
προσέχοντας μὲ δέος τὲς κλίσεις καὶ τὴν προφορά·
κ' ἔπληττεν οὐκ ὀλίγον ἔχοντας
κουβέντες στοιβαγμένες μέσα του.

A SOVEREIGN FROM WESTERN LIBYA

All in all, Alexandria liked him
during the ten days he stayed there,
this sovereign from Western Libya,
Aristomenes, son of Menelaos.
As with his name, his attire too was elegant and Greek.
He accepted honors gladly, but
did not seek them out; he was modest.
He would buy Greek books,
especially history and philosophy.
A man of few words for the most part.
They let it be known he was a deep thinker,
and his type have it in them, by nature, not to say much.

Neither a deep thinker, nor anything of the kind—
he was a nobody, a ridiculous man.
He'd taken a Greek name, dressed as the Greeks do,
he learned, more or less, Greek manners;
and his soul trembled lest he by some chance
undo this tolerably good impression
by speaking Greek with those painful barbarisms,
whereby the Alexandrians would break into mockery
of him, as is their custom, merciless sort that they are.

That's why he restrained himself, the terror of few words,
careful to use the right cases, syntax and pronunciation;
and he was practically driven mad, having
whole conversations bottled up inside him.

ΚΙΜΩΝ ΛΕΑΡΧΟΥ, 22 ΕΤΩΝ, ΣΠΟΥΔΑΣΤΗΣ ΕΛΛΗΝΙΚΩΝ ΓΡΑΜΜΑΤΩΝ (ΕΝ ΚΥΡΗΝΗ)

«Τὸ τέλος μου ἐπῆλθε ὅτε ἤμουν εὐτυχής.
Ὁ Ἑρμοτέλης μὲ εἶχε ἀχώριστόν του φίλον.
Τὲς ὕστατές μου μέρες, μ᾽ ὅλο ποὺ προσποιοῦνταν
πὼς δὲν ἀνησυχοῦσε, ἔνοιωνα ἐγὼ συχνὰ
τὰ μάτια του κλαμένα. Σὰν νόμιζε ποὺ λίγο
εἶχ᾽ ἀποκοιμηθεῖ, ἔπεφτεν ὡς ἀλλόφρων
στῆς κλίνης μου τὸ ἄκρον. Ἀλλ᾽ ἤμεθαν κ᾽ οἱ δυὸ
νέοι μιᾶς ἡλικίας, εἴκοσι τριῶ ἐτῶν.
Προδότις εἶναι ἡ Μοῖρα. Ἴσως κανένα πάθος
ἄλλο τὸν Ἑρμοτέλη νά ᾽παιρνεν ἀπὸ μένα.
Τελείωσα καλῶς· ἐν τῇ ἀμερίστῳ ἀγάπῃ.»—

Τὸ ἐπιτύμβιον τοῦτο Μαρύλου Ἀριστοδήμου
ἀποθανόντος πρὸ μηνὸς στὴν Ἀλεξάνδρεια,
ἔλαβα ἐγὼ πενθῶν, ὁ ἐξάδελφός του Κίμων.
Μὲ τὸ ἔστειλεν ὁ γράψας γνωστός μου ποιητής.
Μὲ τὸ ἔστειλ᾽ ἐπειδὴ ἤξερε συγγενὴς
ὅτ᾽ ἤμουν τοῦ Μαρύλου: δὲν ἤξερε ἄλλο τί.
Εἶν᾽ ἡ ψυχή μου πλήρης λύπης γιὰ τὸν Μαρύλο.
Εἴχαμε μεγαλώσει μαζύ, σὰν ἀδελφοί.
Βαθυὰ μελαγχολῶ. Ὁ πρόωρος θάνατός του
κάθε μνησικακίαν μοῦ ἔσβυσ᾽ ἐντελῶς …
κάθε μνησικακίαν γιὰ τὸν Μαρύλο—μ᾽ ὅλο
ποὺ μὲ εἶχε κλέψει τὴν ἀγάπη τοῦ Ἑρμοτέλη,
ποὺ κι ἂν μὲ θέλει τώρα ὁ Ἑρμοτέλης πάλι
δὲν θά ᾽ναι διόλου τὸ ἴδιο. Ξέρω τὸν χαρακτῆρα
τὸν εὐπαθῆ ποὺ ἔχω. Τὸ ἴνδαλμα τοῦ Μαρύλου
θά ᾽ρχεται ἀνάμεσό μας, καὶ θὰ νομίζω ποὺ
μὲ λέγει, Ἰδοὺ εἶσαι τώρα ἱκανοποιημένος.
Ἰδοὺ τὸν ξαναπῆρες ὡς ἐποθοῦσες, Κίμων.
Ἰδοὺ δὲν ἔχεις πιὰ ἀφορμὴ νὰ μὲ διαβάλεις.

KIMON, SON OF LEARCHOS, 22,
STUDENT OF GREEK LITERATURE (IN KYRENE)

"My end has come   while content and in high spirits.
Hermoteles had me   for his inseparable companion.
In my final days,   though he acted as if
he wasn't apprehensive,   I myself often sensed
his reddened, tearful eyes.   And when he thought for a bit
I'd fallen asleep,   he threw himself distraught
on the edge of my bed.   Yes, we were both
young men of the same age,   twenty-three years old.
What a traitor Fate proves—   it could've been worse: some other
lover might've taken   Hermoteles away from me.
I ended well;   in a love that could never be divided."—

This epitaph, written   for Marylos, son of Aristodemos,
who died only   a month ago in Alexandria—
I received it,   his mourning cousin Kimon,
sent to me by the writer,   a poet of my acquaintance,
sent it to me because   he knew I was
related to Marylos;   he knew nothing more.
My heart overflows   with sorrow for Marylos.
We had grown up   together like brothers.
I'm deeply saddened.   His early death
wipes out completely   all bad feelings …
all bad feeling or malice   for Marylos—even if
he did steal the love   of Hermoteles from me
so that, even if Hermoteles   wanted me again,
it would never be the same.   I know well my vulnerable
nature, my character.   The image of Marylos, his idol,
will come between us,   and I'll imagine him saying to me:
"There, now, are you   pleased with yourself?
There, then, you've got him   back, as you desired, Kimon;
there, you've no more   reason to malign me."

ΕΝ ΠΟΡΕΙΑ ΠΡΟΣ ΤΗΝ ΣΙΝΩΠΗΝ

Ὁ Μιθριδάτης, ἔνδοξος καὶ κραταιός,
μεγάλων πόλεων ὁ κύριος,
κάτοχος ἰσχυρῶν στρατῶν καὶ στόλων,
πηγαίνοντας πρὸς τὴν Σινώπην πέρασε ἀπὸ δρόμον
ἐξοχικόν, πολὺ ἀπόκεντρον
ὅπου ἕνας μάντις εἶχε κατοικίαν.

Ἔστειλεν ἀξιωματικό του ὁ Μιθριδάτης
τὸν μάντι νὰ ρωτήσει πόσα θ' ἀποκτήσει ἀκόμη
στὸ μέλλον ἀγαθά, πόσες δυνάμεις ἄλλες.

Ἔστειλεν ἀξιωματικό του, καὶ μετὰ
πρὸς τὴν Σινώπην τὴν πορεία του ξακολούθησε.

Ὁ μάντις ἀποσύρθηκε σ' ἕνα δωμάτιο μυστικό.
Μετὰ περίπου μισὴν ὥρα βγῆκε
περίφροντις, κ' εἶπε στὸν ἀξιωματικό·
«Ἱκανοποιητικῶς δὲν μπόρεσα νὰ διευκρινίσω.
Κατάλληλη δὲν εἶν' ἡ μέρα σήμερα.
Κάτι σκιώδη πράγματα εἶδα. Δὲν κατάλαβα καλά.—
Μὰ ν' ἀρκεσθεῖ, φρονῶ, μὲ τόσα ποὺ ἔχει ὁ βασιλεύς.
Τὰ περισσότερα εἰς κινδύνους θὰ τὸν φέρουν.
Θυμήσου νὰ τὸν πεῖς αὐτό, ἀξιωματικέ:
μὲ τόσα ποὺ ἔχει, πρὸς θεοῦ, ν' ἀρκεῖται!
Ἡ τύχη ξαφνικὲς ἔχει μεταβολές.
Νὰ πεῖς στὸν βασιλέα Μιθριδάτη:
λίαν σπανίως βρίσκεται ὁ ἑταῖρος τοῦ προγόνου του
ὁ εὐγενής, ποὺ ἐγκαίρως μὲ τὴν λόγχην γράφει
στὸ χῶμα ἐπάνω τὸ σωτήριον *Φεῦγε Μιθριδάτα*.»

ON THE MARCH TO SINOPE

Mithridates, glorious and powerful,
head of great cities,
master of powerful armies and ships,
on his march to Sinope took a route
through an out-of-the-way part
of the country, where a seer made his home.

Mithridates sent forth one of his officers to ask
the seer how much more wealth he would come by,
how much more power, in the future.

He sent on his officer, and then
continued his march to Sinope.

The seer withdrew into a secret room.
Then, in roughly half an hour, he emerged,
uneasy, and said to the officer:
"To my mind, there is nothing here that's clear.
Today is not an appropriate day, it seems.
I made out some shadowy things, I didn't understand.—
But I believe the king should content himself with what he has.
To fight for more, may prove dangerous for him.
Remember to say exactly this, officer:
with so much that's his, for God's sake, let him be content!
Fortune can have sudden reversals.
And tell king Mithridates this: it's very rare
to meet with someone like his ancestor's noble companion,
who, just in time, wrote in the earth with his lance
the very words that saved his life: '*Mithridates, escape.*'"

ΜΕΡΕΣ ΤΟΥ 1909, '10, ΚΑΙ '11

Ἑνὸς τυραννισμένου, πτωχοτάτου ναυτικοῦ
(ἀπὸ νησὶ τοῦ Αἰγαίου Πελάγους) ἦταν υἱός.
Ἐργάζονταν σὲ σιδερᾶ. Παληόρουχα φοροῦσε.
Σχισμένα τὰ ποδήματά του τῆς δουλειᾶς κ' ἐλεεινά.
Τὰ χέρια του ἦσαν λερωμένα ἀπὸ σκουριὲς καὶ λάδια.

Τὸ βραδυνό, σὰν ἔκλειε τὸ μαγαζί,
ἂν ἦταν τίποτε νὰ ἐπιθυμεῖ πολύ,
καμιὰ κραβάτα κάπως ἀκριβή,
καμιὰ κραβάτα γιὰ τὴν Κυριακή,
ἢ σὲ βιτρίνα ἂν εἶχε δεῖ καὶ λαχταροῦσε
κανένα ὡραῖο πουκάμισο μαβί,
τὸ σῶμα του γιὰ ἕνα τάλληρο ἢ δυὸ πουλοῦσε.

Διερωτῶμαι ἂν στοὺς ἀρχαίους καιροὺς
εἶχεν ἡ ἔνδοξη Ἀλεξάνδρεια νέον πιὸ περικαλλῆ,
πιὸ τέλειο ἀγόρι ἀπὸ αὐτόν—ποὺ πῆε χαμένος:
δὲν ἔγινε, ἐννοεῖται, ἄγαλμά του ἢ ζωγραφιά·
στὸ παληομάγαζο ἑνὸς σιδερᾶ ριχμένος,
γρήγορ' ἀπ' τὴν ἐπίπονη δουλειά,
κι ἀπὸ λαϊκὴ κραιπάλη, ταλαιπωρημένη, εἶχε φθαρεῖ.

DAYS OF 1909, '10, AND '11

He was the son of a tormented, poverty-stricken seaman
(hailed from some island on the Aegean sea).
He worked at a blacksmith's; wore threadbare clothing;
torn, too, the shoes he wore for work, and squalid.
His hands were soiled from rust and oil grime.

At twilight, as the shop closed down,
if there were something he dearly liked,
a special tie that was somewhat costly,
some special tie for a Sunday outing,
or something he'd seen in a shop window
that he longed for, perhaps some shirt of pure blue,
he would sell his body for a half-crown or two.

I ask myself if in ancient times
glorious Alexandria had a youth more divine,
a more perfect boy than this—who went to waste:
he was never drawn or sculpted, no statue made of him;
thrown in the grimy shop of a blacksmith,
fingers worked to the bone—then too, the sleazy
debauchery—he was soon used up and discarded.

ΜΥΡΗΣ· ΑΛΕΞΑΝΔΡΕΙΑ ΤΟΥ 340 Μ.Χ.

Τὴν συμφορὰ ὅταν ἔμαθα, ποὺ ὁ Μύρης πέθανε,
πῆγα στὸ σπίτι του, μ' ὅλο ποὺ τὸ ἀποφεύγω
νὰ εἰσέρχομαι στῶν Χριστιανῶν τὰ σπίτια,
πρὸ πάντων ὅταν ἔχουν θλίψεις ἢ γιορτές.

Στάθηκα σὲ διάδρομο. Δὲν θέλησα
νὰ προχωρήσω πιὸ ἐντός, γιατὶ ἀντελήφθην
ποὺ οἱ συγγενεῖς τοῦ πεθαμένου μ' ἔβλεπαν
μὲ προφανῆ ἀπορίαν καὶ μὲ δυσαρέσκεια.

Τὸν εἴχανε σὲ μιὰ μεγάλη κάμαρη
ποὺ ἀπὸ τὴν ἄκρην ὅπου στάθηκα
εἶδα κομμάτι· ὅλο τάπητες πολύτιμοι,
καὶ σκεύη ἐξ ἀργύρου καὶ χρυσοῦ.

Στέκομουν κ' ἔκλαια σὲ μιὰ ἄκρη τοῦ διαδρόμου.
Καὶ σκέπτομουν ποὺ ἡ συγκεντρώσεις μας κ' ἡ ἐκδρομὲς
χωρὶς τὸν Μύρη δὲν θ' ἀξίζουν πιά·
καὶ σκέπτομουν ποὺ πιὰ δὲν θὰ τὸν δῶ
στὰ ὡραῖα κι ἄσεμνα ξενύχτια μας
νὰ χαίρεται, καὶ νὰ γελᾶ, καὶ ν' ἀπαγγέλλει στίχους
μὲ τὴν τελεία του αἴσθησι τοῦ ἑλληνικοῦ ρυθμοῦ·
καὶ σκέπτομουν ποὺ ἔχασα γιὰ πάντα
τὴν ἐμορφιά του, ποὺ ἔχασα γιὰ πάντα
τὸν νέον ποὺ λάτρευα παράφορα.

Κάτι γρηές, κοντά μου, χαμηλὰ μιλοῦσαν γιὰ
τὴν τελευταία μέρα ποὺ ἔζησε—
στὰ χείλη του διαρκῶς τ' ὄνομα τοῦ Χριστοῦ,
στὰ χέρια του βαστοῦσ' ἕναν σταυρό.—
Μπῆκαν κατόπι μὲς στὴν κάμαρη
τέσσαρες Χριστιανοὶ ἱερεῖς, κ' ἔλεγαν προσευχὲς
ἐνθέρμως καὶ δεήσεις στὸν Ἰησοῦν,

MYRES, ALEXANDRIA, A.D. 340

When I heard the tragic tidings, that Myres had died,
I went to his house, although I avoid
entering the houses of Christians,
mainly during times they mourn or have festive holidays.

I lingered in the corridor. I didn't want
to go further inside because I sensed clearly
the relatives of the deceased saw me
with obvious amazement and displeasure.

They had placed him in a large room,
and from the corner where I lingered
I had a good glimpse of it: all precious carpets,
and rich vessels of silver and of gold.

I stood in the corner of the corridor, weeping.
And I thought how our meetings and excursions
without Myres would no longer be worth much;
and I thought how I would not see him again
at our lovely, indecent, all-night sessions,
reveling and laughing and reciting verses
with his perfect feel for Greek rhythm;
and I thought how I'd lost forever
his beauty, lost forever
the youth I'd worshipped so madly.

Some old women close by talked in hushed voices
about the last day of his life—
on his lips incessantly, the name of Christ,
a cross held tightly in his hand.—
Afterward, four Christian priests
entered the room, reciting prayers
and supplications fervently, to Jesus,

ἢ στὴν Μαρίαν (δὲν ξέρω τὴν θρησκεία τους καλά).

Γνωρίζαμε, βεβαίως, ποὺ ὁ Μύρης ἦταν Χριστιανός.
Ἀπὸ τὴν πρώτην ὥρα τὸ γνωρίζαμε, ὅταν
πρόπερσι στὴν παρέα μας εἶχε μπεῖ.
Μὰ ζοῦσεν ἀπολύτως σὰν κ' ἐμᾶς.
Ἀπ' ὅλους μας πιὸ ἔκδοτος στὲς ἡδονές·
σκορπῶντας ἀφειδῶς τὸ χρῆμα του στὲς διασκεδάσεις.
Γιὰ τὴν ὑπόληψι τοῦ κόσμου ξένοιαστος,
ρίχνονταν πρόθυμα σὲ νύχτιες ρήξεις στὲς ὁδοὺς
ὅταν ἐτύχαινε ἡ παρέα μας
νὰ συναντήσει ἀντίθετη παρέα.
Ποτὲ γιὰ τὴν θρησκεία του δὲν μιλοῦσε.
Μάλιστα μιὰ φορὰ τὸν εἴπαμε
πὼς θὰ τὸν πάρουμε μαζύ μας στὸ Σεράπιον.
Ὅμως σὰν νὰ δυσαρεστήθηκε
μ' αὐτόν μας τὸν ἀστεϊσμό: θυμοῦμαι τώρα.
Ἀ κι ἄλλες δυὸ φορὲς τώρα στὸν νοῦ μου ἔρχονται.
Ὅταν στὸν Ποσειδῶνα κάμναμε σπονδές,
τραβήχθηκε ἀπ' τὸν κύκλο μας, κ' ἔστρεψε ἀλλοῦ τὸ βλέμμα.
Ὅταν ἐνθουσιασμένος ἕνας μας
εἶπεν, Ἡ συντροφιά μας νά 'ναι ὑπὸ
τὴν εὔνοιαν καὶ τὴν προστασίαν τοῦ μεγάλου,
τοῦ πανωραίου Ἀπόλλωνος—ψιθύρισεν ὁ Μύρης
(οἱ ἄλλοι δὲν ἄκουσαν) «τῇ ἐξαιρέσει ἐμοῦ».

Οἱ Χριστιανοὶ ἱερεῖς μεγαλοφώνως
γιὰ τὴν ψυχὴ τοῦ νέου δέονταν.—
Παρατηροῦσα μὲ πόση ἐπιμέλεια,
καὶ μὲ τί προσοχὴν ἐντατικὴ
στοὺς τύπους τῆς θρησκείας τους, ἑτοιμάζονταν
ὅλα γιὰ τὴν χριστιανικὴ κηδεία.
Κ' ἐξαίφνης μὲ κυρίευσε μιὰ ἀλλόκοτη
ἐντύπωσις. Ἀόριστα, αἰσθάνομουν

or to Mary (I don't know their religion well).

We'd known, of course, that Myres was a Christian,
known it from the very first moment, when
the year before last he first joined our group—
though he lived exactly as we did.
More given to bodily pleasures than all of us;
he squandered his money lavishly on amusements;
indifferent what the world thought of him,
he threw himself with zeal into night-time brawls
when our gang of friends came to clash
with some rival bunch in the street.
And never did he speak of his religion.
In fact, we even told him once
that we'd take him with us to the Serapeion.
But he seemed displeased, didn't like
our joking that way: I remember it now.
And yes, two other times come back to me.
When we made libations to Poseidon,
he drew apart from our circle, and he looked away.
And when one of us in his excitement said:
"May our companionship be favored and protected
by the great, the most beautiful Apollo"—Myres
whispered (the others did not hear): "not counting me."

The Christian priests were praying loudly
for the young man's soul.
I observed with how much care,
how much intense regard
for the rituals of their religion,
they were preparing the Christian funeral.
And suddenly, an uncanny sensation
overwhelmed me. Indefinably, I felt
as if Myres were leaving me for good;

σὰν νά 'φευγεν ἀπὸ κοντά μου ὁ Μύρης·
αἰσθάνομουν ποὺ ἐνώθη, Χριστιανός,
μὲ τοὺς δικούς του, καὶ ποὺ γένομουν
ξ έ ν ο ς ἐγώ, ξ έ ν ο ς π ο λ ύ· ἔνοιωθα κιόλα
μιὰ ἀμφιβολία νὰ μὲ σιμώνει: μήπως κ' εἶχα γελασθεῖ
ἀπὸ τὸ πάθος μου, καὶ π ά ν τ α τοῦ ἥμουν ξένος.—
Πετάχθηκα ἔξω ἀπ' τὸ φρικτό τους σπίτι,
ἔφυγα γρήγορα πρὶν ἁρπαχθεῖ, πρὶν ἀλλοιωθεῖ
ἀπ' τὴν χριστιανοσύνη τους ἡ θύμηση τοῦ Μύρη.

I sensed a Christian, come to be united
with his own, and that I was becoming
a stranger, a total stranger. I even felt
overcome by doubt: that I may have been deceived
by my passion and had *always* been a stranger to him.
I hurried out of their horrible house, hurried
before my memory of Myres was snatched away,
before it could be corrupted by their Christianity.

ΑΛΕΞΑΝΔΡΟΣ ΙΑΝΝΑΙΟΣ, ΚΑΙ ΑΛΕΞΑΝΔΡΑ

Ἐπιτυχεῖς καὶ πλήρως ἱκανοποιημένοι,
ὁ βασιλεὺς Ἀλέξανδρος Ἰανναῖος,
κ' ἡ σύζυγός του ἡ βασίλισσα Ἀλεξάνδρα,
περνοῦν μὲ προπορευομένην μουσικὴν
καὶ μὲ παντοίαν μεγαλοπρέπειαν καὶ χλιδήν,
περνοῦν ἀπ' τὲς ὁδοὺς τῆς Ἰερουσαλήμ.
Ἐτελεσφόρησε λαμπρῶς τὸ ἔργον
ποὺ ἄρχισαν ὁ μέγας Ἰούδας Μακκαβαῖος
κ' οἱ τέσσαρες περιώνυμοι ἀδελφοί του·
καὶ ποὺ μετὰ ἀνενδότως συνεχίσθη ἐν μέσῳ
πολλῶν κινδύνων καὶ πολλῶν δυσχερειῶν.
Τώρα δὲν ἔμεινε τίποτε τὸ ἀνοίκειον.
Ἔπαυσε κάθε ὑποταγὴ στοὺς ἀλαζόνας
μονάρχας τῆς Ἀντιοχείας. Ἰδοὺ
ὁ βασιλεὺς Ἀλέξανδρος Ἰανναῖος,
κ' ἡ σύζυγός του ἡ βασίλισσα Ἀλεξάνδρα,
καθ' ὅλα ἴσοι πρὸς τοὺς Σελευκίδας.
Ἰουδαῖοι καλοί, Ἰουδαῖοι ἁγνοί, Ἰουδαῖοι πιστοί—πρὸ πάντων.
Ἀλλά, καθὼς ποὺ τὸ ἀπαιτοῦν ἡ περιστάσεις,
καὶ τῆς ἑλληνικῆς λαλιᾶς εἰδήμονες·
καὶ μ' Ἕλληνας καὶ μ' ἑλληνίζοντας
μονάρχας σχετισμένοι—πλὴν σὰν ἴσοι, καὶ ν' ἀκούεται.
Τωόντι ἐτελεσφόρησε λαμπρῶς,
ἐτελεσφόρησε περιφανῶς
τὸ ἔργον ποὺ ἄρχισαν ὁ μέγας Ἰούδας Μακκαβαῖος
κ' οἱ τέσσαρες περιώνυμοι ἀδελφοί του.

ALEXANDER IANNAIOS AND ALEXANDRA

With success on their side and wholly satisfied,
King Alexander Iannaios
and his wife Queen Alexandra,
music leading them, parade through the streets
with all splendor and luxury,
parade through the streets of Jerusalem.
It won a brilliant outcome, the work begun
by the great Judas Makkabaios
and his four prominent brothers—
work relentlessly continued on
amid many dangers and difficulties.
Yet nothing unseemly remains now.
All giving in to the arrogant monarchs
of Antioch is now over. See this
King, Alexander Iannaios,
and his wife, Queen Alexandra, they are
in every way equal to the Seleukids.
Good Jews, pure Jews, devout Jews—above all.
But, as circumstances require,
also skillful with the Hellenic tongue;
and on good terms with Greek or Hellenized
monarchs—as equals, let it be known.
The work begun, then, by the great Judas Makkabaios
and his four prominent brothers
won a brilliant outcome
indeed, a glorious result.

ΩΡΑΙΑ ΛΟΥΛΟΥΔΙΑ ΚΙ ΑΣΠΡΑ ΩΣ ΤΑΙΡΙΑΖΑΝ ΠΟΛΥ

Μπῆκε στὸ καφενεῖο   ὅπου ἐπήγαιναν μαζύ.—
Ὁ φίλος του ἐδῶ   πρὸ τριῶ μηνῶν τοῦ εἶπε·
«Δὲν ἔχουμε πεντάρα.   Δυὸ πάμπτωχα παιδιὰ
εἴμεθα—ξεπεσμένοι   στὰ κέντρα τὰ φθηνά.
Σ᾿ τὸ λέγω φανερά,   μὲ σένα δὲν μπορῶ
νὰ περπατῶ. Ἕνας ἄλλος, μάθε το, μὲ ζητεῖ.»
Ὁ ἄλλος τοῦ εἶχε τάξει   δυὸ φορεσιές, καὶ κάτι
μεταξωτὰ μαντήλια.—   Γιὰ νὰ τὸν ξαναπάρει
ἐχάλασε τὸν κόσμο,   καὶ βρῆκε εἴκοσι λίρες.
Ἦλθε ξανὰ μαζύ του   γιὰ τὲς εἴκοσι λίρες·
μὰ καί, κοντὰ σ᾿ αὐτές, γιὰ τὴν παλαὰ φιλία,
γιὰ τὴν παλαὰν ἀγάπη,   γιὰ τὸ βαθὺ αἴσθημά των.—
Ὁ «ἄλλος» ἦταν ψεύτης,   παληόπαιδο σωστό·
μιὰ φορεσιὰ μονάχα   τοῦ εἶχε κάμει, καὶ
μὲ τὸ στανιὸ καὶ τούτην, μὲ χίλια παρακάλια.

Μὰ τώρα πιὰ δὲν θέλει   μήτε τὲς φορεσιές,
καὶ μήτε διόλου τὰ   μεταξωτὰ μαντήλια,
καὶ μήτε εἴκοσι λίρες,   καὶ μήτε εἴκοσι γρόσια.

Τὴν Κυριακὴ τὸν θάψαν,   στὲς δέκα τὸ πρωΐ.
Τὴν Κυριακὴ τὸν θάψαν: πάει ἑβδομὰς σχεδόν.

Στὴν πτωχική του κάσα   τοῦ ἔβαλε λουλούδια,
ὡραῖα λουλούδια κι ἄσπρα ὡς ταίριαζαν πολὺ
στὴν ἐμορφιά του καὶ   στὰ εἴκοσι δυό του χρόνια.

Ὅταν τὸ βράδυ ἐπῆγεν—   ἔτυχε μιὰ δουλειά,
μιὰ ἀνάγκη τοῦ ψωμιοῦ του— στὸ καφενεῖον ὅπου
ἐπήγαιναν μαζύ: μαχαῖρι στὴν καρδιά του
τὸ μαῦρο καφενεῖο   ὅπου ἐπήγαιναν μαζύ.

LOVELY FLOWERS AND WHITE THAT BECAME HIM BEST

He entered that café   the two used to go to.
It was here his friend   three months ago said:
"We're broke, you see,   two mere boys, penniless,
down-and-out on our luck,   hanging out at cheap places.
I tell you openly   I cannot stay with you
any more. There's   someone else asking for me."
This "someone else"   promised him two suits,
and silk handkerchiefs.   To get him back, he turned
the world upside down,   till he found twenty pounds.
And for the twenty pounds   he came back to him;
but not just for the money,   but for their old friendship,
for their old love, their deep   feeling for one another.
That "someone else" was a liar,   truly a sleazy youth;
only a single suit did he   order for him, and
that under pressure,   after much pleading.

Now he wants nothing   of tailored suits,
nor cares a whit   for the silk handkerchiefs,
or the twenty pounds,   or twenty piasters even.

Sunday they buried him,   at ten in the morning.
Sunday they buried him,   almost a week ago.

On his shoddy coffin   he laid the flowers,
those lovely white flowers,   highly becoming
to his beauty   of twenty-two years.

When this evening he went—   an obligation brought him there,
a job-related affair—   to this same café
they used to go to together: like a knife to the heart,
that seamy café   they used to go to together.

ΑΓΕ, Ω ΒΑΣΙΛΕΥ ΛΑΚΕΔΑΙΜΟΝΙΩΝ

Δὲν καταδέχονταν ἡ Κρατησίκλεια
ὁ κόσμος νὰ τὴν δεῖ νὰ κλαίει καὶ νὰ θρηνεῖ·
καὶ μεγαλοπρεπὴς ἐβάδιζε καὶ σιωπηλή.
Τίποτε δὲν ἀπόδειχνε ἡ ἀτάραχη μορφή της
ἀπ' τὸν καϋμὸ καὶ τὰ τυράννια της.
Μὰ ὅσο καὶ νά 'ναι, μιὰ στιγμὴ δὲν βάσταξε·
καὶ πρὶν στὸ ἄθλιο πλοῖο μπεῖ νὰ πάει στὴν Ἀλεξάνδρεια,
πῆρε τὸν υἱό της στὸν ναὸ τοῦ Ποσειδῶνος,
καὶ μόνοι σὰν βρεθῆκαν τὸν ἀγκάλιασε
καὶ τὸν ἀσπάζονταν, «διαλγοῦντα», λέγει
ὁ Πλούταρχος, «καὶ συντεταραγμένον».
Ὅμως ὁ δυνατός της χαρακτὴρ ἐπάσχισε·
καὶ συνελθοῦσα ἡ θαυμασία γυναῖκα
εἶπε στὸν Κλεομένη «Ἄγε, ὦ βασιλεῦ
Λακεδαιμονίων, ὅπως, ἐπὰν ἔξω
γενώμεθα, μηδεὶς ἴδη δακρύοντας
ἡμᾶς μηδὲ ἀνάξιόν τι τῆς Σπάρτης
ποιοῦντας. Τοῦτο γὰρ ἐφ' ἡμῖν μόνον·
αἱ τύχαι δέ, ὅπως ἂν ὁ δαίμων διδῷ, πάρεισι.»

Καὶ μὲς στὸ πλοῖο μπῆκε, πηαίνοντας πρὸς τὸ «διδῷ».

COME, O KING OF THE LAKEDAIMONIANS

Kratesikleia thought it beneath her to let
the people see her cry and lament;
she kept moving in dignity and in silence.
Her calm appearance betrayed nothing,
none of her agony, her inner torture.
But even so, came the moment she couldn't bear:
before she boarded that miserable ship for Alexandria,
she took her son apart, to Poseidon's temple,
and once they were left alone she embraced him
and kept kissing him, as he suffered "in great pain,"
according to Plutarch, "and in a trembling fit."
But her powerful spirit struggled through;
regaining her dignity, this wondrous woman
said to Kleomenes: "Come, O king
of the Lakedaimonians, when we step outside,
let no one see that we've been crying
or behaving in ways unworthy of Sparta.
This much is still within our power;
as for our future, that lies with the gods."

She boarded the ship, going toward "… that lies with the gods."

ΣΤΟΝ ΙΔΙΟ ΧΩΡΟ

Οἰκίας περιβάλλον, κέντρων, συνοικίας
ποὺ βλέπω κι ὅπου περπατῶ· χρόνια καὶ χρόνια.

Σὲ δημιούργησα μὲς σὲ χαρὰ καὶ μὲς σὲ λύπες:
μὲ τόσα περιστατικά, μὲ τόσα πράγματα.

Κ' αἰσθηματοποιήθηκες ὁλόκληρο, γιὰ μένα.

IN THE SAME PLACE

Home surroundings, familiar centers, neighborhood places,
those I gaze at and walk through; years and years now.

I have created you amid joys, amid sorrows:
out of so many chance occurrences, so many odd things.

Place, fraught with feeling, the whole of you, just for me.

Ο ΚΑΘΡΕΠΤΗΣ ΣΤΗΝ ΕΙΣΟΔΟ

Τὸ πλούσιο σπίτι εἶχε στὴν εἴσοδο
ἕναν καθρέπτη μέγιστο, πολὺ παλαιό·
τουλάχιστον πρὸ ὀγδόντα ἐτῶν ἀγορασμένο.

Ἕνα ἐμορφότατο παιδί, ὑπάλληλος σὲ ράπτη
(τὲς Κυριακές, ἐρασιτέχνης ἀθλητής),
στέκονταν μ' ἕνα δέμα. Τὸ παρέδωσε
σὲ κάποιον τοῦ σπιτιοῦ, κι αὐτὸς τὸ πῆγε μέσα
νὰ φέρει τὴν ἀπόδειξι. Ὁ ὑπάλληλος τοῦ ράπτη
ἔμεινε μόνος, καὶ περίμενε.
Πλησίασε στὸν καθρέπτη καὶ κυττάζονταν
κ' ἔσιαζε τὴν κραβάτα του. Μετὰ πέντε λεπτὰ
τοῦ φέραν τὴν ἀπόδειξι. Τὴν πῆρε κ' ἔφυγε.

Μὰ ὁ παλαιὸς καθρέπτης ποὺ εἶχε δεῖ καὶ δεῖ,
κατὰ τὴν ὕπαρξίν του τὴν πολυετῆ,
χιλιάδες πράγματα καὶ πρόσωπα·
μὰ ὁ παλαιὸς καθρέπτης τώρα χαίρονταν,
κ' ἐπαίρονταν ποὺ εἶχε δεχθεῖ ἐπάνω του
τὴν ἄρτιαν ἐμορφιὰ γιὰ μερικὰ λεπτά.

THE MIRROR IN THE FRONT HALL

The house of great wealth had in its hallway
a mirror of giant size, and very old;
bought at least eighty years before.

A boy of utter beauty, a tailor's clerk
(on Sundays, an amateur athlete)
stood nearby with a package. He handed it
to someone of the house, who took it inside
to fetch him the receipt. The tailor's clerk
was left alone and waited.
He approached the mirror, looking at himself,
and began fixing his tie. Five minutes later
they brought him the receipt. He took it
and went on his way.

But the ancient mirror that had looked into so much,
during the long years of its existence,
that had seen a myriad things and faces;
now this old mirror felt glad,
and proud to have received into itself
such total beauty even for a few moments.

ΡΩΤΟΥΣΕ ΓΙΑ ΤΗΝ ΠΟΙΟΤΗΤΑ—

Ἀπ' τὸ γραφεῖον ὅπου εἶχε προσληφθεῖ
σὲ θέσι ἀσήμαντη καὶ φθηνοπληρωμένη
(ὡς ὀκτὼ λίρες τὸ μηνιάτικό του: μὲ τὰ τυχερά)
βγῆκε σὰν τέλεψεν ἡ ἔρημη δουλειὰ
ποὺ ὅλο τὸ ἀπόγευμα ἦταν σκυμένος:
βγῆκεν ἡ ὥρα ἑπτά, καὶ περπατοῦσε ἀργὰ
καὶ χάζευε στὸν δρόμο.—Ἔμορφος·
κ' ἐνδιαφέρων: ἔτσι ποὺ ἔδειχνε φθασμένος
στὴν πλήρη του αἰσθησιακὴν ἀπόδοσι.
Τὰ εἴκοσι ἐννιά, τὸν περασμένο μῆνα τὰ εἶχε κλείσει.

Ἐχάζευε στὸν δρόμο, καὶ στὲς πτωχικὲς
παρόδους ποὺ ὁδηγοῦσαν πρὸς τὴν κατοικία του.

Περνῶντας ἐμπρὸς σ' ἕνα μαγαζὶ μικρὸ
ὅπου πουλιοῦνταν κάτι πράγματα
ψεύτικα καὶ φθηνὰ γιὰ ἐργατικούς,
εἶδ' ἐκεῖ μέσα ἕνα πρόσωπο, εἶδε μιὰ μορφὴ
ὅπου τὸν ἔσπρωξαν καὶ εἰσῆλθε, καὶ ζητοῦσε
τάχα νὰ δεῖ χρωματιστὰ μαντήλια.

Ρωτοῦσε γιὰ τὴν ποιότητα τῶν μαντηλιῶν
καὶ τί κοστίζουν· μὲ φωνὴ πνιγμένη,
σχεδὸν σβυσμένη ἀπ' τὴν ἐπιθυμία.
Κι ἀνάλογα ἦλθαν ἡ ἀπαντήσεις,
ἀφηρημένες, μὲ φωνὴ χαμηλωμένη,
μὲ ὑπολανθάνουσα συναίνεσι.

Ὅλο καὶ κάτι ἔλεγαν γιὰ τὴν πραγμάτεια—ἀλλὰ
μόνος σκοπός: τὰ χέρια των ν' ἀγγίζουν
ἐπάνω ἀπ' τὰ μαντήλια· νὰ πλησιάζουν
τὰ πρόσωπα, τὰ χείλη σὰν τυχαίως·
μιὰ στιγμιαία στὰ μέλη ἐπαφή.

HE ASKED ABOUT THE QUALITY—

He came forth, at the finish of his miserable workday
in the offices where he's been recently employed
as the menial that's poorly paid
(up to eight pounds a month, with extras),
where all afternoon he hung his head;
he came away at seven, walking slowly
and loitering along the road.—Very handsome;
and interesting: projecting as he did a mature beauty,
having already reached his sensual perfection.
He'd turned twenty-nine the month before.

He loitered on the road, and along the poor
sidestreets that led to the place he lived.

As he passed in front of a small shop
that sold such meagre things,
cheap and fake things for workers,
there he saw a face, he saw a presence inside,
and felt the urge to enter, where he asked,
feigning interest, to see their colored handkerchiefs.

He asked about the quality of the material
and what they cost, in a drowning voice,
the faint sounds of desire.
And the answers came at him in the same vein,
distracted, the voice hushed,
guarded, yet filled with consent.

They went on speaking of the merchandise—but
the motive was one: that their hands might touch
over the handkerchiefs; their faces, their lips,
might for an instant brush the other, as if by chance.
A fleeting touch of their limbs come together.

Γρήγορα καὶ κρυφά, γιὰ νὰ μὴ νοιώσει
ὁ καταστηματάρχης ποὺ στὸ βάθος κάθονταν.

Furtive and quick gestures, so the shop owner
seated at the back would not catch on.

ΑΣ ΦΡΟΝΤΙΖΑΝ

Κατήντησα σχεδὸν ἀνέστιος καὶ πένης.
Αὐτὴ ἡ μοιραία πόλις, ἡ Ἀντιόχεια
ὅλα τὰ χρήματά μου τά 'φαγε:
αὐτὴ ἡ μοιραία μὲ τὸν δαπανηρό της βίο.

Ἀλλὰ εἶμαι νέος καὶ μὲ ὑγείαν ἀρίστην.
Κάτοχος τῆς ἑλληνικῆς θαυμάσιος
(ξέρω καὶ παραξέρω Ἀριστοτέλη, Πλάτωνα·
τί ρήτορας, τί ποιητάς, τί ὅ,τι κι ἂν πεῖς).
Ἀπὸ στρατιωτικὰ ἔχω μιὰν ἰδέα,
κ' ἔχω φιλίες μὲ ἀρχηγοὺς τῶν μισθοφόρων.
Εἶμαι μπασμένος κάμποσο καὶ στὰ διοικητικά.
Στὴν Ἀλεξάνδρεια ἔμεινα ἕξι μῆνες, πέρσι·
κάπως γνωρίζω (κ' εἶναι τοῦτο χρήσιμον) τὰ ἐκεῖ:
τοῦ Κακεργέτη βλέψεις, καὶ παληανθρωπιές, καὶ τὰ λοιπά.

Ὅθεν φρονῶ πὼς εἶμαι στὰ γεμάτα
ἐνδεδειγμένος γιὰ νὰ ὑπηρετήσω αὐτὴν τὴν χώρα,
τὴν προσφιλῆ πατρίδα μου Συρία.

Σ' ὅ,τι δουλειὰ μὲ βάλουν θὰ πασχίσω
νὰ εἶμαι στὴν χώρα ὠφέλιμος. Αὐτὴ εἶν' ἡ πρόθεσίς μου.
Ἂν πάλι μ' ἐμποδίσουνε μὲ τὰ συστήματά τους—
τοὺς ξέρουμε τοὺς προκομένους: νὰ τὰ λέμε τώρα;
ἂν μ' ἐμποδίσουνε, τί φταίω ἐγώ.

Θ' ἀπευθυνθῶ πρὸς τὸν Ζαβίνα πρῶτα,
κι ἂν ὁ μωρὸς αὐτὸς δὲν μ' ἐκτιμήσει,
θὰ πάγω στὸν ἀντίπαλό του, τὸν Γρυπό.
Κι ἂν ὁ ἠλίθιος κι αὐτὸς δὲν μὲ προσλάβει,
πηγαίνω παρευθὺς στὸν Ὑρκανό.

Θὰ μὲ θελήσει πάντως ἕνας ἀπ' τοὺς τρεῖς.

TO HAVE TAKEN THE TROUBLE

I'm reduced to being penniless and practically homeless.
This ill-fated city, Antioch,
has eaten up all my money,
this ill-fated city and its extravagant life.

But I'm still young and in excellent health.
I have a first-rate mastery of Greek
(I know, and more than know, Aristotle and Plato;
orators, poets, and whoever else you care to mention).
I'm familiar, too, with military matters
and have developed friendships among senior mercenaries.
I'm also in the inner circles of administrative affairs.
I spent six months in Alexandria—last year;
and I do know (and this is certainly useful) matters there:
Kakergetes' deviousness, his lawless tactics, and all the rest.

Hence I consider myself to be fully
qualified to serve this country,
my beloved native land, Syria.

Whatever work they give me, I will do my best
to be of benefit to the country. That's my intention.
Again, should they block my way with their methods—
we know them, those clever scoundrels: need we say more?
If they block my way, I can't be the one to blame.

In the event, I'll come up to Zabinas first,
and if that moron doesn't appreciate me,
I'll turn to his rival, Grypos.
And if that stupid man doesn't give me work as well,
I'll march right up to Hyrkanos himself.

One of the three is bound to want me.

Κ' εἶν' ἡ συνείδησίς μου ἥσυχη
γιὰ τὸ ἀψήφιστο τῆς ἐκλογῆς.
Βλάπτουν κ' οἱ τρεῖς τους τὴν Συρία τὸ ἴδιο.

Ἀλλά, κατεστραμένος ἄνθρωπος, τί φταίω ἐγώ.
Ζητῶ ὁ ταλαίπωρος νὰ μπαλωθῶ.
Ἄς φρόντιζαν οἱ κραταιοὶ θεοὶ
νὰ δημιουργήσουν ἕναν τέταρτο καλό.
Μετὰ χαρᾶς θὰ πήγαινα μ' αὐτόν.

And my conscience is at ease
with the uncaring nature of my choice.
All three are equally harmful for Syria.

But I, a ruin myself, cannot be the one to blame.
I only ask—abject man that I am—to find me a livelihood.
They should have taken the trouble, the almighty gods,
to create a fourth, an honest man;
I would have happily gone along with him.

ΚΑΤΑ ΤΕΣ ΣΥΝΤΑΓΕΣ ΑΡΧΑΙΩΝ
ΕΛΛΗΝΟΣΥΡΩΝ ΜΑΓΩΝ

«Ποιὸ ἀπόσταγμα νὰ βρίσκεται ἀπὸ βότανα
γητεύματος», εἶπ᾽ ἕνας αἰσθητής,
«ποιὸ ἀπόσταγμα κατὰ τὲς συνταγὲς
ἀρχαίων Ἑλληνοσύρων μάγων καμωμένο
ποὺ γιὰ μιὰ μέρα (ἂν περισσότερο
δὲν φθάν᾽ ἡ δύναμίς του), ἢ καὶ γιὰ λίγην ὥρα
τὰ εἴκοσι τρία μου χρόνια νὰ μὲ φέρει
ξανά· τὸν φίλον μου στὰ εἴκοσι δυό του χρόνια
νὰ μὲ φέρει ξανά—τὴν ἐμορφιά του, τὴν ἀγάπη του.

»Ποιὸ ἀπόσταγμα νὰ βρίσκεται κατὰ τὲς συνταγὲς
ἀρχαίων Ἑλληνοσύρων μάγων καμωμένο
ποὺ, σύμφωνα μὲ τὴν ἀναδρομήν,
καὶ τὴν μικρή μας κάμαρη νὰ ἐπαναφέρει.»

FOLLOWING THE RECIPE OF ANCIENT
GRECO-SYRIAN MAGICIANS

"What essence can be found, distilled
from magical herbs," said the aesthete,
"what essence, following the recipes
of ancient Greco-Syrian magicians, made so
that it bring back to me for one day, or maybe for
a shorter time (as its strength is not enough for more),
—bring back to me my twenty-third year;
and bring my friend in his twenty-two years,
bring him back to me—his beauty, his love.

What essence can be found, following the recipes
of ancient Greco-Syrian magicians, made so,
as part of this aura of things past,
to bring back again even the little room we shared."

ΣΤΑ 200 Π.Χ.

«Ἀλέξανδρος Φιλίππου καὶ οἱ Ἕλληνες πλὴν Λακεδαιμονίων»—

Μποροῦμε κάλλιστα νὰ φαντασθοῦμε
πὼς θ᾽ ἀδιαφόρησαν παντάπασι στὴν Σπάρτη
γιὰ τὴν ἐπιγραφὴν αὐτή. «Πλὴν Λακεδαιμονίων»,
μὰ φυσικά. Δὲν ἦσαν οἱ Σπαρτιᾶται
γιὰ νὰ τοὺς ὁδηγοῦν καὶ γιὰ νὰ τοὺς προστάζουν
σὰν πολυτίμους ὑπηρέτας. Ἄλλωστε
μιὰ πανελλήνια ἐκστρατεία χωρὶς
Σπαρτιάτη βασιλέα γι᾽ ἀρχηγὸ
δὲν θὰ τοὺς φαίνονταν πολλῆς περιωπῆς.
Ἀ βεβαιότατα «πλὴν Λακεδαιμονίων».

Εἶναι κι αὐτὴ μιὰ στάσις. Νοιώθεται.

Ἔτσι, πλὴν Λακεδαιμονίων στὸν Γρανικό·
καὶ στὴν Ἰσσὸ μετά· καὶ στὴν τελειωτικὴ
τὴν μάχη, ὅπου ἐσαρώθη ὁ φοβερὸς στρατὸς
ποὺ στ᾽ Ἄρβηλα συγκέντρωσαν οἱ Πέρσαι:
ποὺ ἀπ᾽ τ᾽ Ἄρβηλα ξεκίνησε γιὰ νίκην, κ᾽ ἐσαρώθη.

Κι ἀπ᾽ τὴν θαυμάσια πανελλήνιαν ἐκστρατεία,
τὴν νικηφόρα, τὴν περίλαμπρη,
τὴν περιλάλητη, τὴν δοξασμένη
ὡς ἄλλη δὲν δοξάσθηκε καμιά,
τὴν ἀπαράμιλλη: βγήκαμ᾽ ἐμεῖς·
ἑλληνικὸς καινούριος κόσμος, μέγας.

Ἐμεῖς· οἱ Ἀλεξανδρεῖς, οἱ Ἀντιοχεῖς,
οἱ Σελευκεῖς, κ᾽ οἱ πολυάριθμοι
ἐπίλοιποι Ἕλληνες Αἰγύπτου καὶ Συρίας,
κ᾽ οἱ ἐν Μηδίᾳ, κ᾽ οἱ ἐν Περσίδι, κι ὅσοι ἄλλοι.
Μὲ τὲς ἐκτεταμένες ἐπικράτειες,

IN THE YEAR 200 B.C.

"Alexander, son of Philip, and the Greeks, except the Lakedaimonians …"

We can very well envision
how indifferent everyone in Sparta would have been
to this inscription: "except the Lakedaimonians"—
but of course. The Spartans were not those
that could be led blind and ordered around
like invaluable servants. In any case,
a panhellenic expedition without
a Spartan king in command
would not seem to them of high enough standing.
Yes, of course, "except the Lakedaimonians."

That's certainly one position. Understandable.

So, "except the Lakedaimonians" at Granikos,
and afterwards at Issos; then in the decisive
battle, where the splendid army was wiped out,
the very army the Persians had amassed at Arbela:
it set out from Arbela to triumph, and was wiped out.

And from this miraculous panhellenic expedition,
the victorious, wildly brilliant,
everywhere renowned, moved to glory
as no other has ever been glorified,
incomparable, so we emerged:
a Hellenic world, the new, the great one.

We! The Alexandrians, the Antiochians,
the Seleukeians, and the myriad
other Greeks of Egypt and of Syria,
and those in Media and in Persia, and so many more.
With our far-flung dominions,

μὲ τὴν ποικίλη δρᾶσι τῶν στοχαστικῶν προσαρμογῶν.
Καὶ τὴν Κοινὴν Ἑλληνικὴ Λαλιὰ
ὢς μέσα στὴν Βακτριανὴ τὴν πήγαμεν, ὢς τοὺς Ἰνδούς.

Γιὰ Λακεδαιμονίους νὰ μιλοῦμε τώρα!

our adaptable acts of judicious integration
and our common, spoken Greek tongue,
which we brought all the way to Baktria, as far as India.

Should we be talking about Lakedaimonians now!

ΜΕΡΕΣ ΤΟΥ 1908

Τὸν χρόνο ἐκεῖνον βρέθηκε χωρὶς δουλειά·
καὶ συνεπῶς ζοῦσεν ἀπ' τὰ χαρτιά,
ἀπὸ τὸ τάβλι, καὶ τὰ δανεικά.

Μιὰ θέσις, τριῶ λιρῶν τὸν μῆνα, σὲ μικρὸ
χαρτοπωλεῖον τοῦ εἶχε προσφερθεῖ.
Μὰ τὴν ἀρνήθηκε, χωρὶς κανένα δισταγμό.
Δὲν ἔκανε. Δὲν ἤτανε μισθὸς γι' αὐτόν,
νέον μὲ γράμματ' ἀρκετά, καὶ εἴκοσι πέντ' ἐτῶν.

Δυό, τρία σελίνια τὴν ἡμέρα κέρδιζε, δὲν κέρδιζε.
Ἀπὸ χαρτιὰ καὶ τάβλι τί νὰ βγάλει τὸ παιδί,
στὰ καφενεῖα τῆς σειρᾶς του, τὰ λαϊκά,
ὅσο κι ἂν ἔπαιζ' ἔξυπνα, ὅσο κι ἂν διάλεγε κουτούς.
Τὰ δανεικά, αὐτὰ δὰ ἦσαν κ' ἦσαν.
Σπάνια τὸ τάλληρο εὕρισκε, τὸ πιὸ συχνὰ μισό,
κάποτε ξέπεφτε καὶ στὸ σελίνι.

Καμιὰ ἑβδομάδα, ἐνίοτε πιὸ πολύ,
σὰν γλύτωνεν ἀπ' τὸ φρικτὸ ξενύχτι,
δροσίζονταν στὰ μπάνια, στὸ κολύμβι τὸ πρωΐ.

Τὰ ροῦχα του εἶχαν ἕνα χάλι τρομερό.
Μιὰ φορεσιὰ τὴν ἴδια πάντοτ' ἔβαζε, μιὰ φορεσιὰ
πολὺ ξεθωριασμένη κανελιά.

Ἆ μέρες τοῦ καλοκαιριοῦ τοῦ ἐννιακόσια ὀκτώ,
ἀπ' τὸ εἴδωμά σας, καλαισθητικά,
ἔλειψ' ἡ κανελιὰ ξεθωριασμένη φορεσιά.

Τὸ εἴδωμά σας τὸν ἐφύλαξε
ὅταν ποὺ τά 'βγαζε, ποὺ τά 'ριχνε ἀπὸ πάνω του,
τ' ἀνάξια ροῦχα, καὶ τὰ μπαλωμένα ἐσώρουχα.

DAYS OF 1908

In that very year he was out of work;
and so he made his living from cards,
from backgammon, and borrowing what he could.

A job, paying three pounds a month, in a small
stationery store had been offered him—
one he turned down without hesitation.
It would not do. This was no wage for him,
a youth, with some education, twenty-five years of age.

On any day he'd manage to win two or three shillings or so.
What could the poor boy make from cards and backgammon,
at the cafés of his class, those lowly cafés,
however cleverly he played, however mindless the opponents he chose.
As for the loans: no more than a pittance now and again.
Managing a crown was rare, more often half,
sometimes he'd grovel for a shilling or so.

Occasionally for a whole week, sometimes more,
when he managed to escape the horrors of nightlife,
he'd freshen up in early morning at the baths, then have a swim.

His clothes were a frightful mess.
One single suit, he always wore that same suit,
that faded cinnamon-hued suit.

Summer days, days of nineteen hundred and eight,
your discerning gaze upon his beauty
has already erased the ugly cinnamon suit.

Your gaze has him fixed forever
as he disrobed, threw them from his body,
those unworthy clothes, the worn and mended underwear.

Κ' ἔμενε ὁλόγυμνος· ἄψογα ὡραῖος· ἕνα θαῦμα.
Ἀχτένιστα, ἀνασηκωμένα τὰ μαλλιά του·
τὰ μέλη του ἡλιοκαμένα λίγο
ἀπὸ τὴν γύμνια τοῦ πρωϊοῦ στὰ μπάνια, καὶ στὴν παραλία.

And he stood there naked; in perfect beauty; a miracle.
Uncombed, unruly hair;
limbs lightly burned by the morning sun
that caught him naked at the baths, then at the seashore.

ΕΙΣ ΤΑ ΠΕΡΙΧΩΡΑ ΤΗΣ ΑΝΤΙΟΧΕΙΑΣ

Σαστίσαμε στὴν Ἀντιόχειαν ὅταν μάθαμε
τὰ νέα καμώματα τοῦ Ἰουλιανοῦ.

Ὁ Ἀπόλλων ἐξηγήθηκε μὲ λόγου του, στὴν Δάφνη!
Χρησμὸ δὲν ἤθελε νὰ δώσει (σκοτισθήκαμε!),
σκοπὸ δὲν τό 'χε νὰ μιλήσει μαντικῶς, ἂν πρῶτα
δὲν καθαρίζονταν τὸ ἐν Δάφνῃ τέμενός του.
Τὸν ἐνοχλοῦσαν, δήλωσεν, οἱ γειτονεύοντες νεκροί.

Στὴν Δάφνη βρίσκονταν τάφοι πολλοί.—
Ἕνας ἀπ' τοὺς ἐκεῖ ἐνταφιασμένους
ἦταν ὁ θαυμαστός, τῆς ἐκκλησίας μας δόξα,
ὁ ἅγιος, ὁ καλλίνικος μάρτυς Βαβύλας.

Αὐτὸν αἰνίττονταν, αὐτὸν φοβοῦνταν ὁ ψευτοθεός.
Ὅσο τὸν ἔνοιωθε κοντά, δὲν κόταε
νὰ βγάλει τοὺς χρησμούς του· τσιμουδιά.
(Τοὺς τρέμουνε τοὺς μάρτυράς μας οἱ ψευτοθεοί).

Ἀνασκουμπώθηκεν ὁ ἀνόσιος Ἰουλιανός,
νεύριασε καὶ ξεφώνιζε: «Σηκῶστε, μεταφέρτε τον,
βγάλτε τον τοῦτον τὸν Βαβύλα ἀμέσως.
Ἀκοῦς ἐκεῖ; Ὁ Ἀπόλλων ἐνοχλεῖται.
Σηκῶστε τον, ἁρπάξτε τον εὐθύς.
Ξεθάψτε τον, πάρτε τον ὅπου θέτε.
Βγάλτε τον, διῶξτε τον. Παίζουμε τώρα;
Ὁ Ἀπόλλων εἶπε νὰ καθαρισθεῖ τὸ τέμενος.»

Τὸ πήραμε, τὸ πήγαμε τὸ ἅγιο λείψανον ἀλλοῦ·
τὸ πήραμε, τὸ πήγαμε ἐν ἀγάπῃ κ' ἐν τιμῇ.

Κι ὡραῖα τῳόντι πρόκοψε τὸ τέμενος.
Δὲν ἄργησε καθόλου, καὶ φωτιὰ

ON THE OUTSKIRTS OF ANTIOCH

We were at our wits' end here in Antioch
when we heard of Julian's latest conniving.

Apollo made clear the deal with him at Daphne!
He didn't want to give a prophesy (as if we cared!),
he had no intention of speaking prophetically, if we
didn't first purify his shrine found at Daphne.
He was bothered, so he declared, by the neighboring dead.

There are many graves at Daphne.
One of those buried there
was the miraculous, the triumphant martyr Babylas,
a true saint, glory of our Church.

It was him this false god alluded to, him he feared.
As long as he sensed him near, he didn't dare
pronounce his prophesies; not a word.
(They're terrified of our martyrs, these false gods.)

Profane Julian got himself ready to attack,
lost his temper and began to shout: "Raise him up,
take him out of here, away at once with this Babylas.
How rude. To disturb Apollo.
Raise him, grab him at once.
Dig him up, away, bury him where you will.
Take him out, take him away. There'll be no games.
Apollo said the shrine must be purified."

We took it; we took the sacred relic elsewhere.
We took it; we moved it away in love and in honor.

Oh, how the shrine has thrived since!
In no time a huge conflagration

349

μεγάλη κόρωσε: μιὰ φοβερὴ φωτιά:
καὶ κάηκε καὶ τὸ τέμενος κι ὁ Ἀπόλλων.

Στάχτη τὸ εἴδωλο· γιὰ σάρωμα, μὲ τὰ σκουπίδια.

Ἔσκασε ὁ Ἰουλιανὸς καὶ διέδωσε—
τί ἄλλο θὰ ἔκαμνε—πὼς ἡ φωτιὰ ἦταν βαλτὴ
ἀπὸ τοὺς Χριστιανοὺς ἐμᾶς. Ἂς πάει νὰ λέει.
Δὲν ἀποδείχθηκε· ἂς πάει νὰ λέει.
Τὸ οὐσιῶδες εἶναι ποὺ ἔσκασε.

blazed: it was truly a horrible fire;
the shrine burned down, together with Apollo.

The statue in ashes: trash to be swept away.

Julian went wild with anger, and spread the rumor—
what else could he have done?—that we, the Christians,
set the fire. Let him say what he wants.
It was never proven. Let him say what he wants.
The essential thing is he went wild with anger.

Notes

These notes are intended to provide the basic information necessary to situate each poem and its personages chronologically and historically. I believe that the poems as such will not gain from an extended historical commentary.

THE CITY

First written in 1894 and placed in the thematic division "Prisons"; published in its present form in early 1910 in the journal *Νέα Ζωή*, together with "Satrapy."

SATRAPY

Probably written in July 1905 and published in *Νέα Ζωή*, in June 1910.

THE WISE KNOW WHAT HAPPENS NEXT

First written in 1896 under the title "Imminent Things," it appeared in its present form in 1915, in a sheaf of eleven poems—the most published in one year up to that time. The poet averaged about six poems a year.

THE IDES OF MARCH

Written in 1906, it appeared in 1911 in the journal *Κρητική Στοά*, under the present title.

FINISHED

Written in May of 1910 and published in the journal *Γράμματα*, in April 1911.

THE GOD ABANDONS ANTHONY

Some of the information comes from Plutarch's *Life of Anthony*, as does the title.

Plutarch's story has Mark Anthony, before his death, hearing voices singing and music playing, and people wildly dancing. All this commotion was moving toward the Gate where people thought Dionysos had abandoned the Roman General.

Written in 1910; published in 1911 in *Γράμματα*.

THEODOTOS

First written in 1911, titled "Victory," it was published under the present title in 1915. Theodotos was a rhetor from Chios, the teacher of Ptolemy XII. He was the one who convinced the Egyptians to kill Pompey in 48 B.C.—Pompey had gone to Egypt after the battle of Pharsala against Julius Caesar. There is no reliable evidence, however, that it was subsequently Theodotos who brought Pompey's head to Caesar.

MONOTONY

Written in 1898 under the title "Like Time Past."

ITHACA

A first draft was written in 1894, titled "Second Odyssey."

This version was written in 1910 and printed in 1911. Homer's giant cannibals destroy Odysseus's ships on the journey back to Ithaca; the Cyclops, the Laestrygonians, and the god Poseidon, having played a prominent role in Homer, are repeated by the poet, giving them proper importance.

AS MUCH AS YOU CAN

Written in 1905 under the title "A Life" and published in 1913 in *Néa Ζωή*.

TROJANS

Written in 1900, the poem appeared in the journal *Παναθήναια*.
"… Priam and Hecuba weep": the king and queen of Troy.

KING DEMETRIOS

Written in 1900; published in 1906 in *Παναθήναια*.

A quasi-historical poem about Demetrios Poliorketes (The Besieger), king of Makedonia; his army, tired of fighting to increase his wealth, abandoned him and joined his enemy, Pyrrhos, king of Epeiros.

THE GLORY OF THE PTOLEMIES

Written in 1896, and placed in the sheaf of poems titled "Ancient Days," the poem was rewritten in 1911 and published in *Γράμματα*.

Founded in Egypt, this Makedonian Greek Dynasty (323–30 B.C.) were descendants of the general of Alexander the Great, Ptolemy I Soter.

THE FOLLOWERS OF DIONYSOS

Written in 1903; published in *Παναθήναια*, in 1907.

Damon is an imaginary figure, an artist after money so that he might enter politics. The mythological figures are "real" enough.

THE BATTLE OF MAGNESIA

Written in 1913 and published in 1916 in *Νέα Ζωή*.

Though a historically based poem, the scene is imagined: as Philip V of Makedonia was defeated (without receiving aid from his friend Antiochos III of Syria), the poem describes Philip's reaction, as a sometime co-conspirator of Rome, when in 190 A.D. he found out about the catastrophic defeat of Antiochos in Magnesia—which clinched full control over the Mediterranean for the Romans.

THE DISPLEASURE OF SELEUKIDES

Written in February 1910; published in 1916 in *Νέα Ζωή*.

A historically based poem, centering on the son of Seleukos IV, who became king of Syria.

OROPHERNES

Written in February 1904 and first published in *Νέα Ζωή*.

A historically based poem: Orophernes was the doubted son of Ariarathos IV of Kappadokia; he later ascended the throne in 157 B.C.

ALEXANDRIAN KINGS

Written in May 1912 and published in July of that year in *Νέα Ζωή*.

A historically based poem, referring to an occurrence in 34 B.C.—a celebration trumped up by Anthony and Kleopatra so that the various conquered lands that had at one time "belonged" to Alexander the Great should be left to Kleopatra and her four small children.

Cavafy's own note on this poem: "I do not describe the whole of this celebration … I describe only that which, in my view, the Alexandrians rushed to witness. The 'coronation' as kings of the three offspring, the male heirs of the House of the Lagids. That, it seemed to me, is what attracted them, and (in spite of the fact that they knew all those titles were only words,) it is what moved them."

PHILHELLENE

Written in July 1906 and published in April 1912 in *Νέα Ζωή*.

In dramatic monologue style; made to seem historically based.

THE FOOTSTEPS

First written in 1893 as "The Footsteps of the Eumenides" and placed in the sheaf of poems titled "Ancient Days." Rewritten in 1908 as "The Footsteps" and published in 1909 in *Νέα Ζωή*.

A historically based poem.

HERODES ATTIKOS

First written in 1900 and placed among the "Ancient Days" poems; rewritten in June 1911 and published in 1912 in Γράμματα.

A historically based poem: Herodes Attikos, a wealthy Roman, brought up in the Greek tradition, spent half of his time in Athens and half in Rome; he built many monuments, most notably the theatre at the foot of the Akropolis, used to this day for performances.

This is the first and only mention of Athens in Cavafy's mature poetry.

SCULPTOR OF TYANA

First written in June 1893 as "A Sculptor's Workplace"; rewritten in 1903 and first published in Γράμματα in 1911.

Rhea, mother to the Olympian Gods; Marius, Aemilius Paulus, and Scipio Africanus, all of them, Roman Generals; Patroklos, the friend of Achilles in the *Iliad* and elsewhere. Kaisarion was Ptolemy XV Caesar (the son of Julius Caesar and Kleopatra); he was given the title King of Kings by Mark Anthony.

TOMB OF THE GRAMMARIAN LYSIAS

Written in February 1911 and published in 1914 in *Νέα Ζωή*.

The poet attempts to make the poem appear to have a historical base.

Syenite stone: a red granite from upper Egypt.

TOMB OF EURION

Written in 1912; published in 1914 in *Νέα Ζωή*.

THAT WOULD BE THE MAN

A poem made to give the appearance of a historical occurrence.

The title is a phrase from Lucian's *The Dream*, 11. Lucian relates that in his youth he was persuaded to take up a literary career because of a dream he had, in which the personified Paideia promised him that wherever he traveled he would not be a stranger, nor some unknown, but people would point him out and say, "that would be the man."

FRAUGHT WITH DANGER

Published in February 1911 in *Néa Zωή*.
Made to give the appearance of a historical poem.

MANUEL KOMNENOS

Written in March 1905 and published in June 1916 in *Néa Zωή*.
A historically based poem: Manuel died on September 20, 1180.

IN CHURCH

First written in August 1892, rewritten in December 1901, with a final version in May 1906; likely printed in December 1912.

VERY SELDOM

Written in December 1911 and published in January 1913 in *Néa Zωή*.

FOR THE SHOP

Written in December 1912 and published in October 1913 in *Néa Zωή*.

PAINTED

Written in August 1914 and published in June 1916 in *Néa Zωή*.

MORNING SEA

Published in June 1916 in *Néa Zωή*.

IONIC

First written in May 1886 under the title "Memory"; published under that title in 1896 in the newspaper *Tὸ Ἄστυ*. Rewritten again in July 1905 under the title "Thessalia"; finally published as "Ionic" in *Γράμματα* in June 1911.

AT THE CAFÉ ENTRANCE

Possibly written in July 1904 under the title "From the Hands of Eros." Likely to have finally been printed after June 1915.

ONE NIGHT

First written in July 1907 under the title "One of My Evenings," and later again as "One of My Nights." Finally the poem appeared in June 1916 in *Νέα Ζωή* under the present title.

REAPPEAR

First written in June 1904 under the title "Sensual Memory." Rewritten in September 1909 under the title "Reappear," and published in October 1912 in *Νέα Ζωή*.

LONG AGO

Written in March 1914 and published, most likely, in December of that year.

HE SWEARS

First written in December 1905, titled "Libidinousness"; most likely printed after 1915 with its present title.

I WENT

Written in June 1905 and published in October 1913 in *Νέα Ζωή*.

CHANDELIER

Written in April 1895 and published in June 1914 in *Νέα Ζωή*.

SINCE NINE O'CLOCK—

Written in November 1917 under the title "Half Past Twelve"; printed in 1918 under the present title.

UNDERSTANDING

Written in 1915 and published between December 1917 and January 1918 in *Γράμματα*.

BEFORE THE STATUE OF ENDYMION

Written in May 1895 under a slightly variant title and printed in 1916 in its present form.

The poem gives the appearance of a historical monologue: the period is possibly the fourth or fifth century A.D.

ENVOYS FROM ALEXANDRIA

Written in June 1915 and printed in 1918.

A historically based poem: the scene, probably imagined, occurs in 157 B.C.

ARISTOBOULOS

Written in October 1916 and published in July 1918 in *Γράμματα*.

A historically based poem.

KAISARION

First written in December 1914 under the title "Of Ptolemy, a Caesar"; printed in 1918 under its present title.

A historically based poem: the eldest son of Kleopatra and Julius Caesar, Kaisarion ("Small Caesar"), was put to death by Octavius

Caesar in 30 B.C. In 34 B.C. Mark Anthony had conferred on Kaisarion the title "King of Kings"; after the defeat of Anthony, his victorious opponent, Octavius, was now Caesar Octavianus.

NERO'S TERM

Written in December 1915 under the title "Toward the Fall"; printed in its present form in May 1918.

IN THE HARBOR TOWN

Written in September 1917 under the title "Tomb of Doros" and printed in July 1918.

ONE OF THEIR GODS

Written in 1899 and titled, initially, "One of Them"; the poem was first printed in 1917 under the present title.

TOMB OF LANES

Written in December 1916 and published in Γράμματα between December 1917 and January 1918.

TOMB OF IASES

Written in April 1917, the poem appeared in May 1917 in Γράμματα.

A TOWN IN OSROENE

Written in August 1916 under the title "Charmides," it was printed in 1917 under the present title.

TOMB OF IGNATIOS

Written in April 1916 and first titled "Tomb of Hieronymos"; the poem was printed under the present title in 1917.

IN THE MONTH OF ATHYR

Written in March1917 and published in Γράμματα in May 1917.
The poem is made to seem historical.

FOR AMMONES, WHO DIED AT 29, IN A.D. 610

First written in September 1915 under the title "Epitaph for the Poet
Ammones"; printed under the present title in 1917.

AIMILIANOS MONAE, ALEXANDRIAN A.D. 628–655

Likely to have been written in 1898 under the title "Protected";
printed in 1918 under the present title.

WHEN THEY ARE ROUSED

Written in September 1913 and printed possibly just before
November 1916.

TO SENSUAL PLEASURE

Written in September 1913 and printed in 1917.

I'VE FACED HEAD-ON—

First written in October 1911 under the title "For the Lovely";
published under the present title in Γράμματα in 1917.

IN THE STREET

First written in July 1913 and printed in 1916.

THE TOBACCONIST'S WINDOW

First written in September 1907 under the title "The Closed
Carriage"; printed under the present title in 1917.

PASSAGE

Written in January 1914; first printed in 1917.

IN THE EVENING

Written in March 1916 under the title "Alexandrian"; printed in 1917 under the present title.

GRAY

Written in February 1917 and published in Γράμματα in May 1917.

IN FRONT OF THE HOUSE

First written in July 1917 and most likely printed in 1919.

THE NEXT TABLE

Written in February 1918 and most likely printed in 1919.

BODY, REMEMBER ...

Written in May 1916 and published in December 1917–January1918, in Γράμματα.

DAYS OF 1903

First written in 1909 under the title "March 1907"; printed in 1917 under the present title.

VOICES

First written on July 12, 1894 under the title "Sweet Voices," and published in December of that year in Αἰγυπτιακὸν Ἡμερολόγιον.

Rewritten in December 1903 under its present title, and published in its present form on August 15, 1904 in Παναθήναια.

LONGINGS

Written in September 1904 and published in *Κ. Π. Καβάφη, Ποιήματα,* in 1904.

CANDLES

Written in August 1893, it appeared in December 1899 in the *Ἐθνικὸν Ἡμερολόγιον τοῦ Ἔτους 1900.*

AN OLD MAN

Written in October 1894 and placed in the thematic sheaf "Fleeting Years." The poem appeared in *Ἐθνικὸν Ἡμερολόγιον τοῦ Ἔτους 1898,* with the overhead title *"Eheu fugaces"* ("Ah, how swiftly the years glide by"; Horace, *Odes,* II.14).

SUPPLIANCE

Written in July 1896 and printed in November 1898 in a quadruple-page sheaf.

THE SOULS OF OLD MEN

Written in August 1898 and placed in the sheaf entitled "Prisons"; printed in 1901 in *Ἐθνικὸν Ἡμερολόγιον τοῦ Ἔτους 1902.*

THE FIRST STEP

First titled "The Last Step" and included in the sheaf entitled "Our Art." Written in February 1895 and printed in December 1899.

A historically based poem: Theokritos (ca. 270 B.C.) was known for his pastoral poems and dialogues; the scene and the young poet Eumenes, however, are imagined.

INTERRUPTION

Written in May 1900 and printed in December 1901.

The goddesses Thetis and Demeter were prevented (by Peleus and Metaneira, respectively) from completing the fire ritual to make the infants Achilles and Demophon immortal.

THERMOPYLAI

Written in January 1901 and published in 1903, in Gregorios Xenopoulos's article "A Poet," which appeared in *Παναθήναια*.

The poem's base has a historical pretense.

CHE FECE ... IL GRAN RIFIUTO

Written in July 1899 and printed on August 31, 1901.

The title comes from Dante (*Inferno*, III.60).

WINDOWS

Written in August 1897 and placed in the thematic sheaf entitled "Prisons." In November 1903 it appeared in Gregorios Xenopoulos's article "A Poet," in *Παναθήναια*.

AWAITING THE BARBARIANS

Written in December 1898 and printed as an eight-page pamphlet.

The poem pretends to be historical; but it only makes use of history for its internal dialogue and its symbolic, philosophical content.

DISLOYALTY

Written in May 1903 and published in May 1904 in *Παναθήναια*.

THE HORSES OF ACHILLES

Written in July 1896 and placed in the sheaf entitled "Ancient Days." It appeared in 1897 in *Ἐθνικὸν Ἡμερολόγιον τοῦ Ἔτους 1898*.

WALLS

Written on September 1, 1896 and placed in the thematic collection "Prisons." The poem was printed privately in a pamphlet on January 16, 1897, along with an English translation by the poet's brother John.

THE FUNERAL OF SARPEDON

A first version was very likely written at the end of 1892 and placed in the sheaf "Ancient Days"; it appeared in the Ἐθνικὸν Ἡμερολόγιον τοῦ Ἔτους 1899.

The poem was later rewritten, in August 1908, and published in September 1908 in Νέα Ζωή, and again in July–October in the journal Νέα Τέχνη, 1924.

THE AFTERNOON SUN

Written in November 1918 and printed in 1919.

There is nothing ambiguous about the sex of these youths in the original Greek; they are two young men.

COMES TO CLAIM ITS PLACE

Written in March 1918 and printed in July 1919.

OF THE JEWS (A.D. 50)

Written in October 1912 and printed in 1919.

The characters are imaginary: Ianthes, a Jew with a Greek name, while his father—Antonios—had a Roman name. The date (A.D. 50) indicates the reign of Claudius, who gave certain privileges to the Alexandrian Jews.

IMENOS

A version without the second stanza was written in October 1915. The poem was rewritten in February 1919 and printed during that year.

Both the name and the letter are imaginary. The poet places the piece in the time of the Byzantine emperor Michael III (842–867 A.D.).

ON BOARD SHIP

Written in October 1919 under the title "The Ionian Sea"; printed in December 1919.

OF DEMETRIOS SOTER (162–150 B.C.)

First written in 1915 and printed 1919.

As the king of Syria and son of Seleukos IV, he was given the name "Soter" ("Savior"). He spent much of his youth in Rome as a hostage. While he was in Rome there were several usurpers of his throne in Syria, until he escaped from Rome and assumed the Syrian throne in 162 B.C. The poet has written a number of poems from this historical period and on this particular royal family: "The Battle of Magnesia," "Craftsmen of Wine Bowls," "The Displeasure of Seleukides," "To Antiochos Epiphanes," "Temethos, Antiochian; A.D. 400," "Orophernes," "The Favor of Alexander Balas," "Envoys from Alexandria."

IF ACTUALLY DEAD

First written (the first part only) in October 1897 under the title "Absence;" rewritten in July 1910 and printed under the present title in March 1920.

The title comes from the *Life of Apollonios of Tyana* (VIII.29) by Philostratos (third century A.D.); Cavafy was taken by the biography and by the philosopher-magus Apollonios.

YOUNG MEN OF SIDON (A.D. 400)

Written in June 1920 and printed in the same year.

The scene and the characters are imagined. Sidon is the Helle-nized city along the coast of Phoenicia; it began its decline early in the first century A.D. and was taken over by the Arabs in 637–638 A.D. Aeschylus is Cavafy's favorite of the tragedians.

SO THEY MIGHT COME—

Printed in 1920.

DAREIOS

Written in May 1917 and printed in October 1920, though there is some evidence of an earlier version from before 1897.

The scene (imagined to be about 74 B.C.) is of the poet Phernazes (a fictitious Persian character) composing the poem concerning the period of Dareios (559–529 B.C.) of the Battle of Marathon fame. The turbulent period of Phernazes (120–71 B.C.) interferes with his "ancient" days, those of Cyrus the Great and Dareios.

ANNA KOMNENE

Written in August 1917 and printed in December 1920.

It is a historically based poem. The title character was the first-born daughter of the Byzantine emperor Alexios I Komnenos (1081–1118 A.D.). She attempted to usurp the throne from her brother Ioannes II in order to give it to her husband, who died unex-pectedly in 1136 A.D. Following these events she withdrew from any hope of a worldly life to a monastery.

A BYZANTINE NOBLEMAN, IN EXILE, COMPOSING VERSES

Written in March 1921 and printed in the same month.

The poem creates the aura of being a historical poem; the imag-ined, anonymous central character appears to have lived between the reigns of Nikephoros III Botaneiates (1078–1081 A.D.) and that of Alexios I Komnenos (1081–1118 A.D.).

THEIR BEGINNING

Written in June 1915 and printed in March 1921.

THE FAVOR OF ALEXANDER BALAS

The poem is presented as an internal monologue giving the appearance of history; Balas is a historical figure, who became king of Syria (150–146 B.C.) as an impostor and was later murdered.

MELANCHOLY OF IASON KLEANDROS, POET IN KOMMAGENE, A.D. 595

Likely to have been written in August 1918 under the title "Knife"; printed in June 1921.

The character of the title is imaginary. Kommagene, a small independent state northeast of Syria, was part of Byzantium until 638 A.D., when it was taken over by the Arabs. The date of the title of Iason's monologue falls between the plunder by Hosroes I of Persia and the treaty between the Byzantine emperor and Persians.

DEMARATOS

First written in August 1904, rewritten in November 1911, and printed in September 1921.

A historically based poem; the fact that Porphyry enters the picture places the composition of the young Sophist's essay between 263 and 305 A.D.

In the second half of the poem, we are transported to Persia ca. 480 B.C.; Demaratos had lost his throne in Sparta and went to Persia as a defector to the court of Dareios I.

I BROUGHT TO ART

Written in September 1921 and printed in the same month.

FROM THE SCHOOL OF THE RENOWNED PHILOSOPHER

Written in December 1921 and printed in the same month.

A poem made to appear historically based. The anonymous central figure is an Alexandrian ca. 242 A.D.; of the same period as the philosopher Sakkas, who was referred to as "the Sokrates of Neoplatonism." His oral teachings have survived thanks to his two famous students, Plotinos and Origen.

CRAFTSMAN OF WINE BOWLS

First written in 1903 under the title "The Amphora"; rewritten in July 1912, and again in December 1912 under the present title. It was eventually printed in December 1921.

The craftsman and the scene are imaginary. The time appears to be somewhat (perhaps fifteen years) after the battle of Magnesia in 190 B.C.

THOSE WHO FOUGHT FOR THE ACHAEAN LEAGUE

Written in February 1922 and printed in the same month.

The first part is read as an epigram on the disaster of dissolving the Achaean League and the complete Roman conquest at about 146 B.C. Many of Cavafy's early readers of the poem, however, interpret it as alluding to the Asia Minor catastrophe of 1922.

TO ANTIOCHOS EPIPHANES

Possibly first written in November 1911 under the title "Antiochos Epiphanes"; rewritten in February 1922 and printed in the same month.

It is made to seem historical. The scene and the youth, an anonymous favorite of Antiochos, are perhaps placed at around 160 B.C.

IN AN OLD BOOK—

Possibly written in September 1892 under the title "The Book"; printed in December 1922.

IN DESPAIR

Written in May 1923 and printed in the same month of that year.

JULIAN SEEING NEGLECT

Possibly written in September 1923; printed in the same month of that year.

A historically based poem. From the year 1896 to 1932/33, Cavafy wrote seven poems whose subject matter is Julian the Apostate's attitude toward Christianity.

EPITAPH FOR ANTIOCHOS, KING OF KOMMAGENE

Possibly written in November 1923; printed in the same month of that year.

Although the poem is historically based, the epitaph, events, and personages are imaginary.

THE THEATRE OF SIDON (A.D. 400)

Possibly written in November 1923 and printed in the same month of that year.

Appearing to be historical—an internal monologue of an imaginary personage.

JULIAN IN NIKOMEDEIA

A draft was perhaps in the works in 1892. Written in its final form in January 1924 and printed in the same month of that year.

A historically based poem: Julian passed some time in Niko-medeia, first as an orphaned and banished prince (337–342 A.D.), and later as a grown up (351–352 A.D.). There, he began to lean deci-sively toward a mystical paganism. The poem takes place during his second stay in that city. The persons who influence him while there appear in the poem:

1. Chrysanthios, the Neoplatonic philosopher, who along with his friends initiated Julian into the pagan rites.

2. Gallos was Julian's elder half-brother; for a time proclaimed Caesar by their emperor cousin.

3. Constantios II, Emperor; Constantios had Gallos executed (354 A.D.) and gave Julian the throne in 360–361 A.D.

4. Mardonios was Julian's Hellenophile tutor.

BEFORE TIME CHANGES THEM

Written in January 1924 and printed in the same month of that year.

HE CAME HERE TO READ—

Written in July 1924 and printed in the same month of that year.

IN ALEXANDRIA, 31 B.C.

Written first in April 1917; rewritten in July 1924 and printed in the same month of that year.

A historically based poem; the central figure is anonymous and the events imaginary. In September of 31 B.C. in the sea battle of Actium (outside of Preveza), Octavius defeated Anthony and Kleopatra. Yet Kleopatra tried to hide the defeat by returning for a triumphal march into Alexandria.

IOANNES KANTAKOUZENOS TRIUMPHS

Printed on December 9, 1924.

A historically based poem; the story of the anonymous protago-
nist unfolds in ca. 1347 A.D. As he lay dying, Byzantium's emperor
Andronikos III Palaiologos named Ioannes Kantakouzenos his
vice king. A wealthy man, he triumphed over Andronikos's wife
and was crowned emperor, together with his wife Eirene Asan, in
Constantinople.

TEMETHOS, ANTIOCHIAN; A.D. 400

Printed on 20 January, 1925.
A historically based poem; Cavafy creates an imaginary persona
in Temethos who, in turn, "creates" the imaginary Emonides.

OF COLORED GLASS

Printed on February 27, 1925.
A historically based poem; the formal coronation of Ioannes
Kantakouzenos and Eirene Asan took place in 1347 A.D. at the
royal church of Vlachernai, because the Cathedral of Saint Sophia in
Constantinople was half in ruins; and Anna of Savoy, in her battles
with Kantakouzenos, had used up the wealth of the state—and even
had to sell all the jewels of the throne.

THE 25TH YEAR OF HIS LIFE

Likely written in June of 1918 under the title "The 23rd Year of My
Life in Winter"; printed under the present title on June 30, 1925.

ON AN ITALIAN SHORE

A historically based poem, with imaginary characters. The scene
is likely to have taken place in 146 B.C.: the Roman consul Lucius
Mummius, having wasted the Achaean League at Leukopetra, went
on to plunder Corinth by killing all the men, selling the women and
children into slavery, and shipping all the art treasures to Italy. This

was pretty much the beginning of the final act—the usurpation of Greater Greece by the Romans.

IN THE LIFELESS VILLAGE

Written in 1925 and printed on October 20 of the same year.

APOLLONIOS OF TYANA IN RHODES

Written in 1925 and printed on October 20 of the same year.

A historically based poem; Philostratos tells the story of an empty-headed youth of newly acquired wealth, with little or no education. Cavafy is thought to have based his character on Philostratos's story.

KLEITOS'S ILLNESS

Printed in February 1926.

The poem is made to appear historical; the scene and characters are imaginary. It may occur during the fourth century.

IN A TOWNSHIP OF ASIA MINOR

Printed on March 30, 1926.

A historically based poem; both the scene and the decree are imaginary—but they may be dated to 31 B.C., after Anthony's defeat by Octavius at Actium.

PRIEST AT THE SERAPEION

Printed on June 9, 1926.

The poem is made to seem historical, although both the scene and the personages are imaginary.

The scene: the famous Alexandrian temple of Serapis. It was built by Ptolemy I Soter, then opulently rebuilt by Ptolemy III Euergetes (all happening ca. 300 B.C. and 246–221 B.C.). The temple was considered to be one of the great wonders of the world of late antiquity. It was all destroyed by the emperor Theodosios in 391 A.D. Serapis was a confluence of Osiris and Apis, with a mingling of Zeus, Dionysos, Plouton, and Asklepios. The Alexandrians worshipped him at the official behest of the Ptolemies. The god's priests were usually of Greek decent.

IN THE TAVERNAS—

Printed on June 9, 1926.

Imaginary characters in a poem that is made to appear historical, with broken lines that are randomly rhymed.

A GREAT PROCESSION OF PRIESTS AND LAYMEN

A version is likely to have been written in September 1892, under the title "The Cross," and was placed in the thematic sheaf "The Beginnings of Christianity." Subsequently rewritten, perhaps, in March 1917 and printed on August 30, 1926.

A historically based poem; Julian was killed in a battle with the Persians on June 26, 363 A.D. Following those events Jovian, a tolerant Christian, ruled for only seven months. He died suddenly in February 364 A.D.

SOPHIST ABANDONING SYRIA

Printed on November 15, 1926.

Made to give the appearance of a historical poem, with broken lines that are randomly rhymed.

JULIAN AND THE ANTIOCHIANS

Printed on November 15, 1926.

A historically based poem; when Julian confronts Antioch, a Christian city, he berates it for not allowing an aristocratic form of paganism, which he preferred. He was especially harsh during the short time he passed in the city.

ANNA DALASSENE

Printed on January 4, 1927.

A historically based poem; in 1081, Alexios I Komnenos (1081–1118 A.D.), while going off to war, entrusted, *carte blanche*, all of the powers of the empire to his mother, Anna Dalassene.

DAYS OF 1896

Written in 1925 and printed on March 26, 1927.

TWO YOUNG MEN, 23 TO 24 YEARS OLD

Printed on June 14, 1927.

GREEK SINCE ANCIENT TIMES

Printed on September 9, 1927.

A historically based poem; according to one tradition, Io, daughter of the king of Argos, was transformed to a heifer and chased all through the East by Hera. She finally died in Syria, where the Argive colonists built a temple in her honor; at that exact spot, in 300 B.C., Seleukos I Nikator built the city of Antioch.

DAYS OF 1901

Written before October 15, 1927 and printed on October 28, 1927.

YOU DIDN'T UNDERSTAND

Printed on January 16, 1928.

A YOUNG MAN OF LETTERS—IN HIS 24TH YEAR

Printed on January 16, 1928.

IN SPARTA

Printed on April 17, 1928.

A historically based poem; Kleomenes III (236–222 B.C.), in his desperate attempt to change the Lykourgos constitution (because his armies were being depleted), resorted to asking the aid of Ptolemy III in order to fight the Makedonians and the Achaean League. Ptolemy agreed to aid the Spartans, with the condition that Kleomenes' mother, Kratesikleia, and his children be sent to Alexandria as hostages.

A LIKENESS OF A TWENTY-THREE YEAR OLD YOUTH
PAINTED BY HIS FRIEND OF THE SAME AGE, AN AMATEUR

Printed on April 17, 1928.

IN A LARGE GREEK COLONY, 200 B.C.

Printed on April 17, 1928.

Made to seem historical—the place of the Colony is indeterminate.

A SOVEREIGN FROM WESTERN LIBYA

Printed on August 20, 1928.

Made to seem historical, though the main character is obviously imaginary.

KIMON, SON OF LEARCHOS, 22,
STUDENT OF GREEK LITERATURE (IN KYRENE)

Possibly written in December 1913 under the title "Tomb of Marikos"; printed under the present title on August 20, 1928.

ON THE MARCH TO SINOPE

Printed on December 6, 1928.

A historically based poem; the incident with the soothsayer is imaginary, but it suggests some historical occurrences dated to 301 B.C.: the saving of Mithridates I by his friend Demetrios Poliorketes.

In this poem, the central figure is Mithridates V Euergetes of Pontos. He was murdered by his wife in 120 B.C. after his arrival at Sinope; she disagreed with him on his decrees against the Romans.

DAYS OF 1909, '10, AND '11

Printed on December 6, 1928.

MYRES, ALEXANDRIA, A.D. 340

Printed on April 19, 1929.

The longest poem in Cavafy's canon.

Made to seem historical, the scene and personages are imaginary. The time (340 A.D.) is a period of great upheaval, political and religious: civil war between the sons of Constantine the Great, with Constantios being victorious in the East; battles in Alexandria between the followers of Areios and Athanasios—and banishment of the latter to Rome.

ALEXANDER IANNAIOS AND ALEXANDRA

Printed on July 19, 1929.

A historically based poem: Alexander Iannaios was the most ruthless of the kings of Judea. He reigned from 103–76 B.C. Alexandra-Salome, his wife, was the widow of his brother, Aristoboulos I, founder of the Hsmonaean dynasty.

LOVELY FLOWERS AND WHITE BECOME HIM BEST

Printed on October 3, 1929.

Each line consists of two broken hemistichs.

COME, O KING OF THE LAKEDAIMONIANS

Printed on October 26, 1929.

The events of the poem "In Sparta" are here extended and take a tragic turn: Kratesikleia was executed by the successor to her son's

Egyptian patron, Ptolemy IV. The title and the closing quote come from Plutarch, *Life of Kleomenes*, 28.

IN THE SAME PLACE

Printed on December 9, 1929.

One word (difficult to translate): αἰσθηματοποιήθηκες ("fraught with feeling") is indicative of Cavafy's whole corpus.

THE MIRROR IN THE FRONT HALL

Printed on February 3, 1930.

HE ASKED ABOUT THE QUALITY—

Printed on May 15, 1930.

TO HAVE TAKEN THE TROUBLE

Printed on July 8, 1930.

Made to seem historical: the central figure of the poem is fictitious, while most of the other names mentioned are historical figures, who vied for power in the Syrian upheavals ca. 128 B.C. They are referred to by their nicknames: Kakergetes (= "Malefactor") was Ptolemy VIII Euergetes (= "Benefactor").

FOLLOWING THE RECIPE OF ANCIENT GRECO-SYRIAN MAGICIANS

Printed on February 23, 1931.

IN THE YEAR 200 B.C.

Probably written in June 1916 under the title "Except the Lakedaimonians"; printed on September 10, 1931.

The date of the title, and indeed the events, places the poem at an optimal moment of the decline of Hellenism; more than a century after Alexander's victories and only a short time before Philip V (the last of the Makedonian Philips) was so badly defeated by the Romans.

The beginning quote is Alexander the Great's dedicatory inscription he sent to the Athenian Parthenon. And the extolling of the Greeks of the East is a way for the poet to bring in the Greek *koinê*, the common spoken language of the people—the very language that for many centuries after that was spoken in the East and in Christendom. He concludes the extolling with Bactria, the rich Satrapy between northern Afghanistan and southern Uzbekistan, which held on to a fine cultural influence from Alexander's day to, perhaps, 140 B.C. and later.

DAYS OF 1908

Possibly written initially in July 1921 under the title "The Summer of 1895"; printed under the present title on November 17, 1932.

ON THE OUTSKIRTS OF ANTIOCH

Probably written between November 1932 and April 1933.

The body of the Bishop of Antioch and martyr Babylas (after his death in 253 A.D., Saint Babylas) had been moved from his burial place so that he would rest in the precinct of the famous temple of Apollo, in the grove at Daphne, the suburb of Antioch. This was done by Caesar Constantius Gallus one century after the saint's death (in 351 A.D.). But the priests of Apollo reacted against what they saw as pollution to the grove of their god and abandoned the area entirely. The Christians then built a church over Babylas's new grave-site. When Julian arrived in Antioch in 362 A.D., he went to pray at Apollo's temple and, when he saw it had been abandoned, he ordered the destruction of the Christian church, the return of the saint's remains, and the purification of the entire area. Soon after, a great fire was set which destroyed the roof of the temple, together with the famous statue of Apollo, the work of the well-known Athenian sculptor Bryaxis. The fire of October 22, 362 A.D. was attributed to the vengeance of the Christians.

Index of Greek Titles

Index of English Titles

General Index

Achilles (Achilleus), 357, 365

Actium (Aktion), 372, 374

Adonis, xvii

Aeschylus (Aischylos), 368

Alexander the Great (Alexandros), 355, 356, 379–380

Alexandria (Alexandreia), vii, xiii, xiv, xvi, 356, 366, 378

Alexios I Komnenos, 368, 376

Ammonios Sakkas, 370

Andronikos III Palaiologos, 373

Anna Dalassene, 376

Anna Komnene, 368

Anna, of Savoy, 373

Antioch (Antiocheia), 375, 376, 380

Antiochos III, 355

Antiochos IV Epiphanes, xvi, 370

Antoniou, T., xiv

Apis, 375

Apollo, 380

Apollonios, 367, 374

Areios, 378

Argos, 376

Athanasios, 378

Athens, vii, xv, xvi, 357

In the General Index, names of modern poets and prose-writers are provided with basic biographical information, for the readers' convenience. Information about all other names is provided in the Introduction and the Notes. See, further, the relevant entries or discussion in *The Oxford Classical Dictionary*, third revised edition (ed. S. Hornblower and A. Spawforth), Oxford 2003; *The Oxford Dictionary of Byzantium* (ed. A. P. Kazhdan), Oxford 1991; L. Polites, *A History of Modern Greek Literature*, Oxford 1973; and S. Alexiou, Ἑλληνικὴ Λογοτεχνία: Ἀπὸ τὸν Ὅμηρο στὸν Εἰκοστὸ Αἰῶνα, Athens 2010.